THE MIDDLE
ENGLISH MYSTICS

THE MIDDLE ENGLISH MYSTICS

*

Wolfgang Riehle
*Professor of English
at the University of Graz*

translated by Bernard Standring

ROUTLEDGE & KEGAN PAUL
London, Boston and Henley

This translation first published in 1981
by Routledge & Kegan Paul Ltd
39 Store Street,
London WC1E 7DD,
9 Park Street,
Boston, Mass. 02108, USA and
Broadway House,
Newtown Road,
Henley-on-Thames,
Oxon RG9 1BN
Set in 10/12pt Journal
by Columns, Reading
and printed in Great Britain by
Lowe & Brydore Ltd
Thetford, Norfolk
First published in Germany 1977 as
Studien zur englischen Mystik des Mittelalters
unter besonderer Berücksichtigung ihrer Metaphorik
© *1977. Carl Winter Universitätsverlag, gegr. 1822 GmbH., Heidelberg*
English translation © *Routledge & Kegan Paul 1981*

British Library Cataloguing in Publication Data

Riehle, Wolfgang
The middle English mystics.
1 Mysticism
I Title
149' 3   *BL625*   80-41433

ISBN 0-7100-0612-8

To my wife

CONTENTS

*

vii

Contents

PREFACE

*

This book, which is the revised edition of a work originally published in German by Carl Winter, Heidelberg, is a comparative study of the medieval English mystics and an attempt to fill the gap caused by the death of Hope Emily Allen who was the only scholar who consistently applied the comparative method in her research on the English mystics, especially on Margery Kempe. Since the scope of this book is the language rather than the theology of the mystics, it focuses on their use of imagery, as this is one of the most revealing subjects in the field of mysticism.

As any student of medieval mysticism will know, the scholar is confronted with numerous obstacles which an individual person is hardly able to overcome. Therefore I am grateful for having been able to profit by the invaluable advice of specialists, above all B. Bischoff, A.I. Doyle, H. Gneuss, H. Kuhn, J. Russell-Smith and R. Woolf. My thanks are also due to the late E. Salter for having helped me find a translator. B. Standring has my warmest thanks not only for having done the translation, but also for having contributed a number of important corrections and suggestions. V. Lagorio has kindly helped me in many ways and has suggested to me the idea of an English edition. It is, however, especially W. Clemen to whom I am most grateful for his encouraging comments and support.

The preparation of this study was made possible by a scholarship of the Deutsche Forschungsgemeinschaft and by a travel grant from the University of Munich.

I also wish to express my thanks to Miss I. Kalt for having typed the difficult manuscript and to Mr Keiper for assisting me in giving the bibliography its final shape.

Finally, I am obliged to the authors of critical, as yet unpublished, editions of texts of the Middle English mystics for having given me their permission to quote. Recently a few editions of mystical texts have been published, yet unfortunately they have appeared too late for consideration in this study. However, as all my quotations from the unpublished editions are followed by the relevant chapter references in the manuscript, it should be easy for the reader to use the newly published editions in conjunction with this book.

W.R.

University of Graz

November 1979

ABBREVIATIONS

*

Abbreviations for editions and works frequently used

Ancrene Wisse	*Ancrene Wisse*: with an introduction by N.R. Ker, ed. J.R.R. Tolkien, *EETS*, OS, 249, 1962.
Berger	Berger, K., *Die Ausdrücke der Unio mystica im Mittelhochdeutschen*, Germanische Studien, 168, Ebering, Berlin, 1935.
Booke of Gostlye Grace	'The Booke of Gostlye Grace', ed. T.A. Halligan (unpublished dissertation, New York, 1963).
Book of M. Kempe	*The Book of Margery Kempe*, ed. S.B. Meech and H.E. Allen, *EETS*, OS, 212, 1940.
Chastising	*The Chastising of God's Children and the Treatise of Perfection of the Sons of God*, ed. J. Bazire and E. Colledge, Blackwell, Oxford, 1957.
Cloud	*The Cloud of Unknowing and the Book of Privy Counselling*, ed. P. Hodgson, *EETS*, OS, 218, 1944, repr. (with corrections) 1958 and 1973.
Comment on the Canticles	Richard Rolle's *Comment on the Canticles*, ed. from MS. Trinity College Dublin 153 by E.M. Murray (unpubl. diss. Fordham University, New York, 1958).
Deonise HD	*Deonise Hid Diuinite, and Other Treatises on Contemplative Prayer Related to The Cloud of Unknowing*, ed. P. Hodgson, *EETS*, OS, 231, 1955.
Deutsche Werke	*Meister Eckhart. Die deutschen und lateinischen Werke*, ed. J. Quint, Kohlhammer, Stuttgart-Berlin, 1936ff.; Part I: *Die deutschen Werke*; vol 1 (Predigten), 1958; vol 2 (Predigten), 1971; vol 5 (Traktate), 1963.

8 Chapters on Perfection	*Walter Hilton's Eight Chapters on Perfection*, ed. F. Kuriyagawa, Keio Institute of Cultural and Linguistic Studies, Keio University, Tokyo, 1967.
English Prose Treatises	*English Prose Treatises of Richard Rolle de Hampole*, ed. G.G. Perry, *EETS*, OS, 20, 1921.
English Psalter	*The Psalter or Psalms of David and Certain Canticles with a Translation and Exposition in English by Richard Rolle of Hampole*, ed. H.R. Bramley, Clarendon Press, 1884.
English Writings	*English Writings of Richard Rolle Hermit of Hampole*, ed. H.E. Allen, Clarendon Press, 1931.
Fire of Love	*The Fire of Love and the Mending of Life, translated by Richard Misyn, 1434-5*, ed. R. Harvey, *EETS*, OS, 106, 1896.
Handbuch theologischer Grundbegriffe	*Handbuch theologischer Grundbegriffe*, ed. H. Fries, Kösel, Munich, 1970.
Incendium Amoris	*The Incendium Amoris of Richard Rolle of Hampole*, ed. M. Deanesly, Publications of the University of Manchester, Historical Series, 26, London, 1915.
Latin Psalter	*D. Richardi Pampolitani Anglosaxonis Eremitae, Viri in divinis scripturis ac veteri illa solidaque Theologia eruditissimi, in Psalterium Dauidicum atque alia quaedam sacrae scripturae monumenta (quae versa indicabit pagella) compendiosa iuxtaque pia Enarratio*, ed. J. Faber, Cologne, 1536.
Lüers	Lüers, G., *Die Sprache der deutschen Mystik im Werke der Mechthild von Magdeburg*, Munich, 1926.
Meditations (English Writings)	*English Writings of Richard Rolle Hermit of Hampole*, ed. H.E. Allen, Oxford, 1931.
Meditations (Lindquist)	*Richard Rolle's Meditatio de Passione Domini according to MS. Uppsala C. 494*, ed. H. Lindquist, Skrifter utgifna af K. Humanistika Vetenskaps-Samfundet: Uppsala, 19, 3, Uppsala, 1917.
Mending of Life in *Fire of Love*	see *Fire of Love*
Mirror of Simple Souls	' "The Mirror of Simple Souls", A Middle English Translation', ed. M. Doiron, *Archivio Italiano per la Storia della Pietá*, 5, Rome, 1968.

Mysticism	Underhill, E., *Mysticism. A Study in the Nature and Development of Man's Spiritual Consciousness*, Methuen, London, 12th edn, 1930.
Offenbarungen der Schwester Mechthild von Magdeburg	*Offenbarungen der Schwester Mechthild von Magdeburg oder das fliessende Licht der Gottheit*, ed. P. Gall Morel, Wissenschaftliche Buchgesellschaft, Darmstadt, 2nd edn, 1963.
Orcherd of Syon	*The Orcherd of Syon*, ed. P. Hodgson and G. Liegey, *EETS*, OS, 258, 1966, I.
Die Predigten Taulers	*Die Predigten Taulers aus der Engelberger und der Freiberger Handschrift sowie aus Schmidts Abschriften der ehemaligen Strassburger Handschriften*, ed. F. Vetter, Deutsche Texte des Mittelalters, 11, Weidmannsche Buchhandlung, Berlin, 1910.
Privy Counselling	*The Cloud of Unknowing and the Book of Privy Counselling*, ed. P. Hodgson, *EETS*, OS, 218, 1944, repr. (with corrections) 1958 and 1973.
Qui Habitat	*An Exposition of Qui Habitat and Bonum Est in English*, ed. B. Wallner, Lund, 1954.
Revelations (SV) *Revelations* (LV)	*A Critical Edition of the Revelations of Julian of Norwich (1342-c.1416)*, by Sr Anna Maria Reynolds (unpublished PhD thesis, Leeds, 1956).
Ruh	*Altdeutsche und altniederländische Mystik*, ed. K. Ruh, Wege der Forschung, 23, Wissenschaftliche Buchgesellschaft, Darmstadt, 1964.
Sancti Bernardi Opera	*Sermones super Cantica Canticorum*, ed. J. Leclerq, C.H. Talbot, H.M. Rochais, *Sancti Bernardi Opera*, Rome, 1957, I-II.
Scale I	'An Edition of Book I of *The Scale of Perfection* by Walter Hilton', by B.E. Wykes (unpublished dissertation, Ann Arbor, 1957).
Scale II	'An Edition, from the Manuscripts, of Book II of Walter Hilton's *Scale of Perfection*', by S.S. Hussey (unpublished PhD thesis, London, 1962).
Schmidt	Schmidt, M., ed., *Rudolf von Biberach. Die siben strassen zu got. Die hochalemannische Übertragung nach der Handschrift Einsiedeln 278*, Spicilegium Bonaventurianum, Quaracchi, 1969.
Talkyng of þe Loue of God	*A Talkyng of þe Loue of God*, ed. M.S. Westra, Martinus Nijhoff, The Hague, 1950.

Werken	*Jan van Ruusbroec, Werken*, ed. J. van Mierlo, J.B. Poukens, L. Reypens, M. Schurmans, D.-A. Stracke, Ruusbroec Genootschap, Tielt, 1944-48, 4 vols.
Wohunge of Ure Lauerd	Þe *Wohunge of Ure Lauerd*, ed. W.M. Thompson, *EETS*, OS, 241, 1958.
Writings	Allen, H.E., *Writings Ascribed to Richard Rolle Hermit of Hampole and Materials for his Biography*, Modern Language Association of America, Monograph Series III, New York, 1927.
Yorkshire Writers	*Yorkshire Writers*, ed. C. Horstmann, London, 1895, 2 vols.

Abbreviations for biblical texts

S. of S.	Song of Songs
Cor.	Epistles to the Corinthians
Deut.	Deuteronomy
Ecclus.	Ecclesiasticus
Eph.	Epistle to the Ephesians
Exod.	Exodus
Gen.	Genesis
Heb.	Epistle to the Hebrews
Hos.	Hosea
Isa.	Isaiah
Mal.	Malachi
Matt.	Matthew
Phil.	Epistle to the Philippians
Prov.	Proverbs
Ps.	Psalm
Rom.	Epistle to the Romans
Tim.	Epistles to Timothy

(All Bible quotations are taken from *Biblia Sacra iuxta Vulgatam Clementinam Nova Editio*, ed. A. Colunga et C. Turrado, Madrid, 1965.)

Further abbreviations

DSAM	*Dictionnaire de spiritualité ascétique et mystique doctrine et histoire*
DVJ	*Deutsche Vierteljahrsschrift für Literaturwissenschaft und Geistesgeschichte*
EETS	*Early English Text Society*
ES	Extra Series
OS	Original Series
ELH	*A Journal of English Literary History*
E&S	*Essays and Studies*
ES	*English Studies*
JEGP	*Journal of English and Germanic Philology*
MED	*Middle English Dictionary*
MLQ	*Modern Language Quarterly*
MLR	*Modern Language Review*
MP	*Modern Philology*
MS	*Medieval Studies*
N&Q	*Notes and Queries*
OED	*The Oxford English Dictionary*
PL	*Patrologiae Cursus Completus, Series Latina*, ed. J.-P. Migne
PMLA	*Publications of the Modern Language Association of America*
RAM	*Revue d'ascétique et de mystique*
RES	*Review of English Studies*
SP	*Studies in Philology*
ZfdA	*Zeitschrift für deutsches Altertum*
ZfdPh	*Zeitschrift für deutsche Philologie*

INTRODUCTION

*

I

In approaching the theme of medieval English mysticism in this book, it is not our intention to present an analysis and detailed survey of the theological teaching. We are concerned rather with the philological question of how the writers cope with the difficult task of coming to terms linguistically with the theme of the mystical experience of God. The medieval English mystics, like all other mystics, are faced with the problem of having to express the union with the divine in a language which proves to be inadequate because it is limited to earthly things. The mystics stress time and again that the mystical experience of God is an experience which surpasses all other earthly experience, such that it cannot be adequately expressed in language and must therefore ultimately remain an *ineffabile*. But the interesting fact remains that the mystics nevertheless succeed in expressing the theme of the union of man and God in language, and indeed in a language which is some-times creative, since in their attempt to push back the limits of what is expressible they coin new words or give new meaning to terms which already exist in the language. The experience of the mystic may well be of a quite amorphous nature, as G. Scholem maintains,[1] but at the same time we must not forget that it is only through the medium of language that mysticism can become a reality which transcends the individual. Anyone who, like Richard Rolle, is imbued with a very intense mystical experience will wish to communicate it to others, and will therefore make every effort to find a language which is capable of transmitting this intensity as far as is possible, so that the wish for a similar experi-ence will be awakened in the reader. Here the mystics sometimes fall back on the tried and tested figures of speech of rhetoric,[2] but above all they strive to make their mystical themes clear by means of sensual concrete metaphors and images, and this not infrequently yields certain analogies with the attempts of poetry to produce concrete language.[3]

It is this imagery which forms the real object of this study and for which we quite deliberately use the blanket term 'metaphorical language'. We want to examine the metaphorical language of English mysticism in its relationship with the long tradition of the language of Christian mysticism. A few preliminary considerations are, however, necessary. The imagery of mysticism arose from a combination of various factors and influences. A considerable number of mystical images can be traced back to Platonic, particularly neo-Platonic, philosophy and the ancient mystery cults. Plato, for example, had already tried to use a concrete image when speaking of the soul as a winged being.[4] Such concrete images for the soul and for transcendental concepts generally could easily be fitted into the medieval mode of thinking of the *analogia entis*, according to which the function of all things which could be experienced by the senses was ultimately to reflect the spiritual world, thus making it possible for the world to be interpreted as one ordered cosmos, despite the fact that it was experienced in a dualistic manner.

But in the development of a mystical metaphorical language the most important model was the language of the Bible, which was looked upon as the ultimate authority in the question of the mystical relationship between man and God. A good recent study on the understanding of metaphor and tropical language in the Middle Ages[5] has shown that there was a widely held view that the Bible already used a metaphorical language. It has been shown that Thomas Aquinas considered the biblical metaphorical language to be necessary,[6] and that the sensual world which is found in the Bible (the 'sensibilia') was understood as an encoding of the statements of relevation (the 'intelligibilia').[7] The encoding of religious language was explained as being necessary in order to inspire the Bible reader to intellectual activity, and to protect the sacred texts from the ridicule of unbelievers.[8] The method used for decoding biblical language was the well known method of Bible allegory, which was current until the Reformation. Thus a biblical text could be interpreted mystically in the form of a tropological exegesis.[9] Many of the images obtained in this way are signs and symbols for a spiritual content, and since there were no firm guide-lines for allegorical exegesis, the result, as Auerbach has shown, was that in the Middle Ages there was 'an infinite wealth of combinations and allusions, crossed motifs and metaphors'.[10]

The images which relate to the actual mystical *unio*, however, have a special place in mystical metaphorical language. For these images, taken from the field of sensual contemplation and experience, do not merely serve as signs which indicate and suggest, but they contain in themselves an intensive, dynamic effectiveness, since they are to reflect the process and achievement of the mystical *unio*. The mystics realize full well that a language using sensual analogies cannot communicate the full reality of the mystical *unio*, but it must also be noted that this language *does* point in the direction of the achieved experience, since it is only in a sensuality which is, as it were, transposed and sublimated, that man is able to have spiritual experiences at all, which, if they are intensive, will always affect the whole man.

This is seen above all in the fact that mystical language so often falls back on the metaphorical language of love, and in this it reflects biblical usage, where the relationship between man and woman is seen as a worldly counterpart to the love of God for man, and where we have in the *Song of Songs* a text which has been taken to refer to the mystical love of the soul for God. The soul is not simply compared to a bride but actually *is* the divine bride and as such experiences God in a 'spiritualized sensuality'.

The reason why the *Song of Songs* is so important for a philological examination of mystical metaphorical language is because it reveals a very interesting relationship between metaphors used both in mysticism and in the literature of secular love — for the *Song of Songs* is originally a purely secular poem. Consequently it is not always easy to decide in the case of an individual mystical text whether the language of love contained in it is influenced by the *Song of Songs* or by secular love poetry. Comparatively recent theological research has shown that the metaphorical language of the *Song of Songs* is to a quite considerable extent a direct borrowing from the lyrical *topoi* of Old Egyptian love poetry.[11] This throws a very interesting light on mystical metaphorical language: as numerous works fell back again and again on the *Song of Songs* and interpreted it in a mystical manner, there slowly began to emerge a fairly constant metaphorical core of a kind of specialist mystical language containing age-old images such as being sick with love or melting with love-longing. But it would be premature to classify these inherited images as *topoi*. Since they frequently — though not always — communicate a personal experience, it is perhaps better to look upon them as ancient human symbols.

In their attempt to capture the *unio* with God in language, the medieval mystics frequently fall back on such ancient images or on already existing literary metaphors. It would therefore be wrong to assess their works, as indeed to assess any medieval works, using individuality and originality as primary yardsticks. For the specifically medieval relationship between tradition and the individual writer is clearly reflected in this conscious attempt to forge links with an already existing language: There was a deliberate effort to remain within the accepted teachings of the church, and the use of already existing linguistic forms was a kind of theological insurance. Yet, despite a certain tendency amongst the mystics to adapt to the language handed down through tradition, the leading lights amongst them were perfectly capable of changing the emphasis and filling the traditional modes of expression with new life, whilst still remaining within the framework of traditional teaching.

In view of the fact that a medieval author could take the same mystical images and metaphors from a variety of texts, we are here confronted with a very unusual and sometimes virtually insoluble source problem. For this reason no attempt will be made in this work to identify in any systematic way the sources for the individual images in the mystical texts. But since the Bible was the ultimate authority for the mystics,[12] we shall pay special attention to any biblical echoes in the metaphorical language of the English mystics.

A further preliminary consideration in examining the metaphorical language of English mysticism is that late medieval mysticism was a movement which encompassed the whole of Europe and which was sustained by a lay public. The desire for a personal experience of God was still widespread amongst the laity, especially in the fourteenth century. Hence the individual character of the mysticism in any one country can only be adequately appreciated when seen within the context of the whole. Thus, apart from a comprehensive survey of the metaphorical language of English mysticism, the second aim of this work is a detailed comparison with the other vernacular mysticisms, especially the German.

Whilst hitherto, apart from a few exceptions, Latin had been the language of theology and mysticism, a large number of texts written at this time to introduce the laity to contemplation now begin to reject Latin, and so there emerges, especially in Germany, a vernacular mysticism which in range and importance must be considered at least equal to contemporary texts still being written in Latin. But for English mysticism we must modify this statement somewhat. Whilst it is true that we have a considerable number of vernacular mystical texts in England in the fourteenth century, Richard Rolle, although undoubtedly a pioneer in the development of mystical prose in England, still wrote most of his works in Latin, since he clearly felt more sure of himself and less restricted in this medium, for the beauty of his Latin language and imagery far surpasses that of his English texts. Rolle's most important Latin works must therefore be included in any examination of medieval English mysticism.

The new vernacular mysticism and the Latin mysticism with its long tradition must be seen in the close relationship which they had to each other. For in their attempts to find linguistic expressions for their mystical themes, vernacular texts orientate themselves on the forms of expression found in Latin mysticism, and their mystical terms are frequently direct translations into the vernacular of Latin expressions. The importance of the fact that vernacular mysticism is firmly anchored in the Latin tradition was first pointed out about a century ago by Denifle,[13] and in our work, too, we shall have to consider the question of the vernacular imitation of Latin models.

Finally we must not forget that mysticism is in no sense a special religion within Christianity; it is only in a few fleeting moments of ecstasy that it anticipates the union with God, which is also the goal of the ordinary believer. This way to *unio* goes via the stages of *purgatio* and *illuminatio*, for the mystic can only hope to attain his goal when his asceticism is complete.[14] Since instruction in asceticism is often a preliminary task of mystical texts, mysticism must also be seen in conjunction with the relevant pastoral literature and literature of spiritual guidance, including sermons.[15]

II

It is somewhat problematical to speak of *the* medieval English mysticism. If we remember that Rolle was born about 1300 and that Julian of Norwich was still alive about 1416, then the main works of English mysticism were spread over a considerable period of time. This fact in itself must lead to certain differences between the individual authors both in their mysticism and in their linguistic style. Nevertheless there are two remarkable unifying features of English mysticism — a fundamentally affective character and a distaste for theological learning.[16]

These features are particularly pronounced in the work of the first great English mystic. It is conceivable that the specific features of Rolle's mysticism, which constantly revolves round the theme of the love of God, were partly influenced by the dominant theological climate in Oxford during the time he studied there. Since the time when Robert Grosseteste was active, the Franciscans, propagating a mysticism with Christ as its centre which was voluntaristic and which stressed feeling, had played an important role in Oxford. The influence of Duns Scotus, the 'Doctor Subtilis', was still felt. His system, although still scholastic, followed Bonaventure in changing the teaching of Thomas Aquinas in decisive points, notably in giving the primacy in the matter of knowledge of God to the will and love, and not, as Aquinas had done, to the intellect.[17] It is apparent from Rolle's works that he had a very comprehensive theological training, even if he wanted his mystical works to appear anything but theologically learned. The canon of his works has been established by H.E. Allen's extremely valuable work,[18] but it will be necessary at some stage to test the methods she uses to produce this canon.[19]

It has been consistently maintained for a long time that Rolle's mystical teaching was essentially different from that of later English mystics, in that he was conscious of a permanent mystical experience of God, whereas other authors maintain that the union with the divine was restricted to very few moments of ecstasy which alternated with long periods of a night of separation from God. It is possible that Rolle's mysticism has perhaps been misunderstood here and that, as Hodgson has already tried to show, it may well not be so far removed from the tradition of English mysticism.[20] Certainly Rolle cannot merely be considered a hermit preoccupied with his own subjective experiences, for he shows a clearly discernible interest in pastoral instruction, and he had — at least occasionally — an inclination for preaching.[21] His authority in matters concerning the spiritual life was so great in the Middle Ages that numerous manuscripts falsely claimed him as author to add weight to individual tracts.

It has become something of a platitude to criticize Rolle's metaphorical language and see in it one of the causes of mystical heresies and sects.[22] Even if it is true that an English Carthusian monk accused Rolle in the Late Middle Ages of having corrupted the enthusiastic sectarians,[23] this judgment cannot be accepted without examination when we evaluate Rolle's metaphorical language within the whole context of late medieval mysticism. As a mystic with strong poetic leanings he often omits to point out the symbolic character of his sensual metaphorical language. This makes it all the more open to the danger of being misunderstood. But if we attempt a comparison with continental mysticism, we find Rolle, as it were, in the best of company. For the works of writers like Mechthild of Magdeburg and Henry

Suso are full of sensual images whose figurative spiritual meaning is assumed. Rolle in fact at times points out the symbolic character of his metaphorical language and gives us to understand that his imagery is not intended to be an end in itself.[24] In his experience of God in the form of mystical music he emphasizes that this music is not to be compared with earthly sounds: 'non putet quis quod cantus ille sit corporalis'.[25] Rolle's statement in his *Incendium Amoris* where he speaks of having felt a burning inside him as if he were holding a finger into the fire,[26] which is perhaps the most criticized passage in his writings, becomes perfectly understandable in the light of these considerations. Such a statement is indeed not at all unusual in mysticism, as we shall see.[27] Rolle simply wishes to indicate that the intensity of his mystical experiences embraces his whole being. His controversial imagery is thus connected with the fact that the 'unified sensibility', to use Eliot's term, was particularly well-developed in the thirteenth and fourteenth centuries. A well-known example of this from German mysticism is the attempt by Henry Suso, who has a great deal in common with Rolle, to appropriate for himself sensually the symbol for Jesus (IHS) by carving it on his body.[28]

We shall see later the intensity with which Rolle drew on the rich treasure of European mystical language. This lends a certain plausibility to the thesis of M. Noetinger and H.E. Allen, [29] later supported by E. Underhill,[30] that Rolle studied for a time in Paris, the intellectual centre in the Middle Ages. Noetinger and Allen base their arguments for this on certain documents on the history of the Sorbonne in which Rolle's name is mentioned, although these documents only date from the seventeenth century. E.J.F. Arnould has tried to show that the details on Rolle in these documents are forgeries.[31] He is, however, unable to put forward any really convincing arguments to support his case, and we must therefore still reckon with the possibility that Rolle did in fact study in Paris.[32]

The second great English mystic clearly preferred to withdraw behind his works both as a person and as an author and remain anonymous. His most important works, *The Cloud of Unknowing* and *The Book of Privy Counselling*, along with a further work, *Pistle of Preier*, and other related texts edited by Hodgson in *Deonise HD*, together constitute the texts of the 'Cloud Group'. These contain very detailed instruction in mystical contemplation such as is not found in Rolle. The author does not, however, indicate how far his mysticism is based on a personal experience. Particularly characteristic of his mysticism is his great reliance on the pseudo-Dionysius, in that he starts from the premise that, since God is so different, only negative statements can be made about him. Thus the appropriate attitude of man towards God is prefigured in the climbing of Mount Sinai by Moses: just as Moses climbed Mount Sinai and, finally enveloped in a cloud, heard the voice of God, so too the man who wishes to be united with God must enter into the cloud of unknowing. Following the Dionysius commentary of the Augustinian Canon Thomas Gallus and affective mysticism generally, the *Cloud* too sees the unconditional love of God as the only possible way to experiencing the divine. Too little attention has as yet been paid to the fact that on English soil even before the *Cloud* Robert Grosseteste, when writing his commentary on the mystical theology of the pseudo-Dionysius, had already observed in his interpretation the central affective character of this text, and had spoken of man being united with God in a 'caligo' if he approaches him in exclusive love.[33]

The most difficult problem raised by the *Cloud of Unknowing* and its related tracts is the anonymity of the author. Certainly he had a very sound theological training and was acquainted with other works besides the pseudo-Dionysius, notably Augustine, Richard of St Victor, Thomas Aquinas and Richard Rolle. Since he concludes one of his works with a blessing, it is not unreasonable to assume that he was a priest,[34] albeit a priest who quite consciously identified himself with the movement of lay mysticism of the Late Middle Ages, and indeed counted himself one of the theologically untrained laity, not simply out of humility, but because he looked upon theological learning as a danger for the immediacy of the mystical experience.[35]

The fact that the author of the *Cloud* also deals with the problem of mystical language in some detail is very revealing for our context, for in so doing he shows a highly developed linguistic awareness which scholars have not hitherto given him sufficient credit for. Even in the paraphrase of the *Mystica Theologia* of the pseudo-Dionysius — which is very probably to be ascribed to him — he expresses his doubts about man's ability to make valid statements in the area of the divine. When man has entered into the darkness of unknowing, he experiences how language fails him in a 'schortyng of wordes', a 'madnes & . . . parfite vnresonabiltee'.[36] In his own *Cloud* he attacks the problem of mystical language at its very root in what is in fact a highly idiosyncratic manner, by pointing out that human language itself, since it is formed by the tongue which is an organ of the body, is therefore also physical in nature and as such unsuitable for reproducing the spiritual.[37] His first reason for discussing the problem of mystical language is that he wants to show those who are adept what linguistic form they should clothe their mystical love in, and what the nature of their prayer should be. Since language is physical in nature, the linguistic forms used when turning to God should be as short as possible — the shorter they are the more spiritual the language, the most suitable form therefore being the monosyllable:

> ʒif þee list haue þis entent lappid & foulden in o worde . . .
> take þee bot a litil worde of o silable; for so it is betir þen of two,
> for euer þe schorter it is, þe betir it acordeþ wiþ þe werk of þe
> spirite.[38]

Hence the author of the *Cloud* is almost painfully obsessed with his attempts to make the reader aware of the improvised, provisional character of mystical imagery. Like other mystical writers who are influenced by the pseudo-Dionysius, he gives a strong warning against taking literally the spatial dimension of language as expressed in the prepositions 'UP or DOUN, IN or OUTE, BEHINDE or BEFORE, ON O SIDE or ON OþER', where these are used in a mystical context.[39] Since God is a spiritual being, man should not imagine him as living in a spatial heaven situated somewhere above him, and further, since he cannot as a bodily creature enter heaven, he should not imagine his mystical way there as in some way an overcoming of spatial distance.[40] Such statements are rather astonishing in a medieval author, for here, long before Bultmann, we have a highly original mind attempting to demythologize the way we speak about God, for he was aware, in a way that no one else was, of the problem of mystical language. But not even the author of the *Cloud* can manage without using images, indeed his central concept of the cloud of unknowing is itself an unreal way of speaking, and, as we shall show in greater detail later, he frequently falls back on the language of sensual perception when explaining for the reader the possibility of human experience of God.

Amongst the few facts which we know from the life of Walter Hilton[41] is one which has perhaps not received the attention it deserves, namely the colophon from the Marseille Manuscript 729 from the fifteenth century, in which he is described as 'Parisius'. It not only states that he studied in Paris, but as B. Bischoff has pointed out to me, it indicates in a manner quite usual in the Middle Ages that he was awarded the title of Master of Theology in Paris: 'Explicit liber . . . editus a. . . Waltero Hiltonensi Parisius in sacra pagina laureato magistro'.[42] There is no good reason for doubting this statement.

Hilton too concerns himself with the problem of mystical metaphorical language. He points out for instance that the biblical motif
of raising the inner eye upwards is not to be understood literally and
spatially but figuratively.[43] But Hilton too falls back again and again
on a concrete graphic imagery. It may well be that he is thinking
disapprovingly of Rolle's frequent use of mystical metaphors of fire
when he states that whoever talks of the 'fire of love'[44] does not know
that this is merely a figurative expression; but Hilton himself on one
occasion also illustrates the process of *unio* by means of the traditional
image of the transformation of the soul into the fire of mystical love.[45]
It is often maintained that Hilton wrote his *Of Angels' Song* specifically
as a warning against excessive use of imagery in mystical language
such as is found in Rolle.[46] Whether this is true or not need not concern
us. But it must nevertheless be pointed out that Hilton, too, like Rolle
before him, speaks of the possibility of experiencing angelic music
which cannot be described and cannot be compared with earthly things
because it is something spiritual, transcending human understanding
and human powers of imagination.[47] Hilton's warning against an over-
use of metaphor will also have been dictated by his concern about
excesses of enthusiasm.

Like the author of the *Cloud*, Hilton draws on the thought of the
pseudo-Dionysius when in the second part of his *Scale of Perfection*
he says that once man has freed himself from all earthly ties, he becomes aware of a dark night. To illustrate the way out of this night
to the divine light, he introduces his famous allegory of the pilgrimage
to Jerusalem: on this journey (just as in the *Cloud*) it is the love of
God in the double sense of God's love for man and man's love for
God which enables the soul, once it has experienced the night, to see
a glimmering of the divine light, which then leads it all the way to
Jerusalem, i.e. to the immediate vision of God.[48]

The work of Julian of Norwich is different in kind from the mysticism of Rolle, the author of the *Cloud* or Walter Hilton. Julian's work,
too, reflects the influence of the pseudo-Dionysius whom she in fact
mentions directly on one occasion (as 'Seynt dyonisi of france'),[49] and
for her also a knowledge of God is unthinkable without love, which
she praises in a hymn at the end of her work. However, there is an
essential formal difference in that it is written as a report of experienced visions. What raises it well above average medieval visionary
literature is the fact that she does not merely relate the individual
mystical experience of her own soul, but that her theme is the divine
plan of salvation for all mankind, and that in her revelations she receives

answers to fundamental questions of human existence. The real attraction of Julian's *Revelations*, when considered as a literary text, is the very effective blending of the concrete imagery of her visions with thought processes which are often very abstract and sometimes even speculative. Incidentally Julian, who must have had a certain knowledge of mystical texts and biographies of the mystics,[50] also shows an awareness of the problem of mystical language. In her imagery she, too, occasionally prefers the simile to the metaphor: 'I saw ye soule so large as it were an endlesse warde'.[51] Again in her vision of a Lord and his Son who is seated at the right hand she adds that this expression is not to be understood literally but symbolically: 'But it is nott ment that the sonne syttyth on the ryght hand besyde as one man syttyth by an other in this lyfe. for ther is no such syttyng as to my syght in the trynyte'.[52]

The fact that we are including Margery Kempe in our study needs some justification. For the excessive emotional piety of this wife of a citizen of Lynn shows pathologically neurotic traits. Nevertheless some of the mystical passages in her autobiography are of some value. The very fact that Julian, who had a conversation with her, considered her piety to be genuine, forces us to include Margery in our study. Her work is a good example of the late phase in the development of affective devotion, which culminates in Franciscan mysticism, which shows an ever-increasing preoccupation in its devotion with the earthly life of Christ.[53]

Margery Kempe, who could neither read nor write, mentions a number of texts with which she was familiar and also several confessors. But without doubt her greatest model in terms of mystical experience was Richard Rolle with his *Incendium Amoris*, and she repeats almost verbatim his statement that he felt such a burning inside him as if he were putting his finger into the fire.[54] She is no longer capable of separating the sensual from the spiritual, and the former is indeed almost more important to her than the latter, for it is the proof ('tokne')[55] that she has been chosen.

In order to have as wide a base as possible for our comparison of the metaphorical language of English mysticism with the imagery of continental mysticism, we shall take into account certain other texts which are important for the affective spirituality of the English Middle Ages. The most important of these are the *Ancrene Wisse*[56], þe *Wohunge of Ure Lauerd*,[57] and the remaining texts of the 'Wooing Group', *A Talkyng of þe Loue of God*,[58] and *The Chastising of God's Children*.[59] We shall also have to consider Edmund of Abingdon's translation of the *Speculum Ecclesiae*[60] and the more important translations of continental mystical works. We shall, however, only make sporadic reference to religious poetry, since this field has already been well covered in the works of Woolf and Gray.[61]

I

*

The public for mystical literature in England

The reason why so many late medieval manuscripts with a mystical content have been preserved, both on the continent and in England, lies, as we have already indicated, in the religious change which took place in the High and Late Middle Ages. The individual was no longer satisfied with the security of the institutionalized church for his own private certainty of salvation, but was beginning to look for ways of attaining a quite personal and immediate relationship with God.[1] The mysticism of the Late Middle Ages is the clearest expression of this new piety. The effects of this religious fervour can be seen in the great numbers of people who were attracted to the religious life; there were especially many girls and women who determined on a life as a nun or recluse. It was necessary therefore to find ways and means of looking after the pastoral needs of this new public. Ever since the thirteenth century the pastoral needs of the nunneries in Germany had been catered for by the mendicant orders, especially the Dominicans. In England most of the numerous nunneries belonged to the Cistercian order, rather fewer to the Dominican, Franciscan and other orders. Special mention should be made of the Brigittine order which founded the Abbey of Syon early in the fifteenth century, which developed as an important centre of spirituality towards the end of the Middle Ages.[2]

Because of this new public there was a considerable need for contemplative instructional literature which had to be met. A large number of works were thus written, aimed specifically at this lay readership. The first great English text with a theme related to contemplation is the *Ancrene Wisse*, which was originally written as a rule of life for three women who had decided to live as recluses. Richard Rolle wrote his *English Psalter* and his tracts *Ego Dormio*, *The Commandment* and

The Form of Living for nuns or recluses. It is a recluse who asks Richard Misyn to translate Rolle's *Incendium Amoris* into the vernacular for her, and the first part of Hilton's *Scale* is addressed to a nun. The paraphrase of Catherine of Siena's *Dialogo della divina provvidenza* with the title *The Orcherd of Syon* was written specially for the Abbey of Syon. In addition there are numerous tracts, including such important works as *The Chastising of God's Children* and William Flete's *Remedies against Temptations*, where the individual reader is addressed as 'religious sister' or 'sister in God'.[3] A considerable amount of vernacular contemplative literature originated in fact from the pastoral efforts of the Carthusian order.[4]

The mystical literature read in the monasteries was largely in Latin. There were indeed some monasteries where vernacular texts were not even allowed, on the grounds that some essential meaning was inevitably lost in the translation into the vernacular, and that no language was comparable to Latin as a vessel for sacred thought. This explains, for instance, why in one particular Carthusian manuscript the *Cloud* and the *Mirror of Simple Souls* have a Latin translation appended.[5] But even if many mystical texts were written in Latin this does not imply that these texts reveal appreciably greater theological learning than the vernacular texts. For Rolle specifically dedicates his main work to the 'rudibus et indoctis, magis Deum diligere quam multa scire conantibus',[6] i.e. to monks who have no great need for extensive theological knowledge. In this Rolle is of one mind with the author of the *Cloud* who, in a manner very telling for the character of late medieval mysticism, speaks disparagingly of theological learning and compares it unfavourably with the uncomplicatedness of the lay person, the man who is 'lewyd', theologically uneducated.[7]

If, on the other hand, the texts written for the female monastic public choose the vernacular as their linguistic medium, the reason for this is primarily that they had to adapt themselves to the level of education of their readers. Although E. Power's extremely negative pronouncements on the educational level of nuns in medieval England can no longer be accepted,[8] it is nevertheless fairly certain that they could not keep pace with the knowledge of German nuns, which was in some cases very profound. It is true that in the thirteenth century the Franciscan John Peckham dedicates his Latin *Philomena* to a 'soror pia'[9] and that around 1300 Simon of Ghent, Bishop of Salisbury, when looking for a devotional book for his sisters, the nuns of Tarrent in Dorsetshire, translates the *Ancrene Wisse* into Latin,[10] but these are very striking exceptions. Latin was largely an incomprehensible language for English nuns as is shown by *The Myroure of Oure Ladye*, written specially for the nuns of the Abbey of Syon. For in the foreword to this work the author remarks that the nuns could only sing and read but 'ye can not se what the meanynge therof ys'; so that they might be able to understand what was in the liturgical texts which they had before them, the author wanted to translate the content exactly into the vernacular.[11]

What social classes did the readers of mystical texts come from? There was certainly an appreciable section of the public which came from the nobility. The three recluses for whom the *Ancrene Wisse* was originally written came from a noble family. Margaret Kirkeby, to whom Rolle dedicated his *English Psalter* and his tract *The Form of Living*, was from the landed gentry.[12] A considerable part of the readership, however, did not lead a monastic life but continued to live in the worldly situation they happened to be in. We learn a great deal about the interest of the nobility in mysticism from wills and bequests.[13] The widow of the nobleman Sir Brian Stapleton of Carlton had in her possession the tract *The Chastising of God's Children* and bequeathed to every Charterhouse in England the sum of 33s. 4d.[14] But the middle classes too were caught up in the movement, as is shown by the example of Margery Kempe who was from the upper middle class. The manuscript Harley 993, which contains Hilton's *Eight Chapters on Perfection* — the translation of a Latin work — was, according to the colophon, in the possession of a certain R. Holland, a sheepshearer and barber.[15] Religious and especially mystical literature was thus to be found in private libraries as well as in religious houses, these being usually nunneries or Augustinian and especially Carthusian monasteries.[16] The question of the provenance of the individual manuscripts containing mystical texts is one which scholarship still has to solve, and it is outside the scope of this work.

Instead we shall tackle a different problem: can we find fundamental differences between the vernacular texts written for a monastic public and those written for a lay public? N.F. Blake has recently answered this question very decisively in the affirmative.[17] He maintains that those texts written for the monastic reader model themselves on Latin theological writings, whereas those aimed at a general reading public are based on French originals. A text like the *Cloud*, which is written specifically for a reader leading a contemplative life withdrawn from the world, is, according to Blake, modelled on Latin monastic mysticism.[18] But a careful examination of the text shows that it was aimed not only at the specific addressee but also at a wider group of readers who were leading an active life as lay people and could not devote all their time to contemplation.[19] The manuscript tradition, too, shows that a work like the *Cloud* was both widely disseminated and highly esteemed.[20] In his tract þe *Book of Priue Counseling* the author of the *Cloud* expressly states that, although he is indeed writing for a specific reader ('in specyal to þi-self')[21] and not for a 'general'[22] public, he has no objections to his book being read by other readers with similar interests.[23] There can be no doubt that frequently the same works, although primarily written for a public of religious and recluses, were also aimed at a larger lay readership. The choice of English also tended to make the works available to a wider public and helped to blur the boundaries between monastic and lay readerships. Thus W. Flete's tract *Remedies against Temptations*, which we have already mentioned, is addressed in the first instance to a nun, but goes on to speak generally of 'man' and adds: 'quan I speke of man in þis wrytinge, take it boþe for man and woman, for so it is ment in alle suche writinges, for al is mankende.'[24] And what is stated in this text holds true for many vernacular texts.

At first sight an interesting tract like *The Abbey of the Holy Ghost*,[25] which is the English adaptation of a French original, would seem to confirm Blake's thesis that works written for a general lay public were based on French originals and were therefore different from monastic writings. But on closer examination this impression is quickly lost. For this text, in attempting to answer the question which was occupying many lay people at this time, namely how they could devote themselves to contemplation despite their worldly state, falls back on the allegory of the human heart as a spiritual monastery to illustrate its point. But just this allegory was developed in the monastic Latin tradition of Hugh of Folieto and taken over by the pseudo-Hugh of St Victor.[26] The French tract makes this allegory the central point of its whole argument. The readers are shown how they could lead a quasi-monastic life dedicated to the immediate experience of God if they were to build a spiritual monastery inside themselves. It therefore follows that such a text has basically the same aims as a monastic text, the only difference being that for the lay person a quasi-monastic situation has first to be created by way of analogy.

It was a similar occasion which caused Walter Hilton to write the work known as *Epistle on Mixed Life*. A 'wordli lord'[27] approached him and asked his advice on how his worldly duties could be reconciled with his desire for contemplation. Hilton advised him to maintain the social ties which he had and to devote his remaining time to contemplation, i.e. to lead a 'mixed' life. For Hilton, too, instruction in contemplation is essentially the same whether aimed at religious or laity.

With the principal mystical texts the converse question must be asked, namely whether those addressed did in fact devote themselves exclusively to contemplation.[28] Can we say with any certainty that they were addressed to monastic readers, and do the texts give any further details about their way of life? Rolle simply states that the reader is leading a monastic life or the life of a recluse, whereas the author of the *Cloud* goes into rather more detail in his works about the way of life. Of the person who is addressed in the *Cloud*, who is still very young, we learn that he was first an active Christian living in the world ('þou were leuyng in þe comoun degree of Cristen mens leuyng'),[29] but that after a while he embraced a 'more special state & forme of leuyng'[30] – perhaps, as Hodgson assumes,[31] as a lay brother – only to change this form of life later for a 'solitari forme & maner of leuyng',[32] so that he could lead a contemplative life. This may perhaps mean that he lived as a recluse; he is unlikely to have been a monk, for the *Cloud* certainly gives the impression of having been written for the layman: there is never any mention of vows, there are no Latin quotations – even vernacular Bible quotations are not accompanied by the Vulgate text – and even when borrowed terms like 'Lesson, Meditacion, & Oryson' are used they are clarified for the reader by the addition of the more usual terms 'Redyng, þinkyng & Preiing'.[33] If we remember that in the Middle Ages the term 'withdrawal from the world', which is implied by the words 'solitari forme ... of leuyng', could be used in a merely figurative sense to mean that the soul had freed itself from the world,[34] it does not even follow that the person addressed need have been a recluse in the strict sense. His way of life must have afforded him the possibility of being 'contynowely'[35] in a contemplative state, but in the *Book of Privy Counselling* there is an additional remark to the effect that the contemplative attitude is to be adopted in the most varied of activities, 'wheþer þei be actyue or contemplatyue',[36] and there follows a list of daily activities ('ete & drink, sleep & wake, go & sit, speke & be stille, ligge & rise, stonde & knele, *renne & ride*'),[37] a list which is in fact so broad that it could even imply a secular way of life. Furthermore the author of the *Cloud*, like Hilton, stresses that contemplation is only meaningful when coupled with active charity, and he therefore urges his reader to be a 'profiter ... vnto þe comunite'.[38] Thus it is clear that the author does not see the mystic as an esoteric person who has turned his back on the world, but assigns him a firm position and function in society.[39]

It would certainly be false to label the writings of the *Cloud*-author a 'Discipline of the Secret', for he quite clearly anticipates a public which wants to combine its contemplative leanings with active social involvement.[40]

The tract *Pistle of Discrecioun of Stirings*, which was almost cert-tainly written by the author of the *Cloud*, gives us an interesting addition to our picture of the readership of these mystical texts. This tract would appear to be addressed directly to a reader who has deter-mined to lead a life which is partly contemplative, partly active. For in it the author answers the question put to him by the reader about how he can fulfil the double duty of immersing himself in contempla-tion and yet remain socially involved, by saying: 'þou askist me counsel of silence and of speking, of comoun dietyng & of singulere fastyng, of *dwelling in companye* & of only wonyng by þiself.'[41] The answer the author gives to such a question is quite remarkable, because he explains that God is not tied to any specific way of life but is to be found, as it were, midway between the strictly contemplative life and life within human society.[42] The attitude which the author of the *Cloud* adopts here consciously follows the Pauline concept of the 'freedom of the children of God', for he quotes St Paul's statement ' "Vbi spiritus Domini, ibi libertas"; "þere where þe spirite of God is, þer is fredom." '[43] Hence he can leave it to the discretion of the reader to decide when he wants to be alone and when he wants to seek the company of others, etc.:

> And þerfore speke whan þee list & leue whan þee list; ete whan þee list and fast whan þee list; be in companie whan þee list & be by þiself whan þee list; so þat God and grace be þi leder. Late fast who fast wil, and be only who wil, and lat holde silence who hold wil; bot holde þee bi God, þat no man begileþ.[44]

It is clear that such a mystical piety based on Pauline freedom is very unlike the life of the religious which is clearly defined by vows.

Walter Hilton wrote mystical texts for religious as well as for the laity: his *Scale*, for instance, is addressed to a monastic public, whilst the *Epistle on Mixed Life*, which we have already mentioned, is a document reflecting his pastoral concern for the laity. There is one text of Hilton's which is very important in our context, and which we only know about indirectly from the British Library manuscript Harley 2406, f.58-60[v]. This manuscript contains a letter to an unknown addressee from his equally anonymous confessor. The confessor tells

of having received a letter from Hilton on how to instruct the addressee, and goes on to explain the content of the letter. This short text,
which begins with the quite neutral form of address 'My dere frende',
is addressed to a woman – and this should serve as a warning to us
that some of the writings of the *Cloud*-group which are addressed to
a 'gostly frend' may well also have been written to women. Hilton
urges this woman to persist in her newly chosen way of life, even if
'prosperite and welth'[45] should try to tempt her away from it. She
should practise humility towards here 'sesteres' with whom she is
living. She should also not speak much and not overrate her good
works. What evil she might see in the world – for instance two lovers
lying naked together in bed – she should condemn, but at the same
time remember that in the same circumstances she would have sinned
more.[46] As 'reules' for living Hilton also gives her general directions on
how to live a life pleasing to God, stressing especially conscience as the
main guiding principle ('þe reule of a wel sette conscience').[47] This
woman can hardly have been a nun, for she has obviously not yet
cut herself off completely from the world nor taken any vows, and
she is not living permanently with other sisters, for she can see what
happens in the world. Apparently too her riches may still prove to be
a seductive attraction. Perhaps she is a lay sister who has not yet made
her profession. What appears to me to be especially important in this
text is the fact that the duty to follow the dictates of one's conscience
alone replaces the monastic vows, and this again, in a very striking
manner, creates an impression of great spiritual freedom. This strong
emphasis on conscience is reminiscent of the *Abbey of the Holy Ghost*,
a work written for the laity, in which conscience is the foundation on
which the spiritual monastery is built.[48] The fact that the tract *The
Abbey of the Holy Ghost* comes immediately after the text describing
Hilton's letter in the manuscript Harley 2406 can scarcely be mere
chance. And it is therefore perfectly possible that Hilton's letter too
was aimed at a lay readership, perhaps one leading a quasi-monastic
life.

Since Hilton's letter was written to a woman who was possibly
living in a non-monastic community of women, we must ask ourselves what lay communities existed in England for fostering mystical
piety. And here the evidence is very sparse indeed. A community of
contemplative women who have not completely severed their ties with
the world is reminiscent of the Beguine movement which arose in the
Netherlands and to which such great mystics as Hadewych and Mechthild of Magdeburg belonged.[49] Certainly the Vita of the famous Marie

d'Oignies was translated into English – the translation has been preserved.[50] And as early as the thirteenth century Robert Grosseteste
praises the Beguine way of life as the highest stage of Christian perfection.[51] It is interesting in our context that in one manuscript the
French source for the tract *The Abbey of the Holy Ghost* specifically
refers to a 'beguinaige'. The English translator did not take this term
over directly but replaced it with the neutral term 'religione',[52] but
this is not to say that there were no communities of women in England
which were not at least like the Beguines. It is more important to see
that the specific spirituality of the *Abbey of the Holy Ghost* and
Hilton's letter possibly have a certain affinity with the Beguine movement.

It is some time since Jusserand put forward the rather daring thesis
that the three noble women living in seclusion for whom the *Ancrene
Wisse* in its original form was written were Beguines.[53] Scholars have
not given this thesis much support, for in contrast to the Beguines,
these three women no longer had any ties with the world whatsoever.
They took the vows of obedience, chastity and permanence of resi-
dence. It is however questionable whether it is mere chance that we
have to assume that the original version of the *Ancrene Wisse* dates
from around the year 1200,[54] a time which saw the first flourishing
of the Beguine movement. It is safest to reckon with the possibility
that the recluses may indeed not have felt themselves to be Beguines
and that there may never have been a genuine imitation of this form
of female piety in England, but that nevertheless this community of
three women was indirectly influenced by this new spirituality and
that there may well have been communities of women in England
which were like Beguine communities especially in the fourteenth
century.

Unfortunately we do not know much about contemplative
communities of men in England either. Particularly important for us
is the late fifteenth-century Latin translation of the *Cloud* and the *Mirror
of Simple Souls* by the Carthusian Richard Methley which we have
already touched upon. A prologue to this translation contains a brief
introduction to pseudo-Dionysian mysticism. There is a warning against
seeing the *unio* between God and man as a complete fusion of the
divine and the human, and this warning is given 'contra heresim begardorum'.[55] This remark indicates that the male counterpart to the
Beguine movement was also known in England, and that here, as on
the continent, it tended towards excessive enthusiasm. Why else would
Methley have needed to warn against such dangers? This is supported

by the fact that we also find warnings against mystical enthusiasts in other Middle English texts, especially the *Cloud*[56] and the *Chastising of God's Children*. This last-named work is not specifically directed against the Beghards but against another mystical sect – the Brethren of the Free Spirit,[57] who must therefore somehow have become known and also have attracted followers in England. For them the personal freedom of the individual was paramount and could develop to complete quietistic inactivity.

An excellent study of the spread of this religious movement across Europe was written some time ago by R. Guarnieri. She quotes as an English example an enthusiast by the name of William Thorpe from the early fifteenth century, and remarks that he did not join the English Lollards but the continental ones, who considered themselves to be Brethren of the Free Spirit.[58] She also shows that the freedom of the spirit is indeed originally a biblical theme and is therefore frequently echoed in tradition, but that in the movement which takes its name from this idea it is given a much more prominent position and is, as it were, radicalized. Since the author of the *Cloud*, as we have seen, attaches such great importance to the theme of the freedom of the spirit, he must somehow have become familiar with the movement of the Brethren of the Free Spirit. Indeed this theme must have been very topical in England at the time, for it plays a very important role in Hilton, which needs to be examined in some detail: The reader of the *Scale* is given the rather remarkable advice that he should take care to progress beyond religious 'customs'[59] and not to value these more highly than 'þe fredom of þin hert'.[60] And at the same time Hilton attacks dangerous sectarian misunderstandings by people who take 'fredom of spirit'[61] to mean living your life according to your own will. It is quite possible to see in 'fredom of spirit' a reference to the Brethren of the Free Spirit. When treating this theme Hilton too, like the author of the *Cloud*, is concerned to preserve orthodoxy. It is also worth noting in our context that the very interesting *Mirror of Simple Souls*, the French original of which almost constitutes a work of the Brethren of the Free Spirit,[62] has an affinity with the texts of the *Cloud*-group and a certain affinity also with Hilton. It is true that Richard Methley in his Latin translation, and before him the translator who only gives his initials 'M. N.', tried to tone down the extremely daring theses of the original and to reconcile them with orthodox teaching. But it is significant that M. N. wants to make the French mystical text available to English readers who are called to this freedom of the spirit or soul, for he speaks of 'goostli louers, þat ben

disposed and clepid to þis hiȝe eleccion of þe fredom of soule'.[63]
Chastising too expressly warns against a heretical misunderstanding
of the freedom of the spirit.[64]

Let us return to the author of the *Cloud*. Although we know virtually nothing about his person, it is clear from his works that he founded
a circle of pupils[65] with whom he maintained lively oral and written
contact. This is in fact the purpose of his extant writings.[66] Hilton, too,
enjoys writing to his pupils to give them spiritual instruction. This
relationship between the author and public is in some ways reminiscent
of the situation on the continent. For in Germany there was a group of
contemplatives calling themselves 'Friends of God' who maintained
frequent oral and written contact with one another. This group was
mainly under the guidance of Dominicans, and Tauler's correspondence
with Rulman Merswin and Henry of Nördlingen's correspondence with
Margaretha Ebner are particularly well-known examples of the kind of
contact they maintained.[67] Just like the author of the *Cloud*, the
Friends of God are very hostile to theological learning and insistent on
humility. But of course these considerations must remain mere assump-
tions. For we can hardly go so far as to see the form of address 'Goostly
freende in God',[68] which the author of the *Cloud* loves so much, as
proof that the movement of the Friends of God had spread to England,
for the idea of friendship with God has a long tradition going back to
Platonism and is fully developed in the writings of the Fathers.[69] We
have, however, in the *Treatise of Perfection of the Sons of God* the
translation of a text of the Friends of God.[70]

Jusserand also produced an idiosyncratic thesis many years ago
on the question of whether there were Friends of God in England.
He sees the same spirituality which is characteristic of the Friends of
God permeating *Piers Plowman*, though he does not actually go so far
as to postulate any direct influence.[71] But this thesis is not really very
convincing. It is true that *Piers Plowman* cannot be ignored in any
assessment of mystical movements in England, but what is reflected
in this text is quite clearly the *Devotio Moderna*. A particular characteristic of this movement, started by G. Groote and the Brethren of the
Common Life, is an imitation of the cross to be practised in daily life.
The *Devotio Moderna* also includes a call to poverty and humility.
When we see in *Piers Plowman* the radical call to the *Imitatio Christi*
and the demand for humble brotherly love in daily life, there can
scarcely be any doubt that offshoots of this lay movement reached
England. Certainly we have Middle English translations of parts of the
Imitatio Christi, ascribed to Thomas à Kempis, which is the principal

text of the *Devotio Moderna*.[72]

Some time ago in his introduction to an edition of the *Cloud* in German[73] E. von Ivánka saw the special quality of this work in the fact that it unites in a quite original way the negative theology of the Areopagite with the *Devotio Moderna*. He pointed out the call to humility and to loving surrender to God. But this reference is certainly not sufficient proof for the presence of the *Devotio Moderna* in English mysticism. For in a text like the *Cloud* it is not the imitation of the cross which is in the foreground, and a call to humility is not of itself sufficient to prove the presence of the *Devotio Moderna*, for it is a fundamental theme of the Christian religion. But there are nevertheless certain late medieval English texts which are utterly imbued with the spirit of the *Devotio Moderna*. There is first of all the translation of the first three books of the *Imitatio Christi*, then the tract þe *Lyfe of Soule*,[74] in which the necessity for a humble imitation of Christ is put before the reader and impressed upon him — and here the author very frequently goes back directly to New Testament utterances — and finally the *Book to a Mother*,[75] a work which shows similar tendencies and which, like þe *Lyfe of Soule*, dates from the late fourteenth century. The reason why Hilton was later thought to be the author of the *Imitatio Christi*, parts of which were in circulation under the title *Musica Ecclesiastica*, is perhaps because people associated him with the *Devotio Moderna* since he was an Augustinian Canon, and it was this order which initiated the movement. And in fact the pronounced christocentric orientation of Hilton's mysticism and its sound anchoring in the Bible do give it a certain affinity with the *Devotio Moderna*.

Our examination of the question of the public of the mystical literature in England leads us to conclude that the contemplative interest of the non-monastically organized laity was quite considerable, and that E. Underhill's assertion that there were no 'lay-groups' in England[76] needs to be somewhat modified, since various offshoots of the continental mystical lay movement must have reached England. This leads us to the question of the interrelation between continental and English mysticism, which will be the subject of the next chapter.

II

*

The interrelation between continental and English mysticism

Our investigations so far have shown that the mystical movement in England did not occur in complete insular isolation. But before beginning any individual analyses we should perhaps indicate briefly the most important pointers we have from the Middle Ages about possible interrelations between continental and English mysticism.

The first question we must ask ourselves is whether Master Eckhart as the greatest German mystic exercised any influence on English writers, a question which has already occupied scholars on many occasions. D. Knowles for instance in his book on English mysticism in the Middle Ages comes to the conclusion that the anonymous *Cloud* reflects at least some of the characteristic traits of Rhenish Dominican mysticism.[1] But it is not as simple as that. On the contrary the question as to whether English mysticism might possibly have been influenced by German mystical spirituality is a very complex one and one which merits a renewed investigation. Some statements by English mystics where critics have thought to discern Eckhart's influence, reveal on closer examination that they are more probably in the tradition of pseudo-Dionysian mysticism. This pseudo-Dionysian mysticism was not merely familiar to a few individuals in the Late Middle Ages but was known in the most important countries in Europe where it always led to comparably high literary performances. In Italy, for instance, we can discern a familiarity with Dionysius the Areopagite in Dante's *Commedia*[2] or in the mysticism of Catherine of Genoa.[3] Towards the end of the fourteenth century in Spain — at the same time that the *Cloud* and the *Scale* appeared — the Spanish mystic Fra Antoni Canals wrote his principal work, the *Scala de Contemplació*,[4] which shows quite clear pseudo-Dionysian traits: like the *Cloud*, he speaks of the dark night which the soul enters into in its search for God.

Critics have hitherto always been surprised to find that the main thoughts of the *Cloud* are also found in the mystical writings of John of the Cross from the sixteenth century. But, already simultaneously with the *Cloud* and Hilton, the vernacular reception of the pseudo-Dionysius was starting in Spain.

In her edition of the *Cloud*, P. Hodgson, when searching for points of contact between the *Cloud* and Rhenish mysticism, draws attention to the tract *De Adhaerendo Deo* and notes important parallels[5] which are also stressed by Knowles. But Knowles rightly adds that this work by John of Kastl was written *after* the *Cloud* and that it is not an original work but a compilation.[6] It is worth looking at the text from which John of Kastl took his excerpts for *De Adhaerendo Deo* — Rudolf of Biberach's *De Septem Itineribus Aeternitatis*. This text, which in its turn is also a compilation, is of great value for research into mysticism, because, in contrast to many other texts, the author frequently indicates that he is quoting and where he is quoting from.[7] The text is important for our purposes because precisely those sections in *De Adhaerendo Deo* which show great similarity with the *Cloud* are taken from *De Septem Itineribus Aeternitatis*. All the features common to *De Adhaerendo Deo* and the *Cloud* which Knowles noted[8] are already present in Rudolf, including above all the expressly affective interpretation of the pseudo-Dionysius. For central to Rudolf's work is the thought that God can ultimately be recognized only through loving and in a night of not-knowing, and here Rudolf draws on Thomas Gallus and Robert Grosseteste amongst others.[9] It is thus perfectly possible that here we have a point of contact between Rhenish and English mysticism. Certainly, if we wish to postulate an influence of German mysticism on the English mystics, then Rudolf is more likely than Eckhart, whose primary thesis is an intellectual understanding of God.[10] Since the original version of Rudolf's work was written in Latin, we can even reckon with the possibility that the author of the *Cloud* was acquainted with Rudolf's work, 91 manuscripts of which are still extant today.

It is worth noting incidentally that the work of the Franciscan Rudolf of Biberach was mainly disseminated among Carthusians and Augustinians.[11] Thus it seems perfectly possible that the *Cloud* was written by a Carthusian or an Augustinian rather than by a Dominican.[12] And it was in any case, as we have already indicated, the Carthusians who were largely responsible for the dissemination of mystical texts, especially vernacular texts, in England. It is becoming increasingly clear today that the individual orders maintained strong international contacts. But in work on English mysticism hardly anyone has yet seriously considered the possibility that the Augustinians may have played a mediating role. But we should remember that Walter Hilton, whose work shows such strong similarities with the *Cloud* group, was himself an Augustinian and that, as we have already mentioned, he was thought to be the author of the first three books of the *Imitatio Christi* by the Augustinian Canon Thomas à Kempis. It is by no means impossible that precisely his order could have brought Rudolf's main work to England.

We have already seen the great importance of the Carthusians for English mysticism in the manuscript which brings together the *Cloud*, its Latin translation and the *Mirror of Simple Souls*. E. Underhill was the first to recognize the high quality of this text a long time ago. She called it a connecting link 'by which the contemplative tradition of western Europe reached England and affected the development of our native mystical school';[13] indeed she saw it as 'one of the missing links in the history of English mysticism'.[14] Even if the work of Rudolf of Biberach really does represent a connecting link to continental mysticism, this does not make Underhill's conclusions any less valid today. For apart from the theme of freedom which we touched upon in the previous chapter, there is a whole series of clear connections between the *Mirror* and the *Cloud* which we shall go into later. It was only in 1946 that Margherita Porete, who was burned as a heretic in Paris in 1310, was identified as the author of the original of the *Mirror*.[15] As C. Kirchberger remarked in 1927, the work is in some ways reminiscent of Eckhart who, as she pointed out, spent some time in Paris and must have begun preaching there by the time the original of the *Mirror* was written.[16] Since in fact some thoughts of the *Miroir des Simples Ames* seem to echo Eckhart — above all for example the central theme that the contemplative soul must not wish for anything any more, not even God — it is quite possible that Eckhart's mysticism became known in England in this indirect manner. But we must immediately add a cautionary note: on the one hand such important Eckhartian themes as the birth of God in the soul are completely lacking in the *Mirror*, and on the other hand the English translation is very concerned to preserve orthodoxy. Hence we can at best only speak of a partial, indirect acquaintance with Eckhart. It is also particularly noticeable that, unlike Eckhart, the *Mirror* does not postulate the possibility of an intellectual understanding of God, but, like Rudolf of Biberach, the commentary on the pseudo-Dionysius by Thomas Gallus and the *Cloud*, places its emphasis on the affective experience of God.

A connection has often been postulated between Tauler, a disciple of Eckhart's, who was more concerned with the practicalities of pastoral work, and Walter Hilton. But there is no concrete evidence to show that Hilton could have become acquainted with Tauler's mysticism. It is not even certain that texts of Tauler's ever reached England. Allen has maintained that the tract, *The Chastising of God's Children*, draws heavily on a sermon of Tauler's where he warns against the heresies of the Brethren of the Free Spirit.[17] But if we examine Allen's thesis, we find that all the formulations in *Chastising* on the question of heretical mystical movements are to be found, often verbatim, in Ruysbroeck's great work *Die Gheestelike Brulocht*, and that it is without doubt this work which is the source for *Chastising*, since there are also many other passages which are either taken from it or which draw heavily on it.[18]

If we are discussing a possible influence of Rhenish Dominican mysticism on the English mystics, then we must consider the work of Julian of Norwich where critics have claimed to find echoes of German mysticism. The parallels pointed out by Dalgairns,[19] Underhill[20] and Reynolds,[21] which we shall go into later, are certainly not convincing enough. Let us for instance take the conclusion of Sr Anna Maria Reynolds that Julian's concept of God as a mother shows the influence of Eckhart.[22] This is simply not tenable, since here Julian is not taking up an Eckhartian thesis but a traditional teaching of divine motherhood, which, although perhaps relatively rare, is nevertheless certainly not unknown.[23] In our later examinations we shall have similar reservations about the parallels which other critics have thought to discern.

Nevertheless Julian as the one great female English mystic is very revealing for us in other respects. For the way in which she — together with Margery Kempe — fits the pattern of the late medieval female mystic as this pattern developed on the continent is quite remarkable and cannot be due to mere chance. The biographical details contained in her works are sketchy, but even these together with the whole style of her *Revelations* reveal surprising affinities with the continental female visionary mystics. At the beginning of her work she tells us of three requests she has made to God for grace[24]: first for Christ's passion to be made present to her, then for a physical sickness, and finally for three wounds — the wound of contrition, the wound of compassion and the wound of loving desire for God. She adds interestingly that she wishes for these wounds because a cleric has told her of the three wounds of St Cecilia.

These requests of Julian's correspond completely to precise details which we know from the biographies of continental female mystics. The starting point for Julian's vision — the concrete and immediate reliving of the passion of Christ and the christocentric character of her mysticism — is often found among continental female mystics, for instance Christina Ebner and Adelheid Langmann, as well as Elizabeth of Spalbek or Marie d'Oignies, both of whom like Julian chose to embrace the life of an incluse. There are even parallels in specific details: when contemplating the crucifix, for instance, Marie d'Oignies suddenly feels rays emanating from it and penetrating her heart;[25] Julian similarly tells how her cell had become quite dark but the crucifix remained bright.[26]

Julian's wish for a physical sickness also deserves closer examination. For as E. Benz has shown, there is often a correspondence between vision and sickness in that sometimes the visionary is also sick, or a sick person through the gift of vision regains physical health, or sickness is experienced as a cleansing process which as *purgatio* or *mortificatio* is a prerequisite for the experiencing of visions.[27] Margaretha Ebner, for instance, in 1312 receives such a preparatory sickness before beginning her contemplative life. A particularly good example is Gertrud of Helfta for whom the sickness is a way of 'exinanitio'.[28] Gertrud comes to understand it as a "strengthening of the spirit" for the love of God, a "softening of the wax of the soul", such that the divine seal can be impressed upon it when it has been softened through the pain of sickness'.[29] Understood in this way, sickness is nothing less than a gift of divine grace. We read in the *Book of the Sisters of Töss* that the greatest praise of a good man is when one can say of him 'das er ain lidender mensch sy'.[30] From here it is only a small step to the rare explicit request to receive a sickness. And this is the step which Julian takes. She asks for a 'sickness unto death' when she is thirty years old as a gift of grace which she then receives. She becomes ill, feels the parts of her body dying one after the other, but from the moment she begins to experience death onwards she begins to recover and then receives her visions. Benz has pointed out that the fact that Julian wishes this sickness for herself for precisely her thirtieth year is intended as a conscious analogy with the life of Christ. Consequently it is 'the idea and the practice of the imitatio Christi in the sense of a re-living of his passion and death which constitute the religious precondition for this desire for suffering'.[31] Afterwards she is completely restored to health although she would have preferred to be freed from the earthly world. It was because of a surfeit of the world in view of her desire for Heaven that Marie d'Oignies had earlier asked for a sickness — although admittedly only at the end of her life.[32] The related request for wounds is also found amongst continental female mystics. Muschg tells of the wish of Swiss nuns to be granted the five wounds of Christ,[33] and Julian's request for the wound of loving desire for God is to be understood as the attempt to become the beloved of the divine lover in the sense of the *Song of Songs*, a theme which we shall have more to say about later.

It fits into the pattern of the medieval female mystic as we know it from the continent that Julian should style herself 'a Symple creature vnlettyrde'.[34] This formulation has caused problems for critics seeking to discover what level of education Julian had. We can get a clearer idea of how we are to interpret this statement if we consider it alongside information we have from continental female mystics about their level of education. We find an amazingly similar statement from Mechthild of Magdeburg, who says 'wa ich der schrift vngeleret bin'.[35] This is all the more interesting for us in that elsewhere she says 'Nu gebristet mir túsches, des latines kan ich nit',[36] a statement clearly meant to be taken literally. This implies that Mechthild had a certain level of education but not an academic one, and had to 'rely on religious instruction in German'.[37] And Julian's term 'vnlettyrde' hence almost certainly means knowing no Latin and probably also no French.[38] The fact, too, that on one occasion she speaks of the alphabet implies that she had a certain level of education. In Mechthild's case we know that she acquired her considerable familiarity with the tradition of mystical formulations from the confessors who came from the Beguine House in Magdeburg, especially from the Dominican Henry of Halle.[39] Julian's position will have been much the same. She, too, will have become familiar with the important thoughts and motifs of Christian mysticism and with the Bible through father confessors and spiritual directors. These may well have been Augustinians, since there was an Augustinian Friary in the same street where she lived as an incluse.[40] But a Dominican influence cannot be rejected out of hand, as the Dominicans had important houses in the vicinity of Norwich.

The whole pattern of Julian's *Revelations* shows an affinity with the works of continental female mystics: she experiences sixteen 'shewings', in which, or through which, the incluse has theological truths transmitted to her. Thus we have one great example in England of the visionary literature which abounds on the continent. But whereas affective and emotional excesses can be observed in many texts of continental visionary literature, in which the visions degenerate and become an end in themselves, in Julian's case the vision always remains, in a very original and individual way, the medium for a spiritual content.

Possessed of a remarkable self-confidence, Julian dares to oppose the view prevalent at the time that in spiritual matters a woman has to remain silent, and she decides to become an author herself for the edification of others: 'Botte for I am a woman schulde I therfore leve that I schulde nou3t telle 3owe the goodenes of god.'[41] These words reveal a maturity quite remarkable in a lay person and especially in a woman. It has been observed that 'it was precisely in the visionary literature of mysticism that woman in Germany attained her literary independence and maturity',[42] and here we can see very interestingly an exactly parallel process in Julian. Underhill is quite right when she calls Julian 'the first English woman of letters'.[43] In view of all the parallels with continental mysticism which we have been able to observe, we must conclude that her knowledge of continental models must have given Julian a decisive impetus for her literary initiative and her mystical experiences.

Margery Kempe too shows great self-confidence — especially in her dealings with a cleric in an episode similar to the story from the continent of the pious Beguine.[44] Margery also has earned lasting fame — apart from the writing of her mystical experiences — as the author of the first great autobiography in English. Since, in contrast to Julian, she could neither read nor write, her experiences were written down at her request by clerics. A man from 'Dewchlond'[45] wrote down the first version of the first book, which again confirms connections with the continent, where German female mystics had preceded her in writing autobiographies. On the contintent too clerics often undertook the actual writing down, as in the cases of Christina Ebner and Bridget of Sweden to mention just two.[46] The fact that Margery has a sickness before the beginning of her mystical experiences[47] again corresponds to the pattern of female mysticism. Her decision to embrace the contemplative life only comes very late when she is already married — another biographical detail for which there are precedents on the continent.[48] Further parallels with continental female mystics are, amongst others, her wish for the marriage bond to be dissolved so that she can immerse herself unconditionally in the contemplation of God,[49] her outbursts of tears,[50] her awareness that she has been specially chosen,[51] and her gift of second sight which enables her to foretell future events.[52] As far as her mystical experiences are concerned, these manifest themselves, as is the case with some continental women, not only in visions but also in auditions. Whilst it may be true that her visions mirror more strongly than Julian's the morbidly exaggerated sensibility of many continental female mystics, it must also be pointed out that these in some respects surpass what we read in Margery, as for example when in a North German mystical tract the nuns are urged to conceive and give birth to Christ.[53]

We possess certain indications as to which texts Julian and Margery and the other English mystics can have known, not least in the references we find scattered in Margery's autobiography. She expressly mentions Bridget of Sweden, Marie d'Oignies and Elizabeth of Hungary, whom she clearly looked upon as model characters for herself.[54] We have Middle English translations of Bridget's *Revelations*[55] and the Middle English *vita* of Marie d'Oignies, the latter in a manuscript which also contains the *vita* of Elizabeth of Spalbek, the *vita* of Christina Mirabilis and a letter of Steven of Siena about Catherine of Siena.[56] We also have a fifteenth-century translation of the main work of Catherine of Siena,[57] whose pupil and friend was William Flete, an Augustinian living in the Italian town of Lecceto. From here he sent a series of letters to his English brethren for their spiritual instruction.[58] We also have a Middle English translation of Mechthild of Hackeborn's *Liber Specialis Gratiae*. This *Booke of Gostlye Grace*,[59] which may have found its way to England even before the middle of the fifteenth century,[60] was apparently very popular there, since it is often mentioned by name in monastic library catalogues.[61] As Allen suspected, Margery Kempe was probably influenced by the visions reported in this work.[62]

Allen tries to identify the Elizabeth of Hungary whom Margery Kempe refers to, as the daughter of King Andrew II of Hungary and wife of the Landgrave Ludwig of Thuringia, and thus as St Elizabeth.[63] But it is very doubtful whether Margery meant this saint, who was certainly not a mystic and whom Margery does not refer to as a saint. But there is another Elizabeth of Hungary who fits more readily into Margery's context: in the year 1309 Elizabeth of Hungary, daughter of the last Arpád and rightful heir to the throne, entered the famous Dominican nunnery of Töss where she died in 1337.[64] Suso's influence at Töss was very strong, since his soulmate Elsbeth Stagel, who wrote the *vitae* of the sisters of Töss which we have already mentioned, lived there. The book of the Sisters of Töss also contains a *vita* of Elizabeth, who appears to have been the pride of the nunnery,[65] and in this *vita* emphasis is laid on the phenomenon of tears as a special characteristic. It is probably this Elizabeth whom Margery meant. This would

seem to indicate that in England German female mysticism was considered exemplary.

It is also worth noting that it was not merely in Germany that the
mystic Suso had the gift of being able to address mystically inclined
women, for an abridged translation of his *Horologium Sapientiae*
appeared in Middle English, and again it was women who particularly
enjoyed reading it. This early fifteenth-century translation is specifically addressed to a woman and is found incidentally in the same manuscript as the *vitae* of the other female mystics which we have already
mentioned.[66] Wichgraf has shown that there were Suso manuscripts
in England at an even earlier date.[67] The tract *The Chastising of God's
Children*, which was written for a nun, was clearly influenced by the
Horologium Sapientiae,[68] as were the morality play *Wisdom* and the
tract *Speculum Spiritualium*.

The mystical styles of Richard Rolle and Suso are very akin to
each other in the fervour and imagery of their language. It is quite
possible that Rolle, who was a contemporary of Suso's, had learned
about him in some way. Even manuscript illuminations show a remarkable parallel between the two mystics in one particular detail. Just as
the British Library manuscripts, Cotton MS. Faustina B VI, pt. II
(f. 8^v) and Addit. MS. 37049 (f. 52^v) — both from the first half of
the fifteenth century — depict Rolle with a monogram of Christ on
his breast, so too several manuscripts of Suso's *Exemplar* — the earliest
from the second half of the fifteenth century — portray Suso with the
monogram of Christ.[69] This parallel does not of course prove any
relationship between Rolle and Suso, as the manuscripts date from well
after Rolle's death, but it does highlight the important point of affinity
between them, for a deep devotion to the name of Jesus, which arose
in connection with the mysticism of St Bernard, permeates the works
of both men[70]: the monogram of Christ is presumably used in the case
of Rolle because of his *Encomium Nominis Jesu*, his famous exegesis
of the verse 'oleum effusum nomen tuum' from the *Song of Songs*;
the illuminator of the *Exemplar* probably chose the monogram because
Suso explains in this work that he had carved the three letters IHS on
his skin.

We conclude our survey with a quite different and hitherto un-
recognized testimony to the relationship between English and continental mysticism. The great Dutch mystic Hadewych, who perhaps had
a decisive influence on the blossoming of the mysticism of Mechthild
of Magdeburg, tells us that she had contacts with England. Altogether
she had fourteen visions and at the end of them, in a state of ecstasy

lasting for three days and three nights, she sees a large number of those who have attained perfection gathered round the divine throne, including biblical persons like Mary, John the Baptist and John the Evangelist, Fathers of the Church like Augustine, saints, women like St Bridget and Beguines. But she does not merely see the souls of the dead who have attained perfection but also the souls of those still alive who are destined to attain perfection, and in this context she speaks of individual persons from England: 'In England there dwell nine: five hermits, two female recluses and two virgins.'[71] This is incidentally the time when the original version of the *Ancrene Wisse* was written. It is not impossible that Hadewych knew the people the *Ancrene Wisse* was addressed to. But of course, as so often in the question of the relationship between English and continental mysticism, we cannot get beyond mere supposition.

III

*

The Song of Songs *and metaphors for love in English mysticism*

Metaphors for love have a very interesting genesis and are very widely used. Their language therefore provides an ideal starting point for a philological and comparative study of the language of English mysticism. Since the Bible already draws analogies between the love relationship of God and man and the love of man for woman, it was logical for later mysticism to describe mystical love in concrete terms using the language of the passion of earthly love, especially as there exists in the *Song of Songs* a biblical text which almost demands a spiritual interpretation. In Judaism in fact at a very early date this text was given an allegorical interpretation in the sense of ἱερὸς γάμος.[1] The pseudo-Dionysian mystical tradition, too, consciously following Platonic or neo-Platonic philosophy, described the mystical love of God as the desire – ἔρως or *amor* – of imperfect man for absolute perfection. The importance of the erotic language of love has long since been demonstrated for German mysticism, and Grabmann indeed saw the origin of German mysticism in the poetic paraphrases of the *Song of Songs*.[2] There has as yet been no such survey for English mysticism. Nor has one seemed necessary, since a long time ago, in her essay on Walter Hilton and the mystical tradition in England, Helen Gardner came to the conclusion that 'Like the English mystics generally, he [Hilton] makes little use of the metaphor of the spirtual marriage'.[3] It is therefore time to examine this problem in context.

It is precisely in England that the *Song of Songs* was interpreted in a spiritual sense at a very early date. One of the earliest literary products on English soil is Bede's great and important commentary on the *Song of Songs*. Bernard of Clairvaux draws heavily on it for his own sermons on the *Song of Songs*,[4] which in turn had a great deal of influence in England. He himself created the conditions for the spread of his affective Cistercian mysticism on the island by sending to England in 1131 his secretary William and twelve monks from Clairvaux. Gilbert of Hoyland has described very impressively how passionate the mystical ecstasy of the Cistercian nuns in England could be.[5] A pupil and friend of Bernard's, an Englishman who became abbot of the Cistercian monastery of Swineshead in Hoyland, Lincolnshire, Gilbert tried to continue the exegesis of the *Song of Songs* which Bernard had left unfinished on his death. We know too that Aelred of Rievaulx, who also knew Bernard, wrote a commentary on the *Song of Songs* which has not yet come to light.[6] Finally we must remember that Richard Rolle is the author of a Latin interpretation of the *Song of Songs* which was held in high regard in the Middle Ages, and that the Old Testament *Canticum* was so well-known and topical in the Middle Ages that for instance Chaucer was able to parody it so cleverly in his *Miller's Tale*.[7]

The *Song of Songs* is a collection of individual lyric love poems which is not to be understood as genuine folk poetry written by Solomon — as Herder still believed — but as an artistic poetical work with a very deliberate and very subtle structure.[8] Recent stylistic studies have attempted to analyse the unique attraction of this work and to determine its structure. The songs are characterized by a language which is full of 'lyrical sensitivity'[9] and which, as we have already mentioned, has assimilated a whole series of lyrical topoi from Old Egyptian love poetry. Frequent use is made of the stylistic device of the simile, whereby the *tertium comparationis* is often omitted, so that the simile becomes a new independent image.[10] Very typical of the style of the *Song of Songs* are the many repetitions of individual images and formulae, which Bernard of Clairvaux, who has a very fine feeling for the style of this poem, interprets as a linguistic expression of the passion of love.[11] Not infrequently the normal sentence pattern is abandoned and replaced by single words and incomplete sentences. This, too, did not escape Bernard's notice, and he describes such abrupt utterances as spiritual 'belches' ('ructus'),[12] when a heart, overfull with sensation, tries to express its feelings. The *Song of Songs* is made up of numerous dialogues, and it is one of the characteristics of the work that the persons speaking are not introduced, but that each speaker has to be deduced from the context. Indeed in the course of a single poem the author loves to 'oscillate between different speakers'.[13] This explains why we so often find in the mystical exegesis of the *Song of Songs* that some authors attribute certain verses to Christ, whilst others attribute them to the soul. There is no moralizing in this lyric poetry, and the real theme is the 'joyful surrender and pleasure of all the senses, and the naively carefree desire for love and the thirst for beauty'.[14] Whilst in the *Song of Songs* the lovers enjoy their happiness in free love, allegorical interpretations transform them into bride and bridegroom.[15] In the Christian exegesis the bride becomes the church, Mary and finally the individual soul, whilst the bridegroom is usually identified with Christ.

To get a preliminary impression of how the *Song of Songs* affected the style of English mysticism, let us first take a look at Rolle's Latin mysticism before beginning a detailed examination, for it is imbued with the sensual language of the *Canticum* to an extent which has hitherto not been sufficiently appreciated. If Rolle constantly wishes to enter the 'portas ... paradisici pastus'[16] and describes the union with God as reaching the 'paradisica poma'[17] as 'premia ... in pastu parato',[18] then these are to be understood as references to the pastoral-bucolic milieu of the *Canticum*, where we read of the 'pascere' of the groom (1:6 f.) and where we find the image of the 'paradisus malorum punicorom, / Cum pomorum fructibus' (4:13). The *Canticum* uses images of the sweetness of honey to express the qualities of the bride and groom in concrete terms (4:11; 5:1). This imagery had a lasting influence on Rolle's style, and other biblical utterances could be linked with it (especially for instance Ps. 118: 103). The numerous images of sweet flowing which it gave rise to in Rolle, be it the description of heavenly music as 'melos mellifluum',[19] or God's dwelling place on the 'mons mellifluus'[20] or the images of the 'ignis dulcifluus'[21] and the 'laudifluum lumen',[22] give his mystical language that characteristically soft, almost female tone.

A particularly typical example of the way Rolle's imagination, which one might almost call poetic, was influenced by the *Song of Songs* is his interpretation of the words of the sponsus that the beloved has wounded him 'in uno crine colli tui' (4:9). After he has briefly informed the reader that this image is to be understood as an allegory for passionate love for God, he keeps completely to the image suggested to him by the *Song of Songs* and develops it to a very bold statement that God is captivated by a hair: the King of Kings, on seeing the soul adorned with gleaming hair, cannot resist the sight and burns with love for her. Here, as so often, Rolle does not keep to an allegorical interpretation of a given biblical image, but allows the image to develop, as it were, a life of its own, and relies on it having the same suggestive effect on the reader.

In the Early Middle English period words like *derling*,[23] *lemman*[24] and *sweting*,[25] which correspond to the terms *dilectus*, *dilecta* and *amica* of the *Song of Songs*, and which are very common in secular literature, are applied to Christ or the soul in lives of saints and in homiletic and mystical texts.[26] God is even referred to once in the *Cloud* as the 'gelous louer',[27] an obvious reference to biblical texts such as Exod. 20:5. But in the main works of English mysticism God and the soul are almost exclusively interpreted as bride and bridegroom. The *Ancrene Wisse* calls the woman it is addressed to the 'bride of Christ'.[28] Other texts follow suit — the texts of the so-called 'Wooing Group',[29] *A Talkyng of þe Loue of God*,[30] the works of Rolle,[31] the author of the *Cloud*,[32] Hilton[33] and Julian[34]. The author of the *Pistle of Preier* and Hilton use exactly the same formulation when defining the union of God and man as a mystical 'mariage',[35] and the tract *Tretyse of þe Stodye of Wysdome* calls God the 'housbonde of oure soule'.[36]

We can see from the example of Margery Kempe how, towards the end of the Middle Ages, the tendency arose not merely to take over the imagery of the bride, but also to depict the spiritual marriage as an event and even as a dramatic scene which was acted out. In the course of a wedding scene God recites to her the liturgical marriage formula: 'I take þe, Margery, for my weddyd wyfe, for fayrar, for fowelar, for richar for powerar.... And þan þe Modyr of God & alle þe seyntys þat wer þer present in hir sowle preyde þat þei myth haue mech joy to-gedyr.'[37]

The perfection of the divine lover is exalted not only in Latin and German but also in English mysticism as his beauty, about which we shall have more to say later. But the beloved, too, the soul, is called 'beautiful', since in the *Song of Songs* the *amica* had said of herself 'Nigra sum, sed formosa' (1:4). True, the soul only regains its original beauty when it frees itself from its sinfulness and is prepared to live according to God's will. Thus Rolle explains in his *Commandment*: 'For his joy es þat þou be fayre and lufsom in his eghen. Fayrehede of þi sawle, þat he covaytes, es þat þou be chaste and meke ... never irk to do his wille.'[38] Hilton explains this in a somewhat more differentiated way and draws a direct analogy with the soul. He takes the contrast 'nigra' — 'formosa' of the *Song of Songs* and interprets the blackness as representing the 'external' carnal sinfulness of the soul and the beauty as representing the inner disposition towards perfection. For Hilton — and this accords with traditional teaching — the soul is 'Foul withouten as it were a beste, faire withinne like to an aungel. ... Foul for þe flesc(h)ly appetite, faire for þe good wil.'[39] The soul only regains its real beauty, which consists in its being the image of God, as a divine gift.

The *Canticum Canticorum* sings of the 'lectulus . . . floridus' (1:15) as the place of the union of the lovers, and this has become a favourite topos in Western mysticism. An early interpretation of this verse of the *Song of Songs* is found in Hugh of St Victor.[40] An allegorical interpretation of the soul as the bed of God is found in England in the homiletic work *Orrmulum*: 'tin herrte beo þatt bedd þatt God himm ressteþþ inne.'[41] In Rolle's (?) poem *Song of the Love of Jesus* the place of mystical surrender is praised as 'þe bede of blysse',[42] and it is Rolle who is able to adapt this image again and again in a very individual manner, as in his *Melos Amoris* where he has the souls play 'in lectulo leticie'.[43] In the *Mirror of Simple Souls* the spiritual bed of love is transformed into a 'chambre secrete',[44] and in *A Talkyng of þe Loue of God* God is praised in an apostrophe because '[þou] laddest out þi deore lééf. þat is monnes soule. to þi briȝte boure ful of all blisse. to wonen in þi cluppyng'.[45]

It is again Margery Kempe who takes the image of the mystical *lectulus* furthest in her use of sensual concrete terms. She draws a much too forceful analogy between her mystical love and her earlier married sexuality, for she has Christ say to her: 'þu mayst boldly, whan þu art in þi bed, take me to þe as for þi weddyd husbond.'[46] But this drastic bluntness of Margery Kempe's is by no means unique in mysticism. Mechthild of Magdeburg, for instance, in her *Fliessendes Licht der Gottheit* uses the verb *truten* which is normally used to mean the consummation of physical love when she says of God: 'Er trutet si [the soul] mit voller maht in dem bette der miñe.'[47] But Mechthild's almost poetic language is so convincing that even in her extremely erotic imagery the spiritual content is never lost, whereas in Margery there is frequently a crude realism which intrudes in a very embarrassing manner, as when she gets permission from her divine bridegroom 'þu mayst boldly take me in þe armys of þi sowle & kyssen my mowth, myn hed, & my fete as swetly as thow wylt.'[48] Kissing the feet of Christ is a frequent motif in female mysticism for describing mystical surrender, but, as in the translation of Aelred of Rievaulx's *Institutio Inclusarum*, it is taken directly from a typological model — Mary Magdalen's show of reverence to Christ.[49]

The mystical kiss of God and soul which is frequently found in mystical texts and which according to Lüers is found in the Isis cult,[50] is typologically prefigured in the wish of the *amica* at the beginning of the *Song of Songs* to be kissed by the lover. The *Ancrene Wisse* refers directly to this wish for the kiss of the lover. It is described to the 'sustren' as the experiencing of a sweetness which transcends all earthly experience, which Christ gives to them because they have renounced the world:

> þis coss leoue sustren is a swetnesse & a delit of heorte swa unimete swete. þ euch worldes sauur is bitter þer toȝeines. Ah ure lauerd wiþ þis coss ne cusseð na sawle. þe luueð ei þing buten him.[51]

According to the *MED* the *Ancrene Wisse* is the first instance of the occurrence of the kiss-motif in the Middle English period.[52] We meet the mystical kiss most frequently in Richard Rolle: he explains in his *Melos Amoris* that anyone who has experienced the kisses and embraces of the eternal beauty is immune to temptations of voluptuousness.[53] With that easy artistic ability which he has to link several images together in his metaphors, he manages on one occasion to combine several *Song of Songs*-motifs — the girl sitting under a tree, her desire for the kiss of the lover and her joy at his embrace — into one single poetic expression when he says of the soul: 'Apparet exinde quod habet amorem et estuat amplexibus et osculum optatum sub arbore accepit.'[54] We find a no less passionate kiss-metaphor in Mechthild, who says of God that he 'durküsset si mit sinem götlichen munde'.[55]

Like the kiss-motif, the almost synonymous concept of the mystical embrace is particularly common precisely in Rolle: it is often attained in the ecstatic climaxes of his mystical language, as, for instance, in the *Emendatio Vitae* where he addresses the eternal love with the words: 'inflamma animum meum ad amandum deum ut non ardeat nisi ad amplexus eius.'[56] Like Augustine, Hugh of St Victor and Richard of St Victor before him,[57] Rolle here transforms the motif of S. of S. 2:6 into the 'connubium spirituale'. Rolle, however, restricts the motif almost exclusively to his Latin texts. It is only in his *English Psalter* that he attempts to translate this imagery into the vernacular when he explains the verse of the psalm 'Ad te domine leuaui animam meam' (Ps. 24:1) with the words: 'lord i. liftid . . . my saule . . . til the, to hals and see.'[58] When Margery Kempe on beholding the crucifix expresses the wish 'þat þe Crucifix xuld losyn hys handys fro þe crosse & halsyn hir in tokyn of lofe',[59] she is taking up a theme from Bernardian-Franciscan mysticism of the cross, which culminates in the concept of the marriage of the cross and the soul and which had a strong preference for the erotic imagery of the *Song of Songs*. The outstretched arms of the crucified saviour were seen as implying the longing of the suffering lover to receive his beloved, and the gesture of the bowed head was understood as the wish of God for the kiss of the soul.[60]

The highly affective mystical text *A Talkyng of þe Loue of God* closes, for instance, with the words: 'Bi twene·þin armes ley I. me. Bi twene myn Armes cluppe I. þe.'[61] Julian of Norwich, too, works the motif of the divine embrace into her mysticism. In her case it is Christ who embraces man: 'oure lorde god . . . colleth vs and beclosyth vs for tendyr loue.'[62] And here there is a striking tendency in Julian to replace the passion of mystical love with the maternal affection of the creator for his creature, for she refers to Christ as 'oure tender mother'.[63]

The mutual caresses of the lovers in the *Song of Songs* inspired the theme of love-play between God and the soul, which is so important in medieval mysticism. Mechthild of Magdeburg certainly makes a clear reference to the statement of the sponsa 'Laeva eius sub capite meo,/ Et dextera illius amplexabitur me' (2:6), when she describes the union of man and God as mystical love-play: 'Si welle sich rehte muessig und blos / An minen goetlichen arm legen, / Und dc [daz] ich muos mit ir spilen.'[64] We also find the love-play motif in Middle English literature in the poem *Quia Amore Langueo*, an important work of high quality which draws heavily on the *Song of Songs* and its traditional mystical exegesis. In it we read: 'My swete spouse / will we goo play; / apples ben rype in my gardine.'[65]

The earliest example we know where the metaphorical language of love-play is introduced into a mystical context does not, however, apply this imagery to the *unio* but to the change in the state of the soul between the joy of fulfilment in the possession of God and the disappointing feeling of emptiness. It is precisely the feeling of separation from God in the dark night of the soul which so often follows moments of possession of God which mystics like to describe through the image of God playing with the soul: 'Mystics call such oscillations the "Game of Love" in which God plays, as it were, "hide and seek" with the questing soul.'[66] We read in Hilton's translation of James of Milan's *Stimulus Amoris*, the earliest occurrence of this imagery, that God wants to 'absente hym fro þe and pleye with þe þus . . . þis is þe game on loue'.[67] The imagery of the 'ludus amoris' which is found in Suso's *Horologium Sapientiae*[68] is probably[69] taken directly from the *Stimulus Amoris*. Suso's imagery in turn influences the Middle English tract *The Chastising of God's Children* where we read: 'þe pley of loue is ioye and sorwe.'[70] But at the same time the love-play is robbed of its erotic element in this tract, since the temptations of God which the soul has to endure are compared with a mother playing with her child: 'whanne oure lord suffrith us to be tempted . . . he pleieþ wiþ us as þe modir with hir child',[71] a simile probably taken from the *Ancrene Wisse*.[72] The author of the *Cloud* consciously tries to develop this imagery in various ways: on one occasion he uses a very simple but extremely effective image to describe the state of complete relaxation of the mystic, by saying that he wishes to play with a child: 'þi list is likyng to pleye wiþ a childe'.[73] And he also uses the motif of a father playing with his child as a symbol for the complete harmony of man with God, a harmony which is promised in the *Cloud* to those who follow the teachings laid down in the work.[74]

The image of the bride made drunk by her lover is another favourite image of the mystics which they take from the *Song of Songs*. The pleasure which the bride has enjoyed is expressed through the very beautiful metaphor that he has led her into his wine cellars (S. of S. 2:4). The mystical exegesis of this particular verse is supported by a series of other biblical texts.[75] Furthermore, the image of being drunk has been a favourite metaphor for describing mystical ecstasy since Plato and the Ancient Mysteries, especially the Cult of Dionysius,[76] and is found later above all in Philo.[77] A glance at the *Glossa ordinaria* and Richard of St Victor is sufficient to show how widespread this imagery was in Latin mysticism.[78] It has a central place in Sufi mysticism, and is also well-developed in German mysticism, where Mechthild of Magdeburg, for instance, says of God's bride that she is 'trunken worden von der angesihte des edeln antlütes'.[79]

If we examine the English texts to see how widespread the use of this image is, it is apparent that the English texts fall back on this concept to much the same degree as the German mystics. Metaphors to describe ecstasy are found in many different forms. In our context we are interested in those cases where the mystics speak directly of being intoxicated through divine love, for here we find a remarkable parallel with the love-potion motif of contemporary secular literature, particularly as found in the Tristan material. In his edition of *Christus und die minnende Seele* Banz reproduces a medieval book illustration in which Christ is offering the soul the love potion,[80] and we read in Mechthild of Magdeburg: 'ich was vroeliche wan trunken in der minne.'[81] In the English poem *Swete Ihesu, now will I synge* the speaker asks Christ to give the human heart his love potion: 'ȝif hit þi loue to drynke so, þat flessches lustes ben fordo',[82] and in his *Scale* Hilton speaks of the 'precious licour of perfit luf of Iesu'.[83] But we must be extremely wary of making the obvious assumption that such examples are influenced by the motif of the love potion. It is not altogether impossible, but the earliest occurrences of the secular use of this motif in English are not found — according to the *MED* — until the translation of the *Roman de la Rose* and Gower's *Confessio Amantis*,[84] that is *after* English mysticism had reached its peak.

We must also take into account that the motif of the love potion is to all intents and purposes already present in Latin mystical texts, which equate *amor* and *vinum*. Bernard of Clairvaux, for example, explains the spiritual meaning of the verse 'Introduxit me rex in cellam vinariam' (S. of S. 2:4) with the words: 'Secundum spiritum quoque non negat [the sponsa] ebriam, sed amore, non vino, *nisi quod amor vinum est*'.[85] In this connection we also find the following formulation in Richard Rolle's *Incendium Amoris*: 'Amor est uinum spirituale inebrians mentes electorum'.[86] We can safely assume that the verse from the *Song of Songs* itself suggested the identification of *amor* and *vinum*, for the sponsa follows the description of her introduction into the 'cella vinaria' with the abrupt asyndetic sentence: 'ordinavit in me charitatem'.[87] Hilton, too, follows the traditional *Canticum* exegesis when he has Christ say: 'ye shullen be made drunken wiþ þe hiȝest and freshest wyn in My celer, þat is, þe souereyn ioye of loue in þe blisse of heuene.'[88]

But all English examples of mystical wine metaphors are surpassed by the *Mirror of Simple Souls*. For this text really uses this imagery to imply that the spiritual reality it is describing is of an extra-linguistic nature. The soul drinks from the 'diuine tunne of his owen bounte'[89] and also from the 'souerayn fauset, of þe whiche noon drinkeþ but þe Trinite'.[90] The effect of the drink on the soul, however, is so intense, that the language, although it has chosen only an implicit image, begins to fall over itself, as it were, and sentence structure and logical sequence of thought produce a kind of extended *figura etymologica*: 'it is of þis fauset, wiþouten whiche sche drinkeþ, soule nouȝted-drunken, soule fre-drunken, soule forȝeten-drunken; but riȝt drunken and more þan drunke of þat sche neuer dranke ne neuer schal drinke. þis heeriþ, if ȝe vndirstande it.'[91]

The *Song of Songs*, as a collection of love songs, does not merely sing of the joyful union of the lovers in kiss, embrace and ecstasy of love, but also contains the theme of unfulfilled love-longing, which is a basic motif of the love literature of all peoples and all epochs. In Christian mysticism the famous 'amore langueo' of the sponsa (S. of S. 2:5; 5:8) is applied to the soul's wish for the ultimate mystical union with God. And the English mystics are no exception. Rolle often refers to this desire of the sponsa in his Latin texts,[92] and we meet it frequently in the Middle English mystical works. Hilton, for instance, says of God that he 'visiteþ þe soule þat langueshþ in desire',[93] and the *Cloud* speaks of a 'langwishing sekenes'.[94] The synonymous terms *langouren* and *mornen* are similarly widespread and we meet them in a formulation in the *Ladder of Foure Ronges*: 'God is callid & prayed as dere spowse to comme to the moornyng sowle that langurith in love'.[95] Popular, too, is the verbal noun *lufe-longyng* which we find, for instance, in a poem which comes from the Rolle school of mysticism, where we read: 'I sytt and syng of lufe-langyng, þat in my hert es bred.'[96] The same terms which are found in Middle English love poetry are also the ones preferred for these motifs. It is only the author of the *Cloud* who, in expressing the motif of mystical desire in language, uses the rare Middle English term *listines* when he, for instance, calls upon the reader to 'lene wiþ a tristi listines to þe loue of oure Lorde'.[97]

The unique style of the *Song of Songs* where the speakers often change abruptly and where it is not always clear which statements are to be attributed to which speaker, helped cause the exegete to transfer the 'amore langueo' of the bride to the sponsus, and from this Bernard of Clairvaux developed the important theological theme that it is not only the soul which yearns for God but that God also yearns for the soul. But in contrast to German mysticism, the 'deus desiderans' motif is comparatively rare in English mystical prose and is limited almost exclusively to texts of female mysticism. In her autobiography Margery Kempe reports on the sermon of a 'worschepful doctowr of diuinite' in which the words 'Owr Lord Ihesu langurith for lofe' are frequently repeated.[98] The idea of the 'deus desiderans' plays an important role in the work of Julian of Norwich, where Christ has a great yearning to lead the soul into the fullness of heavenly joy.[99] His love-longing is expressed as a spiritual thirst which is only quenched when the soul is eternally united with him: 'For thys is the gostly thyrst of cryst the loue longyng yat lastyth and evyr shall tylle we se that syght at domys day.'[100] In Tauler we find the very concise expression that God thirsts for man to thirst for him: 'Sehent wie die minnencliche guete Gottes mit sinen uzerwelten spilen kan; das er uns herinbringen múge und daz uns harnoch dúrsten welle, darnoch túrstet in mit grossem turste.'[101] The 'deus desiderans' motif is more common in religious lyric poetry — as for example in the poem *Quia Amore Langueo*, where Christ calls out these words as a refrain at the end of each stanza, thus using a quotation from the *Song of Songs*.[102]

But let us return to the use of the words 'amore langueo' as applied to the soul, which is the more common usage. Just as in secular love poetry being sick with love gives rise to all sorts of symptoms, the mystics, too, describe this state more exactly and go into far more detail than their great model the *Song of Songs*. A common motif in English mysticism is the sigh as an image of yearning love, which is fundamental to all love poetry. We read in a poem perhaps written by Rolle: 'My sange es in syghtyng, my lyfe es in langynge, / Til I þe se, my keyng.'[103] But it would be rash to conclude that this theme is directly borrowed from contemporary love poetry, for it, too, had already become part of the general body of mystical love language at the latest with Richard of St Victor, whose important tract *De Quattuor Gradibus Violentae Charitatis* contains the sentence: 'Hec tibi anime vulnerate certa sint signa, gemitus atque suspiria.'[104] And when Rolle complains like an earthly lover that he has become pale in the face from love-longing,[105] this topos too is already part of the mystical language of Richard of St Victor, who in the same passage speaks of the 'vultus pallens atque tabescens' of the mystical lover.[106] Tears of love are also favourite images in mysticism for the soul's yearning for the *unio mystica*. We find them, for instance, in the poem *Swete Ihesu, now wil I synge*,[107] and in Margery Kempe, who reports at great length on her 'teerys wyth lofe'.[108] The importance of tears in Margery has been developed to excess, but on the other hand they do make clear that a very old theological concept, according to which 'terys of compu[n]ccyon, deuocyon & compassyon'[109] were considered to be a gift of divine grace, has been linked with this motif from secular love literature. Just as Troilus in Chaucer's great poem can no longer find sleep once his love for Criseyde begins to develop,[110] so too we find in Rolle's (?) poem *A Song of the Love of Jesus*: 'Lufe us reveth þe nyght rest.'[111] The mystical prose poem *A Talkyng of þe Loue of God*, which has a very strong tendency to take over motifs from secular love poetry, compares the state which passion produces in the soul in a quite drastic manner with the madness of love: 'I. cusse and I. cluppe and stunte oþerwhile. as mon þat is loue mad . . . i cluppe and I. cusse as I. wood wore.'[112] Richard of St Victor, in the tract which we have already mentioned, included this state of soul too in his mystical psychology, when he demonstrated that the vehemence of love can develop into madness. He defined this as a characteristic of *caritas insatiabilis*, the fourth form in his scheme of love typology.[113]

Instead of the motif of love-longing we frequently find in medieval mysticism the concrete image of being wounded by love, which again has its origin in the *Canticum*. In the mysticism of the cross especially the complaint of the sponsus in the *Song of Songs* is taken up, that the beloved has inflicted a wound of the heart on him: 'Vulnerasti cor meum, soror mea, sponsa' (S. of S. 4:9). The wound which Christ had received below the heart from the lance of Longinus is then associated with this. But just like the lovers in secular poetry, the soul herself states that she has been wounded with love-longing. It is true that in the *Song of Songs* the sponsa is satisfied with the aforementioned 'amore langueo', but in the Middle Ages the Latin alternative rendering 'vulnerata caritate ego sum' was current, which is a more exact translation of the Greek 'ὅτι τετρωμένη ἀγάπης ἐγώ'[114] of the Septuagint. We find the resulting motif of the wounded soul very frequently in both German and English mysticism. We need only mention Mechthild of Magdeburg's description of the soul as 'Von warer miñe reht wunt',[115] Richard Rolle's (?) request to Christ: 'Wounde my hert within'[116] or Margery Kempe's characterization of herself as 'a creatur al wowndyd wyth lofe'.[117] But in England the idea that God himself suffers from the wound of love-longing is relatively rare. Although in the *Orcherd of Syon*, the translation of the principal work of Catherine of Siena, we find the marvellous statement which bursts all the bonds of theological dogma: 'O eend[l]ees fadir . . . O al woundid in loue, me semeþ þat þou hast nede of us wrecchide creaturis',[118] we only find similar statements in England in Rolle's Latin mysticism. In his commentary on the 'vulnerasti cor meum' of the *Song of Songs* Rolle attempts to express the mutual love relationship between the soul and God by means of the very concise formulation: 'Vulneratur ergo qui vulnerat, quia amatur qui amat',[119] and supplements this thought with the equally impressive addition that the soul forces God's heart to burn 'ut pateretur Impassibilis et vulneraretur Qui vulnerari non valuit'.[120]

Although in these examples the image of the wound has an evocative, suggestive character in transmitting the idea of the mystical passion of love, the wound did not remain the only motif within the realistic graphic representation of the act of crucifixion as it was developing in the Franciscan tradition of piety, but further motifs were added with ever new connotations. Remarkable amongst these is the metaphorical expression that the soul should look upon the wounds of Christ as its nest, an attempt to illustrate the complete security of the soul in God. This image, too, which takes the modern reader by surprise and which could easily be misunderstood as oversentimentalization, was taken from the allegorical interpretation of the *Song of*

Songs. The verse 'Columba mea in foraminibus petrae' (S. of S. 2:14) tended to be interpreted in the sense that the image of the dove nesting in the clefts of the rock prefigured the soul which finds its refuge in the wounds of Christ. We find this exegesis not only in Bernard of Clairvaux's sermons on the *Song of Songs* but long before him in Bede who, as Bonetti's research has shown, had been influenced by the Spanish bishop St Justin of Urgel.[121] In English, apart from the *Ancrene Wisse*[122] and the poem *Quia Amore Langueo*,[123] it is Rolle and Margery Kempe particularly who use this image. They even expand it into the idea of the wounded Christ as a dovecote.[124] It would be wrong to dismiss such an image as a lapse in good taste, for it is precisely in a metaphor which seems to be so far-fetched that the focal point is not the sensual idea but the spiritual content it conveys, in this case the concept that Christ with his wounds has become a place of refuge not just for the individual soul but for all mankind. When in James of Milan's *Stimulus Amoris*, one of the principal texts of Franciscan mysticism of the cross, the union of the soul and God is described in terms of the joining of both their wounds: 'vulnus vulneri copulatur',[125] this is to be understood in exactly the same manner. Taken for itself alone this image cannot be fully realized sensually unless at the same time the spiritual and affective contents are thought of.

The wound of Christ caused by the lance of Longinus was interpreted as the gateway to his heart and as a precondition for the union with God. This is both a realistic and, paradoxically, at the same time a non-realistic linguistic image: realistic in that here the mystic takes the — for him — real physical body of God made man as the place of the *unio*, but at the same time not realistic in that he is of course aware of the symbolic nature of this image and is only concerned with the fact of the *unio* through the unconditional readiness to suffer with the Saviour. Since the wound in Christ's side is given a new interpretation as an opening through which it is possible for the mystical lover to enter into his beloved and thus become completely one with him, this gives rise in Franciscan mysticism, especially in such an eroticized text as the *Stimulus Amoris*, to a typical and quite consciously intended analogy between this wound of Christ and the female pudenda: the *vulva*, as the place of sexual ecstasy, has, so to speak, been transformed into the *vulnus* of Christ as the place of mystical ecstatic union of the soul with its divine beloved. This is confirmed by the following statement of the Monk of Farne whose fourteenth century text represents the climax of Franciscan mysticism of the cross on English soil: 'latus meum aperio ut osculatum introducam ad cor meum, et simus duo in carne una.'[126] The soul which surrenders to the crucified lover experiences the *unio passionalis* as an ecstatic dying which dissolves the individuality. Long before the verb *to die* came to acquire the connotation of sexual ecstasy which it had in the secular love poetry of the Elizabethan era, it is used in the text *A Talkyng of þe Loue of God* as an expression of ecstatic mystical love.[127] Of course not every author who mentioned the wounds of Christ used this imagery to intend an erotic analogy: In her tenth revelation Julian of Norwich sees Christ, who shows her his wounds and opens them, so that she sees in them a 'feyer and delectable place', which is large enough for all mankind to rest in in peace and love.[128] The erotic element is missing here but we find, as in the examples just cited, the same medieval tendency which is present in all the qualitatively better texts to take a realistic detail of the passion as a starting point, but to use it as a symbol for a spiritual statement which goes beyond the realistic plane.

When considering the wound motif we must not overlook the fact that the very existence of this imagery gave the authors the possibility of drawing an analogy at the same time with the ancient love-arrow motif. The fact that we find the christianized love-arrow as early as the pseudo-Hippolytus shows that this was indeed the case in the early centuries AD.[129] This Christian use of the love-arrow, which is a particularly fine example of the fusing and amalgamating of secular and biblical motifs which started at a very early date, was only to be expected, since the arrow plays an important role in the Old Testament. Augustine was able to take the words of the psalmist: 'sagittae tuae infixae sunt mihi'[130] and make these arrows into words of God which are to move men to love him, i.e. the words of God are understood by Augustine as love-arrows.[131] Rolle clearly has this text of Augustine's in mind when he says very emphatically on one occasion in his *English Psalter*: 'the wordis of haly writ . . . ere dartis, that woundis oure saule til the luf of christ.'[132] The English commentator of the *Mirror of Simple Souls*, whom we only know by the initials 'M. N.', speaks in one of his commentaries of 'rauyschinge dartes', with which divine love visits the soul and 'woundeþ hir so sweteli',[133] It is of course the conventional metaphorical language of courtly love that the arrow wounds should be experienced as sweet. But the attempt of our author to bring together the concept of being pierced with arrows and the experience of mystical ecstasy is remarkable.

It is also very noticeable that English mysticism usually prefers the image of the love-spear, the love-lance or the love-sword to the love-arrow motif. Rolle refers to the soul as 'salubri lancea vulneratam',[134] 'gladio amoris Dei transfixa'[135] and as wounded by 'amoris iaculum'.[136] In his *Scale* Hilton is able to say of love: 'hit woundiþ þe sowle wiþ þe blisseful swerd of lufe',[137] and in a song probably to be ascribed to Rolle the speaker makes the request: 'Thyrl my sawule wyth þi spere'.[138] Does some quite specific intention on the authors' part lie behind this slight modification of the motif? In secular love literature we do have the love-lance as well as the love-arrow, but there can be little doubt that the mystical examples quoted were also intended to refer to the lance of Longinus entering the side of Christ, since medieval authors were fond of interpreting this lance as a love-arrow piercing the heart of the crucified Saviour.[139] This assumption is not only confirmed by a miniature which Banz reproduces,[140] but also by a poem by the Franciscan mystic Jacopone da Todi in which we find the following lines applied to the cross of Christ:

> Ed eo la trovo piena de sagitte
> ch'escon del lato, nel cor me s'ò fitte:
> lo balestrieri en vèr me l'ha ritte,
> onn' arme c' aio me fa perforare.[141]

Dronke is right in assuming that 'the arrows would seem to be a meta-phor for the force of love', and that it appears 'as if the lance that pierced Christ's side had turned into darts of love and remorse that strike the beholder'.[142]

The image of the love-letter has also been developed within the framework of the mysticism of the passion. According to the *OED* the first occurrence of the word 'love-letter' is in a passage from the *Wohunge of Ure Lauerd*, where we read: 'A swe/te iesu þu oppnes me þin herte / for to cnawe witerliche & in to re-/den trewe luue lettres.'[143] But in the *Ancrene Wisse*, too, Christ writes to the soul: 'wiþ his ahne blod saluz to his leofmon. luue gretunge. forte wohin hire wiþ'.[144] This metaphor seems to have been particularly popular amongst female mystics, for as W. Stammler has shown, the spiritual love-letter also occurs in the mysticism of the nuns of North Germany.[145] Indeed time and again we find the attempt to see the whole Bible *expressis verbis* as a love-letter: the English paraphrase of Suso's *Horologium Sapientiae* calls the Bible an 'amorose lettere',[146] and Hilton enlightens the reader of his *Scale* with the words: 'wete þou wele þat swilk . . . knowynges in Holy Writ . . . are not elles bot swet lettre(s), sendynges made atwix a lufende soule & Iesu lufed.'[147]

Within the mysticism of the cross there is a further group of motifs which stands out because love appears in them as a personification and plays an active role. In the courtly era, as we know, Amor, the God of Love of antiquity, became the centre of a secular love religion which developed as a conscious analogy with the divine services of the Christian religion. And in the Middle Ages the God of Love, Amor, gained entry into the actual religious sphere and came into Christian mysticism of love as a motif. Some stimulus for this must certainly have come from the *Song of Songs*, for the expression 'fortis est ut mors dilectio' (S. of S 8:6) which the mystics (including the English mystics) are so fond of quoting, paved the way for an attempt to express the dynamics of mystical love in concrete terms in the form of a personification. On one occasion in his *Incendium Amoris* Rolle says of Christ that he rushed to the cross out of love-longing for the soul and adds: 'sed uerum dicitur quia amor preit in tripudio, et coream ducit'.[148] We also read in one of his poems:

> A wonder it es to se, wha sa understude,
> How God of mageste was dyand on þe rude.
> Bot suth þan es it sayde þat lufe ledes þe ryng;
> Þat hym sa law hase layde bot lufe it was na thyng.[149]

In this rather striking image of the love dance R. Woolf saw a conscious reference to the 'carolling' of the God of Love in the *Roman de la Rose*.[150] But since Rolle never gives any indication in his works of any connection with the *Roman de la Rose*, Woolf's conclusion seems highly improbable. It is perhaps better here to re-examine the tradition of mystical language itself before assuming any direct borrowing of motifs from secular love literature. Mechthild of Hackeborn's mystical work *Liber Specialis Gratiae* contains a particularly fine example of the same concept of the passion of Christ as a ring dance, and we also find there a slight variant of Rolle's formulation 'amor . . . coream ducit' when Christ, referring to the Last Supper, says: 'Recorderis, qualem ego speciosus iuvenis post convivium illud choream duxi.'[151] This special motif of Christ leading the dance attains importance on numerous other occasions in mysticism,[152] and hence it is very probable that Rolle took his dance metaphors directly from the tradition of mystical imagery. If we add to this that the tract *The Chastising of God's Children*, which was so important for English female mysticism, defines the effects of the experience of 'heuenli dew of swetnesse of þe godhede'[153] as a spiritual drunkenness and suggests that these effects can be accompanied by different forms of physical ecstasy including dancing for excessive joy, then there seems no justification for the *MED* not to list a religious and even mystical meaning for the verb *dauncen*. This omission is all the more regrettable as mystical metaphors of dance have a long tradition in European mysticism. It reaches its climax in German mysticism where Christ is often portrayed as a young man playing the musical accompaniment for the soul to dance to, as for instance in Suso who says of Christ: 'als ob er were ein himelsch spilman ... er muesti mit in och himelschlich tanzen.'[154] As has been demonstrated, this metaphorical imagery has its origin in the cult dance of the ancient mysteries, the 'χωρεία πνευματική'.[155] and the *Acts of John* contains a very interesting early Christian example where Christ has his disciples form a ring and dance a hymn of praise to the Father.[156]

But let us return to the imagery of the personified mystical Love: Not infrequently the mystics, above all the texts of female mysticism, go so far as to have Amor personally force Christ into his work of redemption; Hadewych,[157] Mechthild of Hackeborn,[158] Richard Rolle[159] and Julian[160] all agree in this. Rolle's works often show a preference towards including Virgil's proverbial expression 'Omnia vincit amor' from his tenth Eclogue. When Rolle is justifying his call to the reader to boundless unconditional love, he uses this pithy Virgilian formulation which he transfers as a matter of course into the new mystical context.[161] This quotation from Virgil was very widespread in the Middle Ages and we meet it for instance in Provençal love poetry.[162] Bernard of Clairvaux gave it a spiritual interpretation in his sermons on the *Song of Songs* when, in defining Christ as the embodiment of the Christian idea of love he refers to him as 'qui et vincentem omnia vicit mortem',[163] and we read in the *Imitatio Christi* 'Vincit ... omnia divina caritas'.[164]

Rolle's preference for the Virgilian motif is also remarkable when considered from a different angle, for we do not find this quotation in Middle English literature only in Rolle's works, but also in a 'secular' work – Chaucer's *Canterbury Tales*. In his characterization of the Prioress Chaucer works in the famous detail that she wore a brooch on which the inscription 'Amor vincit omnia' could be read.[165] Without knowing the mystical significance of this quotation, it is easy to see this as a splendid example of Chaucerian irony. This sentence, which concludes the characterization of the Prioress, leaves the reader with the impression that she may well with her vows have renounced all earthly pleasures but that she is still just as prepared to recognize the omnipotence of Amor. Scholarship has taken ample account of the fact that this quotation from Virgil was already current in a spiritual context before Chaucer.[166] But we must add that Chaucer's use of this quotation is a particularly clever, subtle form of irony; for because the expression was to be found in spiritual, indeed in mystical language, the real meaning of the term in Chaucer's portrait of the Prioress remains beautifully ambivalent and produces an extremely powerful ironic effect.

In this context it is worth looking at Chaucer's characterization of the Monk in the prologue to the *Canterbury Tales*. In his description of this somewhat secular-minded religious, Chaucer takes up the ironic detail that he wore a 'curious pyn' on which a 'love-knotte' could be seen.[167] The context makes it quite clear here, however, that the monk is following the secular custom of wearing a love-knot as decoration — a ribbon with two intertwined bows — but at the same time the irony is intensified even in this case, because a 'love-knot' could be used in both a secular and a spiritual context. The author of the *Cloud*, for instance, describes the mystical *unio* as 'to knit þe goostly knot of brennyng loue bitwix þee & þi God',[168] and Hilton uses similar words about the soul, that it 'knyttiþ þe knette of loue and deuocion to Ihesu'.[169] In the description of St Francis of Assisi in the *Meditations on the Life and Passion of Christ*, particular attention is paid to the knot in the rope which serves as a girdle round the Franciscan habit, and it is interpreted in a way which is very interesting in our context:

> Þe knotte bytokneþ stedefast loue
> Þat knetteþ him to God aboue.[170]

Rolle's Latin mysticism also knows the image of the mystical love-knot,[171] which is less surprising if we remember that the concept of the 'nodus amicitiae' is already to be found in Aelred of Rievaulx's *Speculum Charitatis*[172] and that it was already possible in antiquity to speak of a 'nodus' of friendship.[173] The image of tying a knot seems almost to stretch back to primitive archaic origins and perhaps to have archetypal status, for it is found in the magic of almost all peoples at all times, signifying both good fortune and misfortune.[174] And the Bible, too, has played a part in the development of this mystical imagery. Amongst the biblical passages which were drawn upon to supplement the erotic metaphorical language of the *Song of Songs* was the statement by the prophet Hosea that God intended to draw his people Israel to him with 'vinculis caritatis' (11:4).

This Bible passage is the basis for the popularity of the mystical love-bond, which appears in English mysticism not only in the special form of the 'love-knot' but also literally translated as 'loue-bondis'[175] or 'bondis of charite'.[176] Just as in secular poetry the God of Love or Frau Minne possesses the love-bond as a sign of his or her power,[177] so too the personified Love possesses it in the realm of mysticism. In English the *Ancrene Wisse* already makes the transition.[178] In the *Meditations on the Life and Passion of Christ* Christ is even bound to the cross through the personified Love with its bond: 'Loue bond so hym he myƷte not fle / Til he were nailed vp-on þe tre.'[179] A good example in German mysticism occurs in Mechthild of Magdeburg who praises the intensity of mystical love with the words: 'o minebant, din susse hant / Hat den gewalt, si bindet beide jung und alt.'[180]

If we survey the examples of the metaphorical language of mystical love which we have examined so far, we can see that in addition to the basic stock of metaphors obtained from the *Song of Songs* several others were borrowed from the language of secular love literature. But in our context we now have the additional question of whether the contemporary courtly love poetry did not in some way 'rub off' on vernacular mysticism. This is certainly the case, for instance, in the works of Hadewych or Mechthild of Magdeburg. But any such relationship that can be observed in England is considerably weaker. This is hardly surprising if we remember that courtly literature did not flourish to the same extent in England as it did on the continent, and 'the divisions between the classes were, on the whole, less rigorous than on the continent'.[181] One of the few exceptions is the famous passage in the *Ancrene Wisse* where Christ is portrayed as a noble wooer, who, after sending many messengers in advance, wants to prove his love to the soul 'þurh cnihtschipe' and goes as a knight in a figurative sense to the 'turneiment'.[182] Even if this is a clear analogy with the knightly courtly culture, we must nevertheless not see other passages in homiletic mystical literature, where Christ is often compared with a knight, as being directly taken from the knightly sphere: for Plato had already compared the life of man with the battle of a soldier, and Paul as well as individual Fathers and certain late medieval tracts had interpreted the life of Christ as a spiritual knighthood.[183] For a very long time it was usual to see the state of the 'miles', the warrior, as a model for a spiritual way of life. This, of course, does not exclude the possibility that in an age of courtly culture it was not least because of their newly acquired topicality that these metaphors were preferred.

Nor must we forget that courtly culture in its turn did not arise without an analogous reference to medieval theology. Not only was the lady seen as the secular counterpart to God as the 'summum bonum', but Hugo Kuhn has further shown that, just as in the Christian religion since the preaching of Jesus man is urged to convert in order to attain grace, so too the lady demands a similar conversion from the knight, a conversion to submission in an unconditional service for the Lady's favour.[184] For this reason we cannot look upon it as an influence of courtly poetry on mysticism, when in the *Ancrene Wisse*, the 'Wooing Group' and the *Talkyng of þe Loue of God* the well-known English petition formulas for grace and mercy are applied to Christ: we frequently find 'A Ihesu þin ore'[185] or 'When wil þou rew on me, Jhesu, þat I myght with þe be'.[186] The important point here is solely the fact that spiritual love and secular courtly love are brought into a relationship with each other by means of an analogy which is consciously drawn.

In the introduction to his edition of the 'Wooing Group' Thompson remarks that in these texts, as earlier in the *Ancrene Wisse* and later in the *Talkyng of þe Loue of God*, courtly concepts like *gentilesse* and *largesse* were transferred to God or Christ and thus acquired an elevated meaning.[187] This is quite right, but we must not overlook the fact that it was not in the flourishing of courtly culture that these terms first came into being: *largesse*, for example, as Curtius has shown, is 'a virtue of rulers dating back to antiquity',[188] and was not first applied to God in the courtly era.

It is not easy to answer the question as to how the term *courteisie* which is the central concept of courtly culture, came to be applied to God in English mystical texts. German mysticism constantly uses courtly ideas and concepts to describe the realm of the transcendental,[189] and Dante defines God as 'sire della cortesia', just as Francis of Assisi is said to have stressed 'cortesia' as a divine attribute.[190] Similarly in England a 'courtesy book' states quite unambiguously that 'courtesy comes from heaven'.[191] In English mysticism one might think first of the author of the *Cloud* whose texts on closer examination reveal a certain courtly attitude, for which he uses the term 'contynaunce'.[192] When he interprets the Mary-Martha episode from St Luke's gospel in the traditional manner as prefiguring the active and contemplative life, he judges the behaviour of the two sisters as decidedly courtly. Martha's rebuke to her sister that she is not helping her is forgiveable, says the author, because 'it was bot curtesly & in fewe wordes'.[193] He adds that Christ himself then replies to her 'curtesly, & as it was semely for him to do bi þe wey of reson'.[194] The existence of a courtly readership for these texts could account for the fact that in the *Pistle of Discrecioun of Stirings* the individual components of a crown are listed and given an allegorical interpretation.[195] But in English texts only Julian of Norwich applies the ideal of 'courtliness' to the mystical love between God and the soul, when she praises the 'curtesse loue of oure god almyghty'[196] and describes the essence of mystical love with the words: 'in loue is gentylle curtesse'.[197] This linking of *loue* and *curtesse* could indicate that here Julian deliberately intends a courtly analogy. As we shall show in some detail later, she demands an attitude of *courtesie* from man towards God, an adoring respectful distance, corresponding to the attitude which the lady requires of the knight.[198] But when the word *courtesie* is applied to God on other occasions in English mysticism, it has undergone an undeniable change in meaning. When courtly culture was on the decline in the fourteenth century, the term went over into common parlance and indeed, according to the *MED* it could be used to denote the epitome of the urban attitude to life. Thus the word could mean much the same as our modern term 'politeness', but it could also have the meaning 'goodness', 'generosity', 'favour',[199] and it is often found amongst the English mystics in precisely this meaning, as for instance when Hilton speaks of 'curteisie and þe merci of Ihesu'.[200]

Scholars sometimes tend to describe Richard Rolle as a spiritual troubadour, a 'troubadour of God'.[201] But we must be very careful in drawing such an analogy and ask ourselves whether it is at all convincing. Certainly Rolle led an unsettled life in poverty and praised in his works the passionate unconditional love of God, reminiscent perhaps of Francis of Assisi who voluntarily dedicated his life to the service of Donna Povertà. But whilst Francis saw his service to Lady Poverty as a conscious parallel with the service of the troubadour to the courtly lady, there is no similar analogous connection with courtly culture in Rolle. Such a connection is indeed a priori impossible, since Rolle always sees woman in a negative light and is only capable of seeing in her an occasion of sin. Clearly by nature susceptible to female beauty, he considers it only dangerous and seductive and, unlike other medieval mystics — Dante for instance — he is incapable of understanding it as an earthly reflection of divine beauty. Comper would thus seem to be right when she says of Rolle that he 'is singularly free from any strong influence of the French lays and love-songs'.[202]

Since there is such scant evidence to show that mystical texts drew concrete impulses from contemporary secular love poetry, it would seem also that the question so frequently asked as to the priority of secular or spiritual literature is wrongly put. Mehl is right to stress that it is more important to recognize the close links between secular and spiritual literature than to attempt to clarify the question of priority.[203] The same is true of the relationship between English mystical prose and contemporary secular love poetry, although in the prose there is a remarkably strong tendency to draw directly on the imagery of the *Canticum*.

IV

*

Metaphors for the preparation for the
unio mystica

Pointing out the need for the soul to prepare itself for the union with God is an important feature of Christian mystical texts. The English mystics make it very clear to the reader that man must fulfil certain conditions in order to be able to experience the mystical *unio*, and when they explain the nature of *purgatio*, the first of the three stages of the mystic way, they show a particularly homiletic concern.[1] We must now look more closely at certain aspects of this first stage of the way to mystical union, examining the linguistic features and drawing comparisons with German mysticism.

Man's withdrawal into himself

The fundamental prerequisite for the mystic is the complete concentration of the soul on itself. This concept, which is so important for Western mysticism, is expressed very vividly by the pseudo-Dionysius when, in his writings on the divine names, he says that the soul describes a circular movement: it withdraws from the outer world, enters into itself with all its powers, and when in this way it has become a One, it can unite with the Beautiful and the Good.[2] Origen taught that sin destroys the unity of man, splits him into parts and separates him from God.[3] For the pseudo-Dionysius, as also for the later mystics, the way into one's inner self is at the same time in a dialectical manner a way to God.[4] In Christian mysticism it was Augustine above all who raised the call for withdrawal into one's inner self to the central theme of the 'intrare ad semet ipsum'.[5] As a mysticism of introversion Christian mysticism aims at experiencing subjective 'inwardness',[6] and indeed the very term 'inwardness', which is both concrete and abstract, reflects

56

the basic character of mystical language altogether, is so to speak a focal point for it. Thus we find in Rolle's *The Form of Living* the very trenchant expression 'Contemplatyfe lyfe es mykel inwarde',[7] and the *Treatise of Perfection of the Sons of God*[8] as well as the *Mirror of Simple Souls*,[9] which are both translations, use the term *inwardness* as a matter of course. In the *Mirror*, for instance, man's abiding in his *inwardness* signifies the complete absence of all wishes and desires pertaining to the outside. The theme of the withdrawal of the soul into itself is translated literally into the vernacular by Master Eckhart when he instructs the soul that it must 'gân ûzer irme ûzersten in ir aller innerstez'.[10] The same image is taken over into English mysticism, where, for instance, Hilton recommends to his reader that she should 'entre wiþinne in to þin owene sowle bi meditacion'.[11]

When man enters into his own soul his undivided attention must be fixed on the object of his contemplation. Plato in his *Phaidon* already uses the image of gathering oneself.[12] In his study on Western mysticism, the gathering of the soul into itself ('se in se colligens') is declared by Bernard of Clairvaux to be the first stage of contemplation.[13] The same thought is also central for German and English mysticism — and this includes Rolle, which we must expressly state, for E. Underhill maintains somewhat unjustifiably in her introduction to Comper's edition of the *Fire of Love* that Rolle is a mystic 'fundamentally of the outgoing type'.[14] English texts use the term *gaderen* as a precise translation of *colligere*: Rolle's description of the mystical attitude as 'Totus intra colligitur'[15] is, for instance, rendered into English by Misyn as 'All inward he is geddyrd'.[16] It must, of course, be added here that on the theme of human attempts at preparation the orthodox mystical texts also indicate unmistakably that such preparation, like the actual *unio*, is only fully realized as a gift of divine grace or love: thus we read in Rolle that by grace man is '*drawne* inwardely til contemplacion of God',[17] and 'M. N.', the commentator of the *Mirror of Simple Souls*, implies that it is love by which 'a soule is drawe into hirsilf from al outward þing'.[18]

It is true that the author of the *Cloud* exhorts his reader: 'gader þi miȝtes & þi wittes holiche wiþ-inne þi-self, & worschip God þere',[19] but only after taking up a critical stance towards this kind of mystical language and making sure that it will not be misunderstood by the reader — a precaution which Hilton also takes as we have already seen.[20]

Most texts are agreed that the withdrawal of the soul into itself only constitutes a real prerequisite for experiencing the mystical *unio* if it is accompanied by a striving on man's part for merciless self-knowledge.

At first sight it may seem surprising that this ancient demand of Socrates should occur in English texts. But on closer examination it becomes clear that this thought is central for the Middle Ages, so much so that St Bernard in his twenty-second sermon on the *Song of Songs* refers *expressis verbis* to Socrates-Apollo. It was possible, too, for the Socratic demand to be fused with Christian teaching to produce a 'Christian Socratism',[21] since knowledge of the soul, which was considered to be the image of God, provided a form of knowledge of God, as we shall see later, and since it was possible to link it with biblical passages. Again it is the allegorizing of the *Song of Songs* which has become important here too, where the sponsus says to the sponsa: 'Si ignoras te . . . egredere' (1:7). Bernard says that here the sponsus is addressing the bride not as a bridegroom but as a 'magister', whose concern is that the soul should purify itself so that it will realize that it is destined for the *unio* and so that it will attain the beatific vision.[22] This call is also widespread in English mysticism and is expressed in some detail in Walter Hilton. In the first part of his *Scale* he refers to Augustine and recommends to his reader:

> þou schalt, if þou wilt, biginne a newe game and a newe
> trauaile, and þat is for to entre wiþinne in to þin owene sowle
> bi meditacion for to knowen what it is, and bi þe knowynge
> þerof, come to þe gostli knowyng of God; for Seint Austyn
> seiþ, Bi þe knowynge of my self, I schal gete þe knowyng of
> God.[23]

And elsewhere he adds that this striving for self-knowledge should only occur when man 'fele hym / stered bi grace'.[24] Later in the same work he interprets the verse from the *Song of Songs* 'Si ignoras te' with the words: 'þou sowle faire bi kinde mad to þe liknes of God, frel as a woman in þi bodi for þe firste synne bi cause þat / þou knowist [not] þi self þat aungeles fode schuld ben þi delices withinne.'[25] He elaborates this by referring to another verse from the *Canticum*: 'Introduxit me [rex] in cellam vinariam', which he allegorizes somewhat surprisingly as: 'þi Kyng of Blis Lord Ihesu led me in; þat is to seien, first in to miself for to biholden and knowyn my self. And after He ledde me in to His celer þat is to seie, a boue my self bi ouerpassinge onli in to Hym'[26] The need for the soul to know itself because it is made in the image of God is discussed in the final chapter.

The soul's 'emptying itself' as prerequisite for the 'unio mystica'

In medieval mysticism a prerequisite for experiencing God which is linked with the withdrawal of the soul into itself is the concept of freeing oneself from the creatural world, the *'abstractio a sensibus . . . indeed a carnali vita* altogether'. It is only this act of becoming free, this 'process of abstraction from the implications and demands of consciously being a person'[27] that enables the medieval mystic to become aware of God. J. Bernhart has drawn attention to the decisive treatment of this theme in Augustine who refers directly to the verse of the psalm 'vacate et videte, quoniam ego sum Deus' (Ps. 45:11), and interprets it as 'We make ourselves empty and see, we *see* and *love*, we love and praise.'[28] From then on the medieval mystics never grow tired of repeating this interpretation of 'vacare', always referring anew to this psalm verse. In his *Melos Amoris* Rolle says of the elect that they 'vacant viriliter a viciis';[29] they should, however, always make themselves available for the pouring in of mystical music, 'vacarent canori contemplacionis',[30] although, of course, many would unfortunately not be well versed in the 'sabatizare in mente.'[31] Bernhart goes on to show that Augustine does not merely stress the need to empty oneself, but actually postulates a direct connection between love and knowledge: '*Amare* and *cognoscere* denote reciprocal values, and in professing this, Platonic and Aristotelian thinkers from Augustine to Nicholas of Cusa ally themselves with mysticism.'[32]

In their efforts to translate these themes into the vernacular, the German mystics performed great feats in the field of language creation, and many of their innovations still exist today, even if the meaning of the individual terms may have changed. We should perhaps mention particularly the concepts *abegescheidenheit, sich lâzen* and *gelâzenheit*, terms of abandonment designed to urge those adept in mysticism to set themselves the goal of a 'state of selfless passivity which transcends sensuality and the idea of wanting something'.[33] We read for instance in Tauler: 'Enkein vernunft enmag daz begriffen waz in diser rehter worer gelossenheit verborgen lit.'[34]

In contrast to German mysticism, no uniform terminology for these terms emerged in medieval English texts, although here, too, as is to be expected, we frequently come across the thought that man must be dead to the world and must feel himself free for God's grace. In his *English Psalter* Rolle uses the word *tome*, which was soon to die out, when translating the psalm verse 'vacate et videte' as 'Takistome and sees for . i. am god'.[35] The translation of this verse in the *Scala Claustralium* of Guigo II is very inexact: 'Beþinke yowe vttyrly and see howe swete God our Sauyoure is.'[36] Hilton, too, gives only a very imprecise rendering of *vacare* when he translates the verse into English with the words 'Cese ȝe & seeþ þat I am God' and adds: 'cese ȝe sumtyme of outwarde wirkynge.'[37] The spatial concept of emptying oneself (of all earthly images and ties) is only rarely retained in translations into English. Richard Misyn, who in his translations of Rolle uses such terms as *to be gyfen to*[38] and *to take hede*[39] for Rolle's *vacare*, only occasionally chooses the adequate adjective *voyde*, as for instance in his translation of the *Emendatio Vitae*, where the psalm verse is: 'be voyde fro wardly vanite & se for I am god.'[40] The author of the *Cloud* uses the same root in his *Pistle of Discrecioun of Stirings*, where he advises the novice in mystical contemplation to renounce everything which is beneath God: 'vtterly voiding fro þi goostly beholding alle maner of siȝt of any þing bineþe him.'[41] This is one of the rare occasions when the author of the *Cloud* uses the verb *voiden*,[42] although the concept of 'emptying oneself' as a prerequisite for the mystical *unio* is fundamental for his mysticism. This is probably because, when he is describing the freeing of the soul from everything sensual, he usually chooses the descriptively more powerful image of the 'cloude of forȝetyng' with which the earthly world has to be covered.[43] The author of the tract *The Chastising of God's Children*, which draws heavily on Ruysbroeck's *Gheestelike Brulocht*, treats this theme in considerable detail. But *Chastising* uses *voide*, *voiden* and *voidaunce* primarily to warn the reader against misunderstanding them as meaning 'comfortable inactivity' and unwillingness to work. The tract thus attacks the pseudo-mysticism of quietism, which came in the wake of the *Devotio Moderna*, by explaining that every man is by nature capable of attaining a state of separation from the earthly world, but that this alone does not deserve to be called divine; for in such a quietistic state God will be forgotten, since the urgent, impatient love of God is not compatible with such a state of rest:

whan a man stondiþ . . . al voide and idel, noþing occupied wiþ (þe ouer) wittis of þe soule, þanne bi verrai kynde he comeþ into reste. Þis reste men mowen fynde bi verrei kynde in hemsilf wiþout worchyng of grace, if þei konne voide and deliuere hem fro al maner imagynaciouns and deedis and werkis; but in þis voidaunce and ydelnesse a goode louyng soule may haue no reste, for goode loue and feruent charite and þe inward worchyng and touchyng of þe grace of god wol nat suffre a man reste in þis maner ydelnesse or voidaunce.[44]

In this context the term *ese* merits special attention. It is a term used by the author of the *Cloud* and by Hilton to convey the effect of *vacatio* on the soul. The reader of the *Pistle of Discrecioun of Stirings* is assured that 'louely and listely to wilne haue God is grete & passing ese',[45] and in the *Scale* we read that freeing oneself in the night of the soul from all creatural ties is 'grete ese for þe soule þat desiriþ þe luf of Iesu'.[46] The fact that Hilton here links *ese* and *luf* is particularly noteworthy, since in courtly love poetry the successful striving of the knight to obtain his lady's favour is also described as the attained state of *ese*. In Chaucer's *Troilus and Criseyde ese* and *disese* amount almost to a leitmotif, and *ese* is used to describe the state of bliss which the lovers achieve through the physical act of lovemaking. At the climax of the poem we read of Troilus and Criseyde: 'And diden al hire myght, syn they were oon,/ For to recoueren blisse and ben at eise.'[47] It is clear then that this seemingly insignificant term *ese* is extremely important for the language of English mysticism and that it should be included amongst the numerous analogies between mystical and secular love language which we have already examined in detail. Because this *ese* of contemplation was taken by outsiders to imply inactivity or even laziness and was used by some as an excuse for a comfortable life, it gave rise to criticism of contemplatives by their contemporaries who were leading an active life. Thus Langland in his *Piers Plowman* includes hermits in his social criticism when he remarks that they had gone to Walsingham with their wenches 'And shopen hem heremites here ese to haue'.[48] Hilton, too, like the other mystics, campaigns against the misunderstanding of quietism. But in the very same breath in which he proclaims mystical *ese*, he makes it clear to those adept at it that the indifference and inactivity of the soul apply only to earthly things, but that the soul is completely occupied with its thoughts of Christ: 'for þawȝ þe soule þink not of ony erþly þinge, nerþeles it is ful bisy for to þinke on Him'.[49]

The laying bare of the soul

The mystics delight in describing the freeing of the soul from all dependence on earthly, non-essential things, the rejection of all ties, as an act of baring oneself. Man's wish to bare himself in order to accept God can sometimes go so far that, as in the case of Francis of Assisi, he wishes to strip off his clothes in order to comply in this radical manner with the command to imitate the crucified Christ. Latin mysticism uses the terms *nudus* and *exuere* to describe this laying bare of the soul. In Richard of St Victor, for instance, we read that the soul 'seipsam penitus exuit, divinum quemdam affectum induit',[50] and in the Alemannic translation of Rudolf of Biberach's *De Septem Itineribus Aeternitatis* we read similarly of the human heart: 'so zuht es sich selben vs und bekleidet sich selber mit einer goetlichen begirde'.[51] In the Eckhart School we find formulations like 'diu sêle muoz als gar enbloezet werden alles des, daz zuogevallen ist',[52] and there is extensive discussion of the need for the 'stripping of the soul' or for its 'nakedness'.[53]

Similar statements are to be found in English mysticism. In the *Book of Privy Counselling* we read that the thinking and willing of the soul must be freed from everything non-essential and must therefore be naked: 'alle corious sechinges . . . fer put back; þat þi þouȝt be nakid'.[54] The human act of will, for which the author uses the term *entent* — which, as Hodgson has pointed out,[55] corresponds to the Scholastic term *intentio* — must be directed nakedly and exclusively to God and his very being: 'þou felist in þi wille a nakid entent vnto God.'[56] This 'nakid entent' is taken up again at the beginning of the *Book of Privy Counselling*, where it is explained somewhat more precisely for the adept mystic to the effect that the important thing in the initial stages of contemplation is a 'nakid þouȝt & a blynde feling of þin owne beyng',[57] a naked consciousness of one's own existence. It is then important to offer up this 'nakid blynde felyng of þin owne beyng' to God.[58] But it must be the goal of the contemplative to get beyond this 'blynde felyng of þi nakid beyng', in order to feel nothing any longer except solely the being of God, for God is in any case the being of the soul.[59]

The repeated assertion by the author of the *Cloud* that man must give himself to God in a naked longing is in line with Hilton's recommendation to his reader that 'al þi trauail schal ben to drawen in þi þouȝte fro alle biholdynges of all erthli þing, þat þi disir miȝte be as it were [made] naked and bar from alle erdli þinges.'[60] In the *Treatise of Perfection* the contemplative souls are 'occupied in the nakede loue of god'.[61] The 'nakede loue' is somewhat reminiscent of Mechthild of Magdeburg's 'nakkende miñe'.[62] Mechthild's use of this figurative expression, however, is unambiguously erotic. G. Lüers, who has undertaken a systematic survey of the metaphors in Mechthild, suspects that the terminology nudus = bloz (naked) = absolutus is somewhat fused with conceptions of the way Amor is depicted in classical antiquity.[63] In the 'nakid entent' of the author of the *Cloud* there is, however, at most a very mild erotic analogy.

The fact that this metaphorical imagery has biblical roots seems to have escaped Lüers. But there is no doubt that it must be linked with the language of St Paul who demands that the Christian must put off the old man and put on the new, i.e. in the last analysis, Christ (Col. 3:9; Rom. 13:14). Suso clearly has these passages from St Paul in mind when he tells souls that they should '[sich] mit Jhesum umbkleiden',[64] and Hilton translates and interprets this same thought with the words: 'Spoile ʒourself of þe olde man . . . þat is, kaste fro ʒow þe luf of þe werld with alle werdly maners.'[65] The author of the *Cloud*, too, is certainly referring to St Paul when he equates the soul's wish to be laid bare with the lover's longing for his beloved, who sees the fulfilment of her love-longing in being clothed with the desired 'object'. Here too he draws heavily on Hilton's translation of the verse from St Paul: '& þis is þe trewe condicion of a parfite louer, only & vtterly to spoyle hym-self of him-self for þat þing þat he louiþ, & not admit ne suffre to be cloþed bot only in þat þing þat he louiþ.'[66] According to Reitzenstein the underlying concept here has its roots in the idea of *transfiguratio* from the Hellenistic Mystery Religions, where the garment was already considered to be an outward sign for this metamorphosis, since it symbolized the $\mu o \rho \phi \dot{\eta}$ $\vartheta \epsilon o \tilde{v}$.[67] Julian, too, uses a linguistically very simple but highly effective formulation which echoes this thought, when she says of God: 'He is oure clothing that for loue wrappeth vs.'[68]

The concept of nakedness for describing the unconditional nature of mystical love is something which the author of the *Cloud*, alone amongst English mystics, applies to God too, when he stresses that the goal of mystical love can only lie in God's naked existence, his very being: 'þof al it be good to þink [a] pon þe kindenes of God, & to loue hym & preise him for hem: ʒit it is fer betyr to þink apon þe nakid beyng of him, & to loue him & preise him for him-self.'[69] Here, too, the author of the *Cloud* is drawing on a very old mystical tradition, which, as has been observed, developed in connection with the use of the word '$\gamma v \mu v \acute{o} v$' in Philo and the pseudo-Dionysius. This tradition was frequently taken up in mysticism, especially in Germany, where, for instance, Master Eckhart explains the process of the intellectual understanding of God in an extremely drastic manner: 'Vernünfticheit ziuhet gote daz vel der güete abe und nimet in blôz, dâ er entkleidet ist von güete und von wesene und von allen namen.'[70]

Mystical annihilation

Preparation for experiencing God in the *unio* includes the consciousness of one's own nothingness in the act of complete surrender, of one's self as *annihilatio*.[71] This prerequisite stems on the one hand from the call to imitate Christ and on the other hand from the apophatic theology of the Areopagite, according to which God is to be understood as a nothing rather than as a something, which was why one had to surrender oneself freely to the nothing. The mystics do not only refer to the New Testament call for self-denial, but also again and again, like Hilton, for instance, to the psalm verse: 'Ego ad nihilum redactus sum' (Ps. 72:22).[72] The use of the perfect passive in this verse could be interpreted allegorically as meaning that God has created man in nothingness.[73] This idea of the annihilation of man by God is expressed particularly effectively in the *Mirror of Simple Souls*, where the soul addresses personified Love with the words: 'he oonli haþ made me noon, and þe nouȝt of þis noon haþ put me in a lowe depnesse vndir lasse þan nouȝt.'[74]

The term *ze nihte werden* and the verb *vernüten* are amongst the central concepts of German mysticism.[75] Tauler for instance exhorts the soul 'du solt dich selber vernúten',[76] and Ruysbroeck even coins the term 'vernieutende leven'.[77] It is very interesting to observe the remarkable agreement that exists on this theme in Hilton, Julian, the *Mirror of Simple Souls* and the works of the author of the *Cloud*, which can scarcely be mere chance. These writers even use identical expressions to make the point that self-denial must stem from a meek and humble attitude. Compare for instance the statement of the author of the *Cloud* on the 'nobil nouȝtnyng of it-self [i.e. the soul] in verrey meeknes'[78] with that of the commentator of the *Mirror of Simple Souls*, of whom we only know the initials 'M. N.': 'þese soules nowten so hemsilf bi uerrey mekenesse.'[79] But Hilton adds a further aspect here — for him the annihilation of the self means at the same time becoming conscious of the darkness of the soul. He supports this argument with an allegorical interpretation of the verse from Isaiah: 'Intra in tenebras tuas, filia Caldeorum' (47:5).[80] A mystical interpretation of this biblical passage is rather unusual, and it illustrates very impressively how the medieval mystics were always seeking to underpin their arguments with references to ever new Bible passages. Hilton praises this recognition of the nothingness of the soul as 'a good mirknes & a riche nouȝt',[81] and his statement is thus very akin to the *Cloud*, which starts from the basic concept that abiding in the nothing leads to the greatest nearness to God. The meek surrender of one's own self makes the complete contemplative experience of God possible: 'þis nobil nouȝtnyng of it-self in verrey meeknes & þis hyȝe allyng of God in parfite charite, it deserueþ to haue God.'[82] The author is here follow- ing the pseudo-Dionysius and has in mind the fundamental mystical paradox that it is precisely in the state of annihilation that the soul experiences the *all* of God: 'What is he þat clepiþ it nouȝt? Sekirly it is oure vtter man & not oure inner. Oure inner man clepiþ it Al.'[83] The *Mirror* shows a particularly close affinity with the *Cloud* when it states: 'And þis nouȝt [i.e. recognition of the creature's nothingness] . . . ȝiueþ hir þe al, and oþirwise myȝte sche not haue it.'[84] Julian adds that Christ has given an example of this 'nouȝtyng' with his passion.[85]

This mystical annihilation is not merely to be understood as humble self-denial but also, as we have already argued, as a rejection of all images from the creatural world and all earthly ties. Julian's famous vision in which she sees the whole of creation in the size of a hazelnut which appears to dissolve into a nothing, has to be seen in this con- text.[86] Here, as we have already seen, the *Cloud* uses the image of the cloud of forgetting with which the soul has to cover the creatural world.[87] In addition the *Cloud* radicalizes this thought at the climax of its stylistically quite masterly argument. After the author has quite deliberately confused his pupil by recommending that he should neither go into himself nor stay anywhere else, the pupil, somewhat perplexed, asks: 'Wher þan . . . schal I be? Noȝwhere by þi tale!' The author then admits that he deliberately tried to elicit this response from him, 'for þere wolde I haue þee',[88] because if one is to experi- ence God it is essential to abide in the nowhere and reject the some- where: 'Lat be þis eueriwhere & þis ouȝt, in comparison of þis [noȝ- where & þis] nouȝt.'[89] At first sight it is very surprising to find an almost verbatim parallel to this statement in Mechthild of Magdeburg's *Flies- sendes Licht der Gottheit*, where this antithesis — typical for German mysticism — is expressed in the corresponding linguistic terminology. Mechthild exhorts her reader: 'du solt minnen das niht. / du solt vliehen daz iht.'[90] There is of course no reason to postulate any direct influence of Mechthild on the author of the *Cloud*. Just as many simi- larities between German and English mysticism do not necessarily indicate any influence but arise simply because both go back to a common tradition, so too the parallel in linguistic terminology here results from the fact that both draw on pseudo-Dionysian mysticism and both use the same linguistic possibilities of the Germanic language.

For the author of the *Cloud* this abiding in the 'nouȝt' as a prerequisite for experiencing the 'al' also implies a rejection of any willing of one's own — apart from the one exception of the loving longing for God for his own sake without having any specific divine attribute in mind.[91] In Germany Rudolf of Biberach argues in the same way as the *Cloud*, following Thomas Gallus' affective interpretation of the pseudo-Dionysius. Master Eckhart is much further removed from the *Cloud*. He takes the lack of will of the annihilated soul to such an extreme that the soul does not actively desire anything any more, not even God. In Eckhart we read: 'Und der geist enmac niht anders wellen, dan daz got wil, und daz enist niht sîn unvrîheit, ez ist sîn eigen vrîheit.'[92] 'Si [the soul] enwil ouch niht got, als er got ist.'[93] 'Her umbe sô biten wir got, daz wir gotes ledic werden.'[94] Amongst the English works there is one text, the *Mirror of Simple Souls*, where this same Eckhartian thought is propounded at some length. In the *Mirror*, just as in Eckhart, the mystic is described as someone who surrenders himself to God like an empty vessel without any will. This is what the author of the French original, Margherita Porete, understood by real spiritual freedom. As we have seen, it was this radical striving for freedom which gave the Brethren of the Free Spirit their name: 'þis soule haþ hir wille yȝouen þat sche haþ not what to wille but þe wille of him to whom sche haþ hir wille yȝoue. Suche folkes lyuen in fredom of charite þat haue noþing of wille. Who þat askide hem what þei wolde, in sooþe, þei wolden seie, noþing.'[95] This theme is so important for the *Mirror* that it is expressed in almost poetic terms when on one occasion there is a reference to the way to the 'contrey of nouȝt wyllynge'.[96] It is easier to see why the author of the *Mirror* was misunderstood and condemned as a heretic than is the case with Eckhart, since, unlike Eckhart, Margherita Porete did not propound practical love of one's neighbour as a counterbalance to her rather quietistic tendencies. Although the *Mirror* is often reminiscent of the *Cloud*, the two texts differ appreciably on precisely this point. In the *Cloud* the abiding in the nowhere is not a state of complete inactivity with no will, but a perfectly active desire for God for his own sake, and hence the reader is expressly urged to this spiritual activity: 'trauaile fast in þis nouȝt & þis nouȝwhere'[97] — a statement which we have already come across in Hilton.

V

*

Metaphors for the way of the soul to God

If the survey in the previous chapter showed that the soul's way into itself is at the same time in a dialectical manner a way to God, the texts
are nevertheless also full of further attempts to overcome the distance
between the soul and God by the use of concrete metaphorical images.
A great variety of images has been used for this since time immemorial.
A frequent and favourite image is that of the journey, which is found in
the title of Bonaventure's *Itinerarium Mentis in Deum* and which is
also basic to the structure of Dante's *Commedia*. The motif of the mystical journey is found in English mysticism only in Hilton's *Scale* where
it takes the form of the famous allegory of a pilgrimage to Jerusalem.[1]
Otherwise English mysticism uses the equally ancient motif of mystical
leading, which goes back to the ancient Mystery Cults. The *Ancrene
Wisse* attempts to interpret Yahweh's promise to Hosea that he will lead
his beloved into solitude (2:14) in this mystical sense.[2] Similarly Rolle
says of the soul that it follows 'ductorem dilectum ad locum in quo
ludat amans cum amato'.[3] Divine grace is often referred to, *expressis
verbis*, as the guide to mystical experience, as for instance by the author
of the *Cloud* who calls it 'þe gide of þi goostly wey'.[4]

The idea of being led by God is present indirectly, as it were, in the
call which occurs time and again in mystical texts to recognize God
from his footsteps in creation. For Augustine,[5] Bonaventure[6] and Franciscan mysticism, observing and following the divine footsteps in created
nature is the lowest stage in knowing or experiencing God: the underlying premise here is that the greatness of the creator can be recognized
from the greatness of his creation. This is why we read in German mysticism, for instance: 'wir menschen erraten dich an dînen vuozsporn, die
wir ûzen sehen an der geschephede.'[7] But in English mysticism this idea
is only seldom found, and indeed the earthly world altogether is scarcely

67

even given any worthwhile mention, although the *Speculum Ecclesiae* specifically describes contemplation 'in Creatures' as the first of the three possible kinds of contemplation.[8] Whenever natural phenomena are mentioned, they usually only have the function of parables to illustrate specific intellectual truths. Of the two ways of attaining a knowledge of God, the positive way of following the divine footsteps in the created world and the negative way of emptying oneself and freeing oneself of all earthly creaturalness, the English authors almost exclusively follow the latter, which, according to the pseudo-Dionysius, is the one which brings us closest to experiencing God. One of the rare occasions when the word *tracen* is used in a figurative, mystical sense — much earlier than the *OED* gives, is a passage in the *Pistle of Discrecioun of Stirings* from the *Cloud*-group, where the author explains to his reader that an intellectual understanding of God is only enough to 'trace how miȝty, how wise, & how good he is in his creatures, bot not in himself'.[9] The only way to experience God as intensively as earthly conditions will allow is through the unconditional love of God.

English mysticism likes to use the image of the 'feet of love' to describe in concrete terms this loving will-power of the soul which enables it to get close to God. In the texts of the *Cloud*-group, Rolle, Hilton and the *Myroure of Oure Ladye*,[10] the soul attempts to reach God by means of the foot of love or the feet of the 'affections'. Apart from the pseudo-Dionysius, Thomas Cisterciensis, Thomas Gallus and Hugh of St Caro,[11] it was above all Augustine who provided the source for these images. In his *Enarratio in Psalmum IX.15*[12] he equates *amor* and *pes animae*. The English translation of Guigo II's tract *Scala Claustralium* then even goes so far as to explain that every mention of a foot in the Bible has to be interpreted allegorically as an image for mystical love: 'By a fote in Holy Wrytte is love vndirstond.'[13] Finally, in the *Ancrene Wisse*, which is the first English homiletic and partly mystical text where foot and love are equated, the allegorical process is extended to the animal world: thus the ostrich, since it usually keeps its feet on the earth, becomes a symbol of the man choosing against God.[14] In Hilton's paraphrase of the *Stimulus Amoris* the reader is encouraged to place the foot of his love into the holes of the tree of the cross,[15] which cannot be understood and acted upon if it is taken literally but only if one mentally adds the symbolic content of both images.

In some cases the movement of the foot of love is described in very concrete terms as a stepping towards God. In this way the author of the *Cloud* illustrates very impressively a concept which is central for him, namely the complete detachment from the world of earthly phenomena.

The world should be completely covered with a cloud of forgetting '& þou schalt step abouen it stalworþly . . . wiþ a deuoute & a plesing stering of loue'.[16] If this gesture expresses very convincingly the process of overcoming what is materially non-essential, yet Rolle, in using this same image of stepping towards God, runs the risk of using mystical language in a purely theatrical manner. The fact that he describes the longed-for divine dwelling as 'granditer gradiens per gradum gloriosum ad sedem supernam',[17] gives rise to the suspicion that with this hypertrophied gesture he wants to make himself the centre of the mystical happening.

Since time immemorial various religions have illustrated how the distance between the soul and God is overcome by describing it as the soul clambering and climbing up. Once again it is without doubt the Bible which is the main source of these metaphors for Christian mysticism, especially the Old Testament. In a dream Jacob sees a ladder (Gen. 28:12) the top of which reaches to heaven, and this has become a prototype for the image of the ladder leading directly to God, an image which has been widespread in mysticism since John Climacus. When Moses in his search for God climbs Mount Sinai, this is applied allegorically first by Philo and later by Richard of St Victor to the mystical ascent of the soul, and, as Hodgson has shown, the *Cloud* here follows Richard's interpretation exactly when it explains to the reader:

> Moyses . . . wiþ grete longe trauayle he clombe up to þe top of
> þe mounteyne & wonid þere & wrouȝt in a cloude six daies. . . .
> By Moises longe trauaile & his late schewyng ben vnderstonden
> þoo þat mowe not come to þe perfeccion of þis goostly werk
> wiþ-outen longe trauayle comyng before.[18]

When we examine the linguistic realization of these metaphors it is quite remarkable that the English mystics in their attempts to translate this image of climbing up to God into the vernacular, only rarely use the borrowed word *ascenden* which already existed in Middle English. The reason for this may well be that it seemed to them too colourless a term to be appropriate for a dynamic movement of the soul towards God. Instead English texts prefer *climben* and another Germanic verb *stien*, which are cognate with the usual words in German mysticism (*uf*)*klimmen* and *stigen*.[19] Richard Rolle gives the word *climben* an extra degree of vividness by adding to it the prepositional phrase indicating the direction *Jhesuwarde*: '[I] wyll þat þou be ay clymbande tyll Jhesu-warde.'[20] In the *Ancrene Wisse* already the readers are exhorted to 'astihen up on ow seolf wið heh þoht toward heouene'.[21] The very vivid use of the verb *stien* by Walter Hilton seems almost to echo this passage when he describes the effect of prayer with the words 'in preier, he felith þe þou3t of his hert . . . vp sti3ende in to Oure Lord bi feruent disir.'[22] It is true that he follows the scholastic definition of prayer which derives ultimately from John of Damascus: 'oratio est ascensus mentis ad deum',[23] but his use of the preposition *in to* is surely rather more intensive than the Latin *ad* and implies the concept of the spatial entering into God, which is also found, for instance, in the title of Bonaventure's work *Itinerarium Mentis in Deum*.

The same suggestion of overcoming a spatial dimension also under-lies the traditional image of stretching oneself out into God, which the author of the *Cloud* chooses when he explains his concept of 'nakid entent', of the unconditional surrender of the soul to God, as a 'streching into God'.[24] It is worth commenting on the fact that the image appears in the form of a verbal noun, for verbal nouns, which are decisive for the dynamic effect of the language of German mysticism, occur with comparable frequency in English texts too, almost as a stylistic element. Walter Hilton, however, feels himself obliged to give a clear warning against possible misunderstandings of this metaphor of the mystical climb, and this warning amounts to a partial retraction of the image content of the metaphor: the human 'ymaginacioun' must not visualize this climb in any sensual, concrete manner, otherwise man will fall back into the world of the material, and such an aid to under-standing is only permitted in the case of inexperienced 'symple soules'.[25]

The more passionate the language of the mystic becomes, the nearer it necessarily gets to the language of earthly love, and hence the *Song of Songs* once again assumes importance in the metaphorical descrip-tion of the soul's way to God. In one of the first verses of the *Canti-cum*, for example, we read how the girl hurries to her lover,[26] and the mystics are particularly fond of using this as a motif. Hugh of St Victor and Dante, for instance, provide examples for the popularity of this metaphor,[27] nor does it elude German mysticism where we find for example that the soul 'îlet ûf ûber sich in got'.[28] The English texts constantly modify this motif. Thus the author of the *Cloud* explains to his reader how to find the shortest route to heaven: 'þe hi3e & þe nexte wey þeder is ronne by desires, & not by pases of feet.'[29] And Richard Rolle confesses in a poem in the tract *Ego Dormio* that Jesus taught him love when he went running to him, and that now he is capable of love and is growing pale with longing for his beloved:

> Now wax I pale and wan for luf of my lemman.
> Jhesu, bath God and man, þi luf þou lerd me þan
> When I to þe fast ran; forþi now I lufe kan.[30]

But this kind of figurative language only attains its full development in Rolle's Latin mysticism, where his metaphorical description of the way to God is quite unthinkable without the terms *currere*, *festinare* and *ruere*. Such terms provide the spark for the poetic strength of his imagination and enable it to produce ever new images. He speaks of the soul's rushing to the 'festum futurum'[31] and to the 'forum futurum',[32] and that the soul 'in sponsi amplexus ruet reverenter'.[33] But in Rolle the soul is above all searching in great haste for the sounds of heavenly music.[34]

It was at the latest with Bernard of Clairvaux that it became usual in mysticism to reverse the motif of hurrying into the *unio mystica* and to apply it to Christ, who, as a *deus desiderans* — we have already mentioned this motif — hastens to the end of his passion in order to redeem mankind.[35] And again it is particularly Richard Rolle among the English mystics who introduces into his texts a common motif from affective mysticism, when he says of Christ that his love for the soul made him run to the cross: 'Ipse uero Christus quasi nostro amore languet, dum tanto ardore ut nos adquireret ad crucem festinauit.'[36]

The haste with which the soul strives for its goal is expressed even more dynamically in the sensual concrete metaphor of the soul leaping to God. German mysticism has both the 'leap' of man 'an die blozzen gotheit'[37] and the leap 'in das herze Godis'.[38] This imagery can be compared with Rolle's attempt to define the first degree of his scale of mystical love, which he took from Richard of St Victor, as 'spryng-and on heght'.[39] In the course of his meditations on the passion the author of the *Talkyng of þe Loue of God* expresses his longing for God in a very concrete image, which is only rarely to be found in German mysticism: 'I. lepe on him raply. as grehound on herte. al out of my self. wiþ loueliche leete.'[40] Sister Elsbeth Hainburg of Villingen uses a similar image when she compares herself with a hound which will run itself to death on the trail rather than desist from its prey.[41] The short tract *The Art of Dieing*, however, shows us that this imagery is not so much to be understood as a very bold metaphor but as a continuation of the traditional animal allegory of the bestiaries, for in this non-mystical tract we read:

The hare renneth and the greyhound renneth: that oon for drede, that other for gret desyr. That on fleeth, that other chaseth. The holy men renneth as greyhoundes for thei have evere here eighen to hevene, for there thei seen the praie that thei honten and chaseth after.[42]

It is interesting at this point to draw comparisons with the *Cloud*, for once again it is precisely its author who is somewhat critical of this kind of metaphorical usage. In his view an attitude expressed in such imagery does not reveal any true understanding of the process of the opening up of the soul to God, but lays itself open to the charge of being immature ('rude'[43]). He recommends that the adept mystic should not experience the eagerness of a greyhound ('lache not ouer hastely, as it were a gredy grehounde'),[44] but should practise a certain amount of secrecy towards God. For God should, as it were, not notice how much he is loved by his mystical lover.[45]

The image of the soul soaring up to God in contemplative flight is one of the basic concepts of mysticism. It was inspired by a whole series of biblical passages, above all the frequent occurrences of metaphors of flight in the psalms.[46] But Plato, too, endows the soul with wings, with the help of which it soars up into the realm of ideas.[47] It has been shown that in Latin mysticism it is chiefly the Victorines who favour this imagery.[48] The same tradition is common too in German mysticism, and is found in English mysticism as early as the *Ancrene Wisse*. Here the words of Jesus that foxes have holes and the birds of the air have nests (Matt. 8:20) are developed along the lines of the bestiaries into a lengthy and highly idiosyncratic allegory, in which the physical form and the way of life of the birds are taken as a model and symbol for the life of a recluse: just as a bird in flight keeps its head low — note the exactness of the observation — and in doing so forms the shape of a cross, so too the recluse should be humble and take on herself the cross of Christ. It is only to maintain her physical health that a recluse may come into contact with earthly things, for a bird only comes down to earth for food, but looks round anxiously whenever it does so, for it feels itself in danger.[49] This is very reminiscent of a similar allegory of the flight of a bird in Mechthild of Magdeburg's *Fliessendes Licht der Gottheit*, where she says:

Dc [daz] der vogel lange bi der erden ist, da mitte verboeset er sine vlúgel und sine vedern werdent swere... Je lenger er vlúget, je er wuñenklicher swebet, kume als vil dc er dc ertrich berueret dc er sich labe ... glicher wis sollen wir vns bereiten.[50]

Amongst the English mystics of the fourteenth century it is primarily Rolle who takes up the metaphor of the bird in flight: when considering the bee the thought occurs to him that some men are 'of gude flyeghynge, for thay flye fra erthe to heven, and rystes thaym thare in thoghte, and are fedde in delite of Goddes lufe'.[51] In his *Melos Amoris* it is the 'supernas sedes'[52] or the divine 'cithara'[53] that the soul wishes to reach by its swift flight. Later in the same work Rolle interprets a passage from Revelations in a very individualistic manner in order to illustrate the goal of the mystic: the birds who are summoned by an angel in the sun to come and gather for the great feast of God are taken by Rolle as a symbol for the contemplatives, for 'omnibus sanctis qui agiles sunt in volatu contemplacionis'.[54]

Apart from these concrete images of the mystical climb of the soul to God, there are other concepts reflecting the movement of the soul towards God in a very general way, which deserve closer examination in our context. There is first of all the language of the author of the *Cloud*, a prose which frequently proves to be remarkably dynamic. This is clear from his individualistic use of the verb *put(ten)* which he has a special liking for. When he teaches his young pupil that he must turn to God in active surrender he uses words like 'meekly put apon him wiþ preier, & sone wil he help þee. . . . Put on þan. . . . Bot what schalt þou do, & how schalt þou put?'[55] In these sentences the word *put(ten)* has the meaning *to push forward to*. The late fifteenth century translation of the *Cloud* by the Carthusian Richard Methley is a great help in coming to an understanding of this mystical term. Where the *Cloud* states that 'a blynde steryng of loue vnto God for him-self & soche a priue loue put vpon þis cloude of vnknowyng'[56] is beneficial to the soul and pleasing to God, the Latin translation renders this very precisely with the words 'in cognita mocio amorosa ad deum pure propter seipsum et talis misticus ictus super hanc ignorancie caliginem'.[57] *Put(ten)* thus expresses the meaning of the Latin *ictus* which plays such an important role in Augustine to denote intentional desire. Just as Augustine demands that mystical surrender to God must be 'toto ictu cordis',[58] with all the will-power of the heart, so too the author of the *Cloud* explains that 'in þis lityl loue put ben contenid alle þe vertewes of mans soule'.[59]

Another of the author of the *Cloud*'s favourite verbs, *smyten*, is also somewhat more dynamic. He demands of his reader that 'þou schalt smite doun al maner þouȝt vnder þe cloude of forȝeting.'[60] He also uses the same word when advising his reader to try to break through the cloud of unknowing which separates him from God: '&

smyte apon þat þicke cloude of vnknowyng wiþ a scharp darte of longing loue'.[61] Sometimes he uses the no less expressive verb *beten* as a synonym for *smyten*, as for instance when he says, 'bete euermore on þis cloude of vnknowyng . . . wiþ a scharpe darte of longing loue'.[62] The love dart referred to expressly in these last two quotations as an instrument for pushing forward to God, and as a sensual concrete image for the way the mystic is compelled to beat his way into what is only half certain, is included with very telling effect in the author's meta- phorical imagery on another occasion when he says, 'bi loue we may [fynde] him, [fele] him and hit him euen in himself.'[63] It is clear from the context that *hit* has the meaning *to strike with a missile*, for the pushing forward of the soul towards God is described as a 'blinde schote', which 'may neuer faile of þe prik, þe whiche is God'.[64] This example is typical of the remarkable ability of the author of the *Cloud*, despite his scepticism towards the use of metaphors in mysti- cism, to use verbs with an active content and apply them figuratively to spiritual situations. As a concrete image it also compares favourably with similar images in German mysticism, and seems at first sight to be no less bold than Mechthild of Magdeburg's magnificent image that 'diu ingende minne . . . spannet iren bogen und Schüsset got in sin hertze'.[65] But on closer examination we see that the author of the *Cloud*, as a kind of theological insurance, indicates that his metaphors derive ultimately from the Bible — in fact from the verse from the *Song of Songs* which we have already discussed, where the sponsus says to the sponsa, 'Vulnerasti cor meum' (4:9).[66] The tract *Eight Chapters on Perfection* would seem to be drawing on the *amor violentus* of Richard of St Victor when it states that Christ is 'þoru violence drawen in-to a louynge soule'.[67] In the *Mirror of Simple Souls* Mary Magdalen, doing penance and 'nouȝting' herself in the wilderness, is held up as a model for the mystic, because she thus 'drewe God to hir'.[68]

Mysticism uses the series of images we have just examined to illustrate the soul's way to God, but also uses a second category of metaphors in which the dynamic movement leading to the *unio mystica* originates from God. This imagery, certainly partly inspired by the request of the sponsa in the *Song of Songs* that her lover should draw her to him (S. of S. 1:3), is modified in a great variety of ways by the individual mystics. In Mechthild we find the constant request, 'So sol mich gotz aten in sich ziehen sunder arbeit.'[69] In Richard Rolle, too, we come across the image of being drawn by God. His partiality for applying a concrete image to an abstract concept and thus giving it life, is demonstrated, for instance, in the way he says in *Ego Dormio* that heavenly sweetness will draw up the soul: 'thou sal fynde swetnes þat sal draw þi hert up.'[70] Elsewhere for the same idea he uses a simile which may appear rather drastic to the modern reader, but which was quite common in mysticism: 'drawe me euer to þee and wiþ þee as a nett draweþ þe fysshe til it comeþ to þe banke of deeþ.'[71] The author of the *Cloud* advises the neophyte that he should let himself be drawn up by God into the cloud of unknowing, 'lat God drawe þi loue up to þat cloude'.[72]

The movement of God and the soul towards each other is sometimes illustrated in mysticism by the idea of God sliding down to the soul. Banz has drawn attention to an axiom of the mystics which they took from the scholastics, 'Illabi menti convenit soli Deo.'[73] Amongst the English mystics Richard Rolle includes this image in his *Incendium Amoris*, where he asks God to slide down to him, using a language which differs in style from the rest of the *Incendium*, in that at this point it goes over into the poetic language of the hymn: 'O Deus meus, O amor meus: illabere mihi, tua caritate perforato, tua pulchritudine uulnerato; illabere, inquam, et languentem consolare.'[74] Rolle's request for God to slide down to him is expressed with such passion, and the repetition of *illabere* lends it such an impatient, urgent note, that his wish for God to come down to him attains an intensity typical for the metaphorical description of the mystical way of the soul to God.

VI

*

Metaphors for speaking about God in English mysticism

It is considered a fundamental fact in theological scholarship that religion is always related to a transcendental opposite, and that it has life because this opposite has a name and can be addressed in the second person.[1] Since the religious act is in the form of a dialogue, it necessarily follows that 'every living religion has a personal concept of God and divinity.'[2] Obviously this fundamental religious characteristic will manifest itself particularly intensively in mysticism. Mystical language is inconceivable without its constant attempts to describe God, the goal which the mystic has before him, in the most varied terms, and, by the use of ever new images and similes, to make God more accessible to the human imagination. Hence discovering what choice the Middle English mystics make from the wealth of traditional images available to them when they speak about God, is very revealing for the unique character of their mysticism.

How far do the mystical texts go in personalizing God? Indeed, is it at all their aim to make God personal and tangible? In the German mystical texts of the Middle Ages we can observe very clearly just how far such a tendency to personification can be taken: we read frequently of God's countenance, breath, heart, eyes, hands and feet and even clothes,[3] all details which are frequently found in biblical references to God. It is therefore strange that English mysticism only rarely makes use of such anthropomorphic images, and in general seems not to be concerned with such a detailed depiction of God in concrete terms. English mysticism regularly makes use of the common biblical image of the divine countenance, and there is an occasional reference to God's helping hand or his inclined ear,[4] but, apart from this, it is only the divine heart which has any real importance, and even this is limited to very few examples. It is found, for instance, in the popular, sensual mysticism of someone like Margery Kempe, whose mysticism shows a strong Franciscan influence. Margery puts the words 'I haue drawe þe lofe of þin hert . . . in-to myn hert'[5] into Christ's mouth. This formulation is reminiscent of Mechthild of Magdeburg, who describes the *unio mystica* with the image that God places the human soul 'in sin gluegendes herze'.[6] In a poem ascribed to Richard Rolle which is also inspired by affective devotion, personified love is praised on one occasion as being able to conquer the heart of Christ, 'Lufe þe keynges hert may wyn.'[7] It is Richard Rolle who takes this image furthest by robbing the very old motif of the burning heart of its usual association, and applying it to God instead of to man, thus achieving a completely original and therefore very impressive image, which is effective because the images are poetically so closely interwoven: the soul, over-shadowed by the scents of love, inflames the heart of the creator: 'Anima utique obumbrata amoris odoribus cor Creatoris cremare coegit.'[8]

A characteristic ingredient of the religious language of the most varied religions is the use of a large number of names for God. And in this there is no mystic whose language can compare with that of Rolle's Latin mysticism. In the exuberance of his hymns of praise he never tires of using more and more new names for God and even of inventing them. This tendency is most marked in his *Melos Amoris* — a work still singularly ignored by scholars — where he uses about ninety synonyms. His divine names, some of which like 'Conditor'[9] or 'Radix'[10] have a long tradition going back to the Bible, are many times more numerous than those found in the classical work on the divine names by the pseudo-Dionysius. As has often been observed, Rolle was certainly influenced by Bernard of Clairvaux, who in his famous fifteenth sermon on the *Song of Songs* praised the name of Jesus in extravagant terms, thus paving the way for the medieval devotion to the name of Jesus.[11] Although it has become usual in research into English mysticism to see in Rolle the first great representative of this cult, it must nevertheless be stressed that many of these metaphorical descriptions apply to God the Father or the Holy Trinity, and that Rolle frequently speaks of 'God' rather than 'Christ'. It is only names like 'Vita',[12] 'Salvans',[13] 'Pastor potentissime'[14] and 'panis perpetuus'[15] which expressly apply to Christ. His passion for more and more new names for God was undoubtedly ultimately inspired by the Bible, especially the psalms, which often present the name of God as the embodiment of his glory and fulness of power.[16]

In comparison with Rolle the other English mystics are much more economical in their choice of metaphorical names for God. They mainly use biblical terms like 'king', 'father' and 'our lord'.[17] Julian is the only English mystic who attempts to represent the name 'lord' realistically, and in doing so uses an impressive vision which she succeeds in interpreting spiritually in a quite magnificent manner. Let us look at some details from this vision. It should be noted first that Julian does not attempt to give an immediate representation of God in concrete terms, but explains that she has been granted knowledge of God in a vision, which took the form of an *exemplum* ('example'), showing the behaviour of a 'lorde' and his 'servaunte' towards each other.[18] This *exemplum* is in tableau form, for the characters do not speak to each other but behave rather according to some strict courtly ritual. This inspires Julian to a spiritual interpretation, for she is clearly familiar with the meaning of courtly decorum. She observes carefully that the lord is seated and that the servant stands to his left. She notes the appearance of both lord and servant, how they are dressed and how they behave towards each other. But she has difficulty initially in grasping the significance of this *exemplum*, and it is only twenty years later, as she herself tells us, that she reaches a full understanding of all the 'points and Properties'. Now she realizes: this lord 'is god'.[19] She thus makes a conscious identification between the subject of the parable and the God he symbolizes. The fact that the lord is seated, as is often the case in medieval paintings of God, illustrates that God, whose true dwelling place is the human soul, is completely at rest in himself. She says of the lord's external appearance,

> his cloþing was wyde and syde and full semely as fallyth to a lorde. The colour of the clothyng was blew as asure most sad and feyer. . . . The colour of his face was feyer brown why te with full semely countenaunce. his eyen were blake most feyer and semely.[20]

The colours in this vision have, of course, a symbolic function. They indicate divine attributes: blue signifies 'stedfastnesse', and the brown of the face together with the black of the eyes symbolizes 'his holy sobyrnesse'.[21] A comparison at this point with German mysticism reveals Julian's originality and at the same time her affinity with the German women mystics. G. Lüers has shown that the colour brown is used in German mysticism to describe the lower powers of the soul.[22] According to O. Vértes brown is only found once in a positive context — in a description of a vision of heaven by the sisters of Töss.[23]

Huizinga has also pointed out the negative symbolic significance of this colour.[24] But it could be used as a symbol for *humilitas* or to express sadness,[25] although these two properties cannot easily be reconciled with Julian's *sobyrnesse*. Blue, however, is frequently a colour of God and signifies fidelity. It is used in this way by Julian and also by the German women mystics in their descriptions of visions.[26] It is very striking that Julian never uses the colours green and red, which are very popular amongst mystics for describing God in concrete terms.[27]

After twenty years Julian becomes aware of the full significance of the servant. She recognizes in him Adam and at the same time Christ as the second Adam. His standing to the left of God is an expression of his respect for him. The lord's glance, which rests on him, expresses generosity, goodness and love. The fact that the servant's only garment is a short, white, well-worn and sweaty work-smock, indicates for Julian that as well as Adam, Christ is represented, who takes on human form and suffers the Passion. This is made even more clear by the servant appearing as a gardener tilling the soil, who deserts his post and falls, but who is finally seated, crowned, at the right hand of his lord. All in all a remarkable attempt by a medieval mystic to depict the theological facts of salvation in concrete terms.

Ever since the New Testament the term 'doctor of souls' has regularly been applied to Christ (e.g. Luke 5:31), and is particularly valued in homiletic literature.[28] Its popularity in English mysticism is thus symptomatic of its homiletic character. In keeping with the devotion to the Passion found in the tradition of the mysticism of St Bernard and St Francis, the wounds of Christ are praised in the language of Christian paradox as healing medicine.[29] The author of the *Cloud* succeeds in giving these *medicus*-metaphors, so popular in Augustine[30] and in patristic writings generally, a remarkable and highly personal slant when he advises the sick soul to place God upon itself as a healing plaster: 'Take good gracyous God as he is, plat & pleyn as a plastre, & legge it to þi seek self as þou arte.'[31] Hodgson's remark that 'This type of imagery is common in patristic writings'[32] is somewhat misleading, for the author of the *Cloud* here takes the conventional image of God or Christ as a doctor and changes it in his own particular way, giving it new life so that it will affect the reader directly. This is all the more surprising since in his work the author of the *Cloud* never tires of stressing how impossible it is to make any concrete statement about God. It is true that in our example there is no direct statement made about God, but nevertheless the carefree familiarity with which the author speaks about him in this passage is rather surprising.[33] It is quite possible that he meant his comparison to have some topical significance, and so he may well have been referring to the medicine known as 'goddes grace',[34] which was in common use in English in the Middle Ages.

Depicting God in concrete terms in religious texts is inconceivable without ample recourse to the symbolism of light, for light is an archetypal symbol 'which occurs in some form or other in almost all religions'.[35] Christianity took over numerous motifs from the Cults of Light of Late Antiquity, transferring for example the Cult of Helios to Christ who was signified by the cosmic symbol.[36] As Lüers has shown, German mysticism likes to use the sun in a figurative sense for God, the soul and the *unio mystica*.[37] There are appreciably fewer examples in English mysticism of the use of the sun as a symbol. Walter Hilton uses this image in the second part of his *Scale*, where the reader is informed that the soul which has been through the stage of *purificatio* is ready to receive the 'gracious liȝt of gostly knowynge & þe perfeccioun of luf, þat is trewe sunne'.[38] Immediately after this he cites Mal. 4:2 as the source for this image, where God is called 'sol iustitiae'. And this metaphor occurs again and again in mystical literature, including the English.[39] Hilton argues further that the divine sun does not merely illumine the soul so that it can perceive the truth, but also inflames its affective powers ('affeccioun') so that they burn with love: '& þan schal þei boþ brennen & schynen. Þei schul þurw vertue of þis heuenly sunne bren in perfit luf, & shynen in knowyng of God.'[40] The same thought lies behind a passage in Rolle's *Melos Amoris* and is derived directly from the verse in the *Song of Songs* where the sponsa says of herself that she is dark but comely, for the sun has scorched her. Rolle logically allegorizes: 'Christus est sol qui nos succendit', and the intense heat of his love has scorched the soul brown.[41]

Metaphors of light are not only widespread in German mysticism,[42] but occur with comparable frequency in English mysticism too. This imagery runs through Rolle's Latin writings almost like a leitmotif And he achieves highly poetic images by introducing the concept of light as a sort of metaphor for God. We read for instance that the souls 'in radius respirant Luminis regnantis'.[43] The divine light is a 'lumen letificans'[44] transporting man into the state of joy. In Rolle's mystical language the aim of mystical longing is to arrive in the 'land of lyght'.[45] In an important article J. Koch has shown that the writings of the pseudo-Dionysius were so important for medieval mysticism that they must be considered almost a 'Handbook or Primer of Light Symbolism', especially the work *De caelesti hierarchia*.[46] Hence we find amongst those English mystics who are in the pseudo-Dionysian tradition — the author of the *Cloud*, Hilton and Julian — a particularly pronounced use of metaphors of light. In his own unique symbolical language the pseudo-Dionysius takes up the thought of 1Tim. 6:16, and refers to the inaccessible light in which God lives as a divine dark, for 'it is invisible because of its overbright brightness and inaccessible because of the excess of supernatural light it emits'.[47] The author of the *Cloud* and Hilton speak the same language — for them the unapproachableness of God is a 'liȝty derknes'[48] or a 'liȝty mirknes'.[49] The author of the *Cloud* almost translates the words of the pseudo-Dionysius quoted above when he says, 'a soule is . . . bleendid in felyng of it for habundaunce of goostly liȝt.'[50] We read, too, in Hilton that it is only possible for man in his earthly life to experience individual 'bemes of gostly liȝt',[51] but that the totality of the fullness of divine light is not accessible to creatural man. Hilton illustrates this with a very beautiful and particularly apt comparison: the mystical soul is like a man who looks at the sun, but has to close his eyes because he is unable to withstand its light — he is then only able to perceive through his eyelids a glimmer of the light which is essentially overbright.[52]

Metaphors of light are also an integral part of the work of Julian of Norwich. She speaks, for instance, of the 'swete gracious lyght of hys [God's] kynde loue',[53] and this corresponds to an expression of Hilton's, who on one occasion praises the 'liȝt of blessud luf',[54] calling it 'boþe luf & liȝt'.[55] Julian adds the property 'lyfe' to her statement on God, and this creates the quite splendid alliterative triad 'lyfe. loue and lyght'.[56] This is derived ultimately from passages in St John's Gospel, where Christ is referred to as 'life', 'love' and 'light'.[57] In her *Revelations* Julian also uses a very simple and for that very reason highly effective image when she calls God 'oure endlesse day'.[58] This image, too, is probably inspired by the language of St John's Gospel, and it is reminiscent of Hildegard of Bingen's interpretation of the prologue of this gospel, where she has God say: 'I am of my own self the day, the day which did not come from the sun but which indeed ignited the sun.'[59] But, unlike Hildegard, Julian prefers language which is concise, suggestive and easily remembered.

The Old Testament already identifies God with fire — God appears to Moses in the burning bush (Exod. 3:2), and in Deuteronomy we read: 'Dominus Deus tuus ignis consumens est' (4, 24), an image taken up by St Paul in his Epistle to the Hebrews (12:29). It was especially the pseudo-Dionysius who helped to ensure that metaphors of fire became so widespread in Western mysticism, for he saw fire as a suitable symbol for expressing God's 'supernatural and formless being'.[60] The image of fire is frequently found above all in attempts to express the intensity of mystical love in concrete terms. In English mysticism it was Rolle who set the standards for the use of these metaphors by attempting to exploit all the possible expressions they afforded: God, whose speech is fiery ('ignitum'[61]) and who inhabits the 'igneum celum',[62] the Empyreum, makes the mystical souls 'ignicoma',[63] i.e. 'gives them fiery trails like comets' — an extremely original and effective image. The metaphor of the fire of mystical love is so central for Rolle that it furnishes the title for his main work, the *Incendium Amoris*, in which the reader or hearer is told that mystical love is an 'ignis . . . igneas faciens animas, ut sint lucentes et urentes'.[64] Although the remaining English mystics follow Rolle in using metaphors of fire to express the intensity of mystical love in concrete terms,[65] they are not interested in a more individual application of such metaphors, and their works reveal no attempts of any note to describe God's being through the image of fire.

The ways of speaking about God which we have so far considered have not been specifically concerned with God's infiniteness. Highly concrete metaphors have always been used to express this concept effectively in language. Thus St Paul for instance attempted to illustrate the limitlessness of God by describing it as the optimal fulfilling of the dimensions of length, breadth, height and depth.[66] The mystics take up this thought too. But it is interesting to observe that in German mysticism Tauler interprets this passage from St Paul, using each individual dimension to highlight in an abstract manner the infiniteness of God,[67] whereas in English mysticism the author of the *Cloud* and Hilton go a somewhat different way, interpreting breadth, height and depth as the divine attributes 'love', 'might' and 'wisdom'. This is rather surprising since they usually hold that man should not love God with special reference to any one particular divine attribute — yet traditionally these properties each represent one person of the Holy Trinity: Might = Father, Wisdom = Son, Love = Holy Spirit.[68]

Cloud	*Scale I*
Þe euerlastyngnes of God is his lengþe; his loue is his breed; his miȝt is his heiȝt; & his wisdam is his depnes. (75, 17 ff.)	þat ȝe mihte knowe and fele . . . whilk is þe lengþe of Þe endeles beinge of God, þe brede of þe wundirful charite and þe goodnesse of

> God, þe heiþ of þe almiȝti
> magestie of Hym, and þe
> grundles depnesse of þe wis-
> dam of God. (ch. 12, p. 104,
> 17ff.)

A very old image for describing the infiniteness of God, which can be traced back to the Mystery Religions of Antiquity,[69] is the circle, and the point which is frequently taken as the midpoint of the circle, often serves the same purpose. Thus Master Eckhart says that the soul which has left all things behind it, throws itself 'in das punt des zirkels'.[70] Amongst the English mystics it is only Julian who draws on this tradition in her famous image 'I saw god in a poynte',[71] which she interprets as meaning that God is 'in the myd poynt of allthynges',[72] and that creation is being led back by divine grace 'in to the blessyd poynt from thens it cam. that is god'.[73] Sr Anna Maria Reynolds would seem to be right in assuming that the inspiration for these metaphors in Julian comes from the pseudo-Dionysian comparison of the Divine with the centre of a circle where all the radii meet.[74] There is a similar statement in Ruysbroeck who also applies metaphors of the point to God, whom he describes as 'dat eewighe Punct daer alle onse Liniën [in beginnen ende inden] '.[75]

The more one looks for metaphors for infiniteness in English mysticism the more evident it becomes that the English writers did not attach the same importance and relevance to this aspect as the German mystics did. This is clear from the fact that comparisons of God with the sea are relatively rare, although they were so popular in the mysticism of the High Middle Ages. In his sermons on the *Song of Songs*, for instance, Bernard of Clairvaux praises the 'divinae claritatis tam ingens pelagus',[76] and similarly Ruysbroeck uses the memorable image of the 'vloyende en ebbende zee'[77] for God. The German mystical work, the *Buch von geistlicher Armut*, extends the image by including man, who 'ertrincket . . . in dem grundelosen mer der gotheit und swimmet in got als ein fisch in dem mere'.[78] It is surprising that images of this kind are not found in English mysticism, especially when one remembers how popular metaphors of the sea are in English literature. To find anything in Middle English which is at all comparable to these expressive metaphors one has to have recourse to translations of continental works — like the *Orcherd of Syon*, where we read of the soul, 'þei casten forþ þe nett of holy desier into me, þat am þe pesible see'.[79] or the *Mirror of Simple Souls*, where personified Love says of the soul that it has 'yentred into þe floodis or wawis of diuine loue'.[80]

The motif of the wilderness is also rarely found in English mysticism, a motif which German mysticism again uses in its attempts to illustrate the otherness of God, the 'Arcanum' or 'ἄδυτον'. Here Lüers correctly points out that this image which derives from the Mystery Religions and which was a favourite image of the pseudo-Dionysius, was also 'partly supported'[81] by biblical allegory. For when German mysticism speaks of the 'wilde wustenunge dô inne got phliget zu sprechene mit der sêle',[82] this is a conscious reference to the verse in Hosea 'ducam eam in solitudinem et loquar ad cor eius' (2:14). Whilst it is true that in English mysticism the wilderness is sometimes chosen as the place where God and man meet, thus illustrating the intimate nature of such a meeting,[83] one will nevertheless search in vain in the English texts for a parallel to, say, Master Eckhart's reference to the pseudo-Dionysius: 'her ûf sprichet Dionysius: gotes wüestenunge ist gotes einvaltigiu natûre',[84] i.e. the wilderness illustrates God's infinite being. Underhill is rather wide of the mark in maintaining that the author of the *Cloud* wishes to express this same thought of the divine wilderness when he states that God is hidden from the soul behind a cloud of unknowing.[85] She fails to take into account the basic difference in the teaching of the two authors. The author of the *Cloud* sees creatural man as able to overcome the cloud of unknowing and attain a knowledge of God, if at all, only through unconditional loving surrender, whereas Eckhart teaches that an *unio* of recognition between God and man occurs in the ground of the soul. If one is looking for a parallel for this in German mysticism, it can be found, as we have already said, in Rudolf of Biberach's main work. The Alemannic translation, *Die siben strassen zu got*, follows Thomas Gallus in telling us that Moses went into the 'geislichen "vinstri" ', where 'got sich bloeslich erzovgt',[86] and Rudolf also teaches that only unconditional love can enable man to know God.

In addition to the concept of the wilderness, German mysticism is also familiar with the concept of the infinite unfathomable depth of God. It has been pointed out that this metaphor grew out of the Pauline thought of the 'βάθη τοῦ θεοῦ' ('profunda dei'[87]) as well as the allegorical exegesis of the psalm verse 'abyssus abyssum invocat' (Ps. 41:8) and the pseudo-Dionysian concept of the ἄδυτον or *arcanum*.[88] In Latin mysticism the term *abyssus* from the above psalm is very popular: Anselm of Canterbury, for instance, speaks of man being swallowed up in the abyss of divine love,[89] Suso talks of the 'wild abgrunt der götlichen tougenheit'[90] and Rudolf of Biberach takes the formulation 'abgrund des gotlichen liechtes'[91] from Richard of St Victor. If we compare this with the way God is depicted in English mysticism we find very interestingly that the English mystics dispense almost completely with the theme of the infinite unfathomable depth of God; at most they speak of the bottomless depth of a divine attribute. Instead the English authors prefer to confine themselves to the idea of divine seclusion, an idea contained in the motif of the unfathomable depth of God and conceptualized by the pseudo-Dionysius. Thus Rolle in his commentary on the *Song of Songs* explains that in his mystical ecstasy man can perceive the 'archana dei',[92] and Hilton promises his reader that God will 'schewe to þe His priuetee'[93] if she imitates him in humility and love.

Just how far the traditional metaphor of the abyss is changed in English mysticism is apparent from the meaning of the commonly used metaphor *grounde*. At first sight it would seem to correspond to the Middle High German *grunt*, a synonym of *abgrunt* (abyss).[94] But when the English authors speak of the divine *grounde* they leave aside the element of infinite unfathomable depth and tend rather to concentrate on another meaning which the word has, namely the meaning 'solid ground' in the sense of the Latin *fundamentum*. We shall treat this metaphor in more detail later when we discuss the theme of the ground of the soul.

The further question now arises as to what the relationship is between these metaphors and the linguistic attempts to speak about God in conceptually abstract terms. The answer is that when English mystics talk about God they often attempt to express themselves in concrete terms. But on the other hand in English texts we constantly come across attempts to dispense with metaphorical descriptions for God altogether, and to speak instead of God and the divine being exclusively in abstract terms. The term *godhed* is frequently used — it is only in the *Mirror of Simple Souls* that it is replaced by the borrowed word *deite*.[95] Whilst the German mystics, according to K. Ruh, can use *wesunge*, *wesen* or more rarely, *wesen(t)heit* to translate the Latin term *essentia*,[96] there is only one term available in English — *being*. The author of the *Cloud*, Hilton and Julian all demand of man that he surrender to the divine *beyng*.[97] But at the same time it is remarkable that both the author of the *Cloud* and the *Mirror* on one occasion do not use a philosophical term but instead choose a simple verbal expression which draws on Yahweh's description of his own name as 'I am who I am' (Exod. 3:14): 'þer is no name ... more acordyng vnto euer-lastyngnes, þe whiche is God, as is þat þe whiche may be had, seen & felt in þe blinde & þe louely beholding of þis worde IS.'[98] Hodgson is not quite right when she maintains that in giving such a definition of God the *Cloud* is here departing from the pseudo-Dionysian tradition which held that the first name for God was 'the Good'.[99] For the same definition, coupled with a reference to the above-mentioned passage from Exodus is also found in other important works in the pseudo-Dionysian tradition — for example in Master Eckhart[100] and in the Alemannic translation of Rudolf of Biberach's great work, where God is given the name 'der ist' or 'das "wesende" '.[101] In addition Rudolf gives a direct indication that he had recourse to Thomas Gallus, John Damascene and Augustine in modifying the pseudo-Dionysian description of God.[102]

In English mysticism, as we have already seen in a different context, the reader is urged again and again to love God not for the sake of any one of his attributes but for his own sake. Rolle recommends to the adept mystic that he should be satisfied with the knowledge *that* God is, without asking *what* God is,[103] a recommendation which is reminiscent of the author of the *Cloud*'s call for surrender to the 'nakid beyng'.[104] Yet even in the work of the pseudo-Dionysius on the divine names individual divine attributes are mentioned time and again, something which can be observed occasionally in English mysticism, too. Hilton, for instance, describes God with the statement that he is 'an vnchaungeable beynge, a souereyn miȝt, souereyn soþfastnes, souereyn goodnes, a blissid lif, an endeles blis'.[105] In mysticism the quality of ideal beauty is often used to illustrate divine perfection. Elements of Platonic-neo-Platonic philosophy are here mixed with the praise of the beauty of the beloved in the *Song of Songs*. When Rolle tries to explain the nature of love to his largely female public as 'Lufe es thoght, wyth grete desyre, of a fayre lovyng'[106] and urges them to 'thynk ay to come to þe syght of his fairehede',[107] he is interpreting divine beauty as the beauty of the ideal lover. But the way the author of the *Cloud* interprets Mary's sitting at the feet of Christ is remarkable and extremely revealing: starting from his teaching of an unconditional surrender to God, he interprets her behaviour as implying that she was so preoccupied with her readiness to surrender herself unconditionally that she was unable, as it were, to have any time left for a 'specyal beholdyng unto þe beute of his precious & his blessid body'.[108]

We can get a clear insight into the specific nature of English mysticism if we ask the question what importance is attached to the relationship of the three divine persons to each other, i.e. how far does English mysticism concern itself with theological speculation at all and attempt to express it in language? The author of the *Cloud* aims at the unity of the three persons,[109] and Rolle too strives to illustrate this for the readers of his *Incendium Amoris*.[110] But there is no term in English as there is in German which expresses the unity of three in one in a single word (*Dreieinigkeit*). Consequently English texts speak almost exclusively of the *trinitie*. Only William Nassington, as far as I know, uses the Germanic word form *threhed*.[111] English authors in fact show a distinct unwillingness to make any kind of speculative statements on inner-trinitary processes or on the functions of the individual persons in the Story of Salvation which go beyond biblical statements, and precisely this fact makes English mysticism essentially different from German mysticism. A statement like Eckhart's 'Der êrste ûzbruch und daz êrste ûzsmelzen, dâ got ûzsmilzet, dâ smilzet er in sînen sun, und dâ smilzet er wider in den vater',[112] which is so characteristic of him, would be quite unthinkable in an English text. It is only in Rolle's Latin *Psalter* that we find such a speculative statement as the assertion that the Son has flowed from the Father from all eternity ('fluit continue a patre'),[113] and even this is not a bold thought on Rolle's part but a thesis which goes back to Anselm of Canterbury.[114] Mystical speculation altogether is very fond of using the neo-Platonic metaphors of flowing, pouring and gushing. K. Ruh has shown how important they become in the German mystical texts.[115] There is little in English mysticism which can be put alongside this. But there are some remarkable exceptions which are applied not to inner-trinitary processes, but to the Story of Salvation. Thus on one occasion Rolle applies the image of melting directly to God. In his allegorical interpretation of Ps. 113:8 ('Qui convertit petram in stagna aquarum') which is based on Peter Lombard, he explains that at first God seemed to man to be as hard as a mountain rock as long as man did not know him; as soon as man begins to love God, however, God melts into him: 'when we bigyn to luf him he meltis him in vs, and wonys in oure hertis as well of life.'[116] And Rolle constantly uses the image of the pouring in of heavenly music to illustrate this mystical gift of grace.[117]

The second important exception is found in the work of Julian of Norwich who is the only English mystic to include in her work the neo-Platonic concept of the world as a divine emanation: God has made creation ('alle kyndes') 'to flowe out of hym to werke his wylle',[118] and this creation is redeemed by the pouring out of divine grace, which in turn is illustrated with emanatistic imagery. For Julian speaks of the climax of the Story of Salvation, the Crucifixion, in a very similar way to Catherine of Siena, referring to the blood of Christ flowing over heaven and the whole earth.[119] In addition there are occasionally in her writings some lines of thought which can certainly be called speculative, as for example the idea of Jesus as mother, which critics have often commented on and which is sometimes found in Latin theology: 'Iesu crist that doth good agaynst evyll is oure very moder. we haue oure beyng of hym. where the ground of moderhed begynnyth with alle the swete kepyng of loue that endlesly folowyth.'[120] This quotation is a very nice example of Julian's particular ability to combine abstract thought with a language derived from the realm of everyday experience; for the image of Jesus as mother is supplemented by the highly individualistic abstract formulation of the loving and world preserving 'ground of moderhed'.

If a certain shifting of emphasis towards the Second Person of the Blessed Trinity can be observed in Julian, the same tendency is also found in the second part of Hilton's *Scale*, in Rolle and in Margery Kempe. But it is doubtful whether this trait can be described as particularly typical of English mysticism, as is generally held. For it must be remembered that even Rolle designates not only Christ but also the Trinity as the true goal of the mystical search for God,[121] and that Julian as early as the fourth chapter of her *Revelations* lays unmistakable emphasis on the motif of the Trinity: 'the trinitie is god. god is the trinitie. the trinitie is our maker. the trinitie is our keper. the trinitie is our everlasting louer. the trinitie is our endlesse ioy. and our bleisse by our lord Iesu Christ.'[122] She also explains unambiguously that whenever she uses the name Christ she intends this to stand for the whole Trinity: 'for wher Iesu appireth the blessed trinitie is vnderstand as to my sight.'[123] If we also remember that in theological terms Christ has to be described in any case as 'the foundation of all Christian mysticism'[124] and that in German mysticism, too, the Second Person of the Trinity is extremely important, then the 'christocentric' tendency of English mysticism can no longer be regarded as a special characteristic. It serves rather to show how firmly English mysticism is rooted in the tradition of St Bernard and St Francis, from which it derived so many decisive impulses.

VII

*

Technical terms for the mystical union and for ecstasy

We shall now discuss the question of how far English texts use conceptual terminology to help them in their attempts to express the union of soul and God in linguistic terms. The discussion will take the form of a survey and lays no claim to completeness. Here too our starting point must be the Latin tradition, where the terminological definition of ecstasy – especially in the terms *unio*, *unitas*, *extasis*, *excessus* and *raptus* – has been discussed and analysed in great detail by scholars.[1] A systematic theological discussion of the phenomenon of ecstasy in the English mystics lies outside the framework of our philological approach, which is concerned with the rendering of Latin terms, based on such imaginative concrete ideas as man's stepping out of himself and his being violently carried off.

'Unio' and 'unitas' of man and God

Expressions for the becoming one of God and soul which have a formulaic directness about them, are in Latin principally the terms *unio*, *unitas*, *unitio* and *unire*, in German mysticism the terms *(ver)einunge*, *vereinen* und *einekeit*, and in the English texts the terms *oonhed*, *oonnes*, *union*, *unicion*, *unite*, *onyng*, *unithing* and *onen* or *unyen*. The first observation to be made is that the borrowed word *unyon* is only very rarely used as a term for translating the central Latin concept *unio* – it is basically used only in translations of continental works like the *Orcherd of Syon*,[2] the *Booke of Gostlye Grace*[3] and the *Mirror of Simple Souls*.[4] *Unio* is usually rendered by the verbal noun *onyng*. Just as in Master Eckhart *einunge* as the equivalent of *unio* contains the idea of 'movement towards the one',[5] so too the Middle

English *onyng* is aimed at the process of becoming one — for instance in the *Book of Privy Counselling* we read that God works in man and that man lets this happen to him so that he will become united 'to oure grete perfeccion & goostly onyng of oure soule vnto hym in parfite charite'.[6] Julian expresses the wedding of man and God in the words 'And in the knyttyng and in the onyng he is oure very tru spouse',[7] which almost suggests an echo of Hilton's 'soþli in þis onynge, ys þe mariage mad, a twyx God and þe soule'.[8] This situation corresponds exactly to the frequent use of the term *einunge* in German mysticism.[9]

A synonym for *unio* in Latin theology is the term *unitio*, a concept which Thomas Aquinas defines with the words: 'unitio vero designat viam ad unitatem';[10] he attempts to distinguish it from *unio*: 'unio importat relationem quandam',[11] 'unitio autem est quaedam actio vel passio, qua ex multis efficitur aliquo modo unum',[12] i.e. *unitio* refers to the concrete process through which *unio* is attained. Similarly the *Orcherd of Syon* on one occasion puts the words *vnicioun* and *vnioun* alongside each other: 'in þe staat of vnicioun þe vnyoun of a parfiȝt man is as wele in þe bodi as in þe soule.'[13] The term *vnicioun* acquires an iterative function in the *Treatise of Perfection*, because it means here the union of man with God which must constantly be renewed: 'in wirkynge the spirit ascendys into newe vnyciouns, and so alwaye the werke and the oned ar renewed.'[14] Whilst Ruysbroeck's original text here speaks of the *vereenighen* of the spirit,[15] the English text chooses the rare borrowed word *vnycioun*, although *union* might have been a more obvious choice since a Latin version — the immediate source for the text — uses the term *unio*.[16]

To express the attained state of union of God and soul Latin mysticism normally uses the term *unitas*, which as a rule corresponds to *einekeit* in the German texts. As is to be expected, *unitas* is usually translated into English as *onheed*. Thus there is a formulation in the *Book of Privy Counselling*: 'þou schalt gracyously rest in þis louely onheed of God & þi soule.'[17] But it must at the same time be noted that the mystical texts do not by any means always make a strict semantic distinction between *onyng* and *onheed*. There is another passage in the *Book of Privy Counselling* in which *onheed* is used where *onyng* could just as well stand: 'he wol make þee . . . so bliþely bowyng . . . to þe perfeccion & þe goostly *onheed* to his owne wille (þe whiche *onyng* is parfite charite).'[18] The *Treatise of Perfection* speaks of the 'indrawynge oned of god'[19] where one would expect *onyng* because of the active content. On one occasion, too, the Latin translation of the *Cloud* does not translate *onheed* as one might have expected with *unitas* but with *unio*.[20] The borrowed word *unite* is, however, only rarely used as a translation for *unitas*. It is a word which Julian [21] and the *Mirror of Simple Souls*[22] prefer when they are attempting to express in language the inner-trinitary union of God.

The verb *onen* occurs fairly frequently in the English texts. However, it does not often mean the actual process of the *unio mystica*, but refers rather to the harmonizing and fusing of the human will with the divine will which precedes the mystical union. Man is urged to ensure that all his thinking is 'onid in hym þat is al'.[23] Only when the soul no longer has any feeling for itself at all, only then 'it may be onyd to God in goostly felyng of him-self'.[24] The verb does, however, play an important role in Julian's *Revelations*. She attempts to find a basis in the Story of Salvation for the mystical meaning of the uniting of God and soul and at the same time to extend this meaning; by dint of the fact that it is created as 'kynde made' ('natura creata') the soul is already 'ryghtfully onyd to the maker whych is substauncyall kynde vnmade yat is god'.[25] On its creation it was already united with God, 'whych knott is so suttell and so myghty that it is onyd in to god'.[26] Nevertheless its creaturalness still separates the soul from God, so that it can only find rest when it is 'substantially vnyted to him'.[27]

In accordance with widespread theological teaching Julian maintains that prayer unites the soul with God, since it bears witness to the unity of the human and divine wills.[28] She is thinking here not just of the individual mystical soul but of all the faithful, for in a vision she sees how they 'enIoye with an hygh myghty desyer to be alle onyd in to hym'[29] − note the dynamic effect of the preposition 'in to'. In addition, there is in Julian a further eschatological component which is typical of her: she is shown in her visions how at the end of time 'we be endlesly onyd to hym in loue'.[30] However, if we compare this terminology for the mystical union with that found in German mysticism, we cannot fail to note that, whereas the terms *vereinen, einunge, einekeit* have passed into New High German, the Germanic terms *onen, onyng, onheed, onness* have not attained the same importance in the historical development of the English language, since they have been replaced by synonyms of Romance origin − the beginnings of this tendency can already be observed in the mystical works of the Middle Ages. But in their terminology for the mystical union the English mystical texts do indeed reveal a certain dynamic quality. This is clear from the fact that, of the remaining words which are used as synonyms for *onen* − chiefly *binden, fastnen, knitten, couplen* and *joinen*[31] — the verbs which are of Germanic origin are far and away the most popular.

'Extasis' and 'excessus mentis'

In the pseudo-Dionysius the mystical attitude of man towards God is already explained not only as a withdrawal of man into himself but, in true mystical paradox, also as an ecstatic stepping of man out of himself, as the action of an 'ἔρως θεῖος ἐκστατικός',[32] The term *extasis* is, however, rarely found, especially in Late Latin mysticism.[33] More often than not it is replaced by the synonym *excessus* — Hugh of St Victor for instance writes: 'Extasim, id est mentis excessum'.[34] In English mystical texts the term *extasis* only occurs towards the end of Rolle's *Emendatio Vitae*, where he says of the mystic that he 'quasi in extasim rapitur'[35] by the sweetness of heavenly love. Rolle does not give a more precise definition of *extasis* in his work, but his formulation shows that he takes it as a synonym for *raptus*. Tradition, however, separates the two terms, and we shall discuss this later when we deal with the theme of *raptus*. Rolle's translater, Misyn, does not take over the term *extasis*, but resorts to other means. He replaces it with the word *trans*[36] and, according to the *OED*, this is the only occurrence of the word in the Middle English period in the meaning of mystical ecstasy, which still has some of the flavour of *transitus*,[37] a term also occasionally found in Latin mysticism to denote the ecstatic trans-formation of the soul. Rolle's remark is very aptly rendered by Misyn, since *trance*, in its original meaning of 'impotency', adequately captures the moment of being carried off by God. As the examples quoted in the *MED* show, the word *extasie* was not yet normal usage in the sense of mystical ecstasy; indeed the *OED* cites Thomas Browne's *Urne Burial* as the earliest occurrence of the word in this sense. But there is at least one exception which should not be overlooked. The tract *The Doctrine of the Hert*, with its homiletic and on occasion mystical thoughts, dates from the same time as the works of Hilton and the author of the *Cloud*. This tract discusses the concept of 'extatik loue' in great detail:

> Extatik loue is suche a þing þat it alieneth þe soule fer fro hire mynde vnto þe loue of þat þing þe whiche it loueth . . . Seynt Denyse . . . clepith extatik loue suche loue þe whiche bryngeth a louer alle hole into þe vse and profit of þat þing þat is loued.[38]

One reason why the Latin writers so often use *excessus* rather than *extasis* is that, like Bernard of Clairvaux,[39] they are referring to St Paul's 'mente excedere' (2 Cor. 5:13). They could also consider the Latin term *excessus* to have the authority of the Vulgate behind it. For the Vulgate translates Ps. 67:28 with the words 'Ibi Beniamin adolescentulus, in mentis excessu', whilst the sense of the original Hebrew would be 'Ibi est Beniamin, minimus natu, praecedens eos.' On the strength of this mistranslation, Benjamin was interpreted in allegorical exegesis as prefiguring the mystical soul, which is granted the grace of 'excessus mentis' as the highest stage of contemplation. It is Richard of St Victor above all who refers to Benjamin as a model. He has the following three stages of contemplation: *dilatatio*, *sublevatio* or *elevatio*, *excessus* or *mentis alienatio*. For Richard *excessus* implies that divine grace draws the soul which has freed itself from the world into the realm of the divine, the soul thus attaining a new form of experience of God in which love and knowledge coincide.[40]

According to Hodgson the *Book of Privy Counselling* draws most closely on Richard of St Victor's *Benjamin Minor* in its interpretation of mystical *excessus*.[41] And in fact, just as in Richard, Benjamin's 'excess of mynde' is interpreted as an 'excess of loue', in which man becomes 'rauisc[h] id abouen mynde'.[42] Again there is formally an imitation of Richard in that the author says at the same time that when the soul has attained true contemplation, 'þan diȝeþ alle mans reson'.[43] Nevertheless there are on this point certain differences between the author of the *Cloud* and Richard, for Richard does not propound an exclusively affective knowledge of God, but he attributes to the powers of the human intellect a considerable degree of ability to understand the transcendental, — although the ultimate enlightenment in contemplation is provided by God himself.[44]

Apart from the above-mentioned quotation the term *excess* is not very widespread in Middle English texts. Even the author of the *Cloud*, who is probably responsible for the translation of the *Mystica Theologia* of the pseudo-Dionysius, translates the phrase 'excessu tui ipsius' which occurs there, as 'þorou þe ouerpassyng of þiself'[45] — an attempt to use a loan translation which will be more readily intelligible to his readers. If we remember that Rolle, too, in his *English Psalter* translates this passage from the psalm as 'out passynge of thoght',[46] and that in his translation Misyn on one occasion translates the 'excessum mentis' as 'passynge of mynde be contemplacion',[47] then it is clear that the authors are here trying to find a way of translating a technical term from Latin mysticism into a concrete image in the vernacular: the

Germanic prefix 'ouer-' and the verbal noun ending '-ing' help to produce an almost graphic effect.

Let us return again to the stage of contemplation of *dilatatio* which we have already mentioned, for the idea of the heart being extended through its desire for God and through the working of divine grace is one of the most important motifs in Christian mysticism, where writers have recourse above all to Ps. 118:32 ('Viam mandatorum tuorum cucurri, / Cum dilatasti cor meum'). In Rolle the soule is 'totus in diuinis desideriis dilatatur',[48] but this motif is rendered into the vernacular in quite different ways. Thus Rolle in his *English Psalter* translates the 'dilatasti mihi' of Psalm 41 with the expression 'thou made brade til me my hert'.[49] But he characterizes this broadening as 'brede of gostly joy', and adds 'this brede of hert charite makis'. Elsewhere in his *English Psalter* Rolle is able to say of the soul: 'i enlargid it til luf of god.'[50] In his translations of Rolle Misyn often uses the verb 'spreden' to translate 'dilatare'; the soul for instance appears as 'All-to-gidyr in godis desiris spreed.'[51] In the *Booke of Gostlye Grace* we find the rather impressive passage: the more man 'peerseth the deppenesse of þe godhede þe more es his sowle spredde wyde'.[52] On one occasion in the *Orchard of Syon* the *dilatatio cordis* is linked with another biblical concept, that of the soul's becoming fat through divine love (cf. Ps. 62:6), for we read of the faithful that they 'maken her soulis fatt in spredynge hemsilf abroad in þe depþe of my charite'.[53] It is only after Middle English mysticism has passed its peak that the word 'dilaten' is used in a mystical sense – in the translation of the *Imitatio Christi*, where the soul asks 'Dilate me in loue.'[54]

The mystical 'raptus'

In Latin mysticism apart from the word *extasis* we frequently come across the term *raptus*, and the two terms are often very clearly distinguished from each other. To express ecstasy the English texts seem to use almost exclusively the verb *ravishen*, which is etymologically related to *rapere* or *raptus*. Thus they frequently blur the distinction in meaning between *extasis* and *raptus*. The mystics often speak of *raptus* or *rapi* instead of *extasis* to imply that mystical ecstasy is a divine happening which man experiences as a being carried off.[55] For Bonaventure *extasis* is the *elevatio* towards God, albeit only as far as the *caligo*, the darkness in which God is hidden, so that man nevertheless remains in a 'docta ignorantia'.[56] This is very similar to the following comment of the *Cloud*:

> þer was neuer ȝit pure creature in þis liif, ne neuer ȝit schal be,
> so hiȝe rauischid in contemplacion & loue of þe Godheed, þat
> þer ne is euermore a hiȝe & a wonderful cloude of vnknowyng
> bitwix him & his God.[57]

But whilst Bonaventure adds that for a very few chosen ones there is
a still higher stage of ecstasy — *raptus* — where the true vision of God
as the 'visio beatifica' is possible,[58] the author of the *Cloud* does not
mention this, and he uses the term *ravisching* where Bonaventure
speaks of *extasis*.

It is the element of violence which distinguishes *extasis* from *raptus*
for Thomas Aquinas. For him *raptus* is a violent ecstasy.[59] In the New
Testament account of Paul being snatched up into the third heaven
(2 Cor. 12:2), which mystical texts frequently allude to,[60] the verb
'ἁρπάζειν' — 'to carry off' — is used. It is interesting that the English
authors should use the verb *ravishen* so often, for it certainly contains
this element of violence, as it can mean 'to carry off', 'to be passion-
ately in love' and 'to assault sexually'. It is used very much in the
sense of Aquinas when Hilton tells us how the soul is taken from the
creatural world through grace and — Aquinas includes this too in his
definition — how it is transported into a state of ecstasy so that it
can thus become one with God: 'A mannys soule . . . is taken in fro
alle erþly and flescly affeccions . . . and . . . bi rauischinge of lufe, þe
soule is oned for þe time and conformed to þe ymage of þe Trinite.'[61]

English mysticism is not only familiar with the idea of the soul
being carried off to God, but also with the converse idea of God being
captured by the soul. This is in line with Augustine's idea that 'anima
capit Deum'.[62] In his *Emendatio Vitae* Rolle has personified Love clasp
Christ to itself: 'Tu audacter intras cubiculum eterni regis; tu sola
Christum rapere non vereris.'[63] True love of God can be recognized
in that it forces Christ into the heart of Man: 'Hic est amor qui
Christum rapit in corda nostra.'[64] This image is so important to him
that he introduces it into his English lyric poetry: 'Luf ravysches
Cryste intyl owr hert.'[65]

But let us return to the definition of ecstasy in Latin mysticism.
Two different views were current about the way God is experienced in
ecstasy. Whilst Bonaventure, as we have already mentioned, argues
that ecstasy very rarely leads to the direct vision,[66] Thomas Aquinas
on the contrary quite definitely includes the vision in ecstasy. For him

the vision is a concrete expression of ecstasy; ecstasy occurs 'cum aliquis etiam actu ab usu sensuum et sensibilium rerum abstrahitur ad aliqua supernaturaliter videnda.'[67] The English mystics too are divided on this point. For the author of the *Cloud* and for Hilton the ecstatic vision is not of primary importance, but it is extremely important in the work of Rolle, Julian and Margery. Rolle experiences such a *raptus* in contemplation, and in it he sees the divine countenance after the gates of heaven have been opened.[68] He experiences this *raptus*, which is the culmination of a vision or audition, in the way Thomas Aquinas describes it, namely as being violently carried off, and he indicates that the agent responsible for this is divine love: the soul is 'tanto amore raptum'.[69] He expresses his thanks to this love for the number of times he has experienced this delight, and in doing so speaks in very passionate terms: 'Eia ergo, O eterna et amabilis dileccio, que nos . . . diuine maiestatis conspectui tam crebro raptu representas!'[70] The transporting of the soul in the imaginative vision is described in *Chastising* as 'swounyng'.[71]

Julian's ecstatic vision will be discussed in detail elsewhere (cf. pp. 125 ff.), but here we should perhaps look again at Margery Kempe. In a way which is typical for her sick, neurotic psyche she uses the verb *ravishen* in both an erotic and a mystical meaning: she admits that she is constantly afraid of being ravished and can trust no man: 'sche was euyr a-ferd to a be rauischyd er defilyde.'[72] But she is overjoyed to report that her lover Jesus has 'rauysched hir spyryt'[73] and has appeared to her in a vision, or that her 'mende' was so 'rauesched in-to þe child-hod of crist'.[74] Again and again Margery Kempe expresses her mystical ecstasy with the word *draught*, and here she too, like Rolle — the model she admired so much — is striving to express the element of violence in the ravishing. She finishes the tale of how one night she heard wonderful heavenly music with the words: '& euyr aftyr þis drawt sche had in hir mende þe myrth & þe melodye þat was in Heuen'.[75] In exactly the same way Mechthild of Magdeburg on one occasion renders the *raptus mentis* into German as 'zuge des geistes'.[76] But in the *Cloud* on the other hand *draught* appears as an expression of the irresistible attraction of divine love: 'What weri wrechid herte . . . is þat, þe whiche is not waknid wiþ þe drawȝt of þis loue.'[77] It also has the same meaning in the *Booke of Gostlye Grace*, where it is used in direct connection with the translation of the 'Trahe me post te' of the *Song of Songs*: 'In this worde, drawht, þynke howe myghty his luffe was ande withow-ten mesure.'[78]

The 'familiaritas cum Deo'

Although the idea of an intimacy between the soul and God is not un-important in the Bible, and although the idea was developed in connection with the allegorical interpretations of the *Song of Songs*, it was not until Gregory the Great that the term *familiaritas* was introduced into theological language.[79] In the Latin mystical tradition this term then underwent a series of changes in meaning. It was often used – and this is why we are discussing it here – as a synonym for the mystical *unio*, although it was liable to individualistic interpretations depending on how the author saw the possibility of the mystical union being realized. But the idea of intimacy between the soul and God was problematical. Above all in Franciscan piety, which was already extemely affective, aiming as it did at visualizing the Childhood and Passion of Christ and immersing oneself in them – as is shown in exemplary fashion in the pseudo-Bonaventurian *Meditationes Vitae Christi* – there was a danger that the faithful would develop a purely sentimental relationship to the person of Christ. Huizinga has shown very vividly how in the Middle Ages, as the everyday world became more and more imbued with religion 'the people were in constant danger of losing sight of the distinction between things spiritual and things temporal.'[80] Where the possibility of an intimate familiarity with God becomes something commonplace, there emerges 'a dangerous state of tension, for the pre-supposed transcendental feelings are sometimes dormant, and whenever this is the case, all that is meant to stimulate spiritual consciousness is reduced to appalling commonplace profanity'.[81]

How widespread is the concept of *familiaritas* in English mysticism? We do not find the loan-word *familiarite* in mystical texts until the fifteenth century, and even then not very often – presumably because it was felt to be too abstract.[82] Usually the motif of intimate familiarity with God is expressed through the more concrete Germanic words *homli* or *homlihed* and *homlines*. Rolle's work is something of a sur-prise in this respect for he rarely uses the term *familiaritas* or *homlines*, although his work is extremely rich in images based on this idea.[83] When the other English authors use the term *homeliness*, they have in mind the intimacy of the personal contact between man and God. This intimacy was lost for a time after the Fall, as we read in Ranulph Higden's *Polychronicon*: 'Man in his bygynnynge . . . fel . . . out of homlynesse.'[84] The reunion with God is made possible through Christ, as Hilton puts it, and he who believes in Christ can experience a 'homli presence of Ihesu Crist'[85] in his soul. The author of the *Cloud* explains that in mystical immersion it can happen for a few moments that man becomes 'homely wiþ God in þis grace of contemplacion',[86] and so the term *homeliness* appears then, say, in Hilton's *Eight Chapters on Perfection*, as a synonym for the mystical union: 'to be transfoormyd . . . þat is, whanne his soule is oonyd wiþ Crist, and riȝt hoomly with him'.[87] When the English mystics use the *familiaritas* motif, there is often a slight analogy with the erotic intimacy of worldly love. Thus the reader of the tract *A Tretyse of þe Stodye of Wysdome* is told in a description of spiritual *affeccioun* that out of this *affeccioun* there arises 'a maner of homlynes for to growe bitwix God & mans soule, and also on a maner a kyndelyng of loue. . . . Pe trewe spouse of oure soule is God.'[88] But it is left particularly to Margery Kempe to imply a sexual connotation, which the word had before it was used in a mystical connection. She has Christ say to her: 'it is conuenyent þe wyf to be homly wyth hir husbond. . . . Ryght so mot it be twyx þe & me. . . . Perfore most I nedys be homly wyth þe & lyn in þi bed wyth þe . . . take me to þe as for þi weddyd husbond.'[89] Margery herself indicates indirectly how much she is indebted to popular Franciscan piety, for she tells us that she met a Franciscan ('Frer Menowr') in Assisi to whom she revealed her contemplative leanings and in whom she confided. This man does not consider her inner spiritual life to be in any way abnormally extravagant, but tells her: 'he had neuyr herd of non sweche in þis worlde leuyng for to be so homly wyth God be lofe . . . as sche was.'[90]

If the examples we have just looked at understand *homeliness* as a personal love relationship between man and God, the same thought is behind the popular mystical interpretation of the disciple John resting on the breast of Christ at the last Passover Feast. John, who according to one apocryphal tradition became the favourite disciple of Jesus because he broke off a betrothal for his sake, becomes a favourite symbol for the pre-eminence of mystical love, mystical *familiaritas*, over earthly love. The Middle English tract on the Twelve Fruits of the Holy Ghost for instance discusses this in great detail: 'because þat he lefte his bodily spousayle for oure lord: þerfor he made him more famylier and homly with him to fore al oþer apostelis.'[91] Similarly in the *Meditations on the Supper of Our Lord* the reader is urged: 'Byholde how homely Ion lyþ sleping On crystys brest, as hys derlyng.'[92] In the above examples the authors manage to avoid the danger of a sentimental watering down of the mystical symbolism, but the author of the *Meditations on the Life and Passion of Christ* which, like the *Meditations on the Supper of Our Lord*, draws heavily on the

Meditationes Vitae Christi, no longer makes any effort to avoid this danger. Here we find popular sentimental distortion of the idea of the *homeliness* of man and God — especially in the devotional motif of Mary caring for the Child Jesus with motherly tenderness, whom the author addresses with the words: 'þou hast set him up-on þy barm / And homly halsed hym in thin arm.'[93]

In the mysticism of Julian of Norwich the idea of the intimacy of God with men plays a key role and it is one of the topics she brings up in her conversation with Margery Kempe.[94] She manages to avoid a false sentimentality when she equates the divine *familiaritas* with the tenderness which a mother shows to her child: 'oure tender mother Iesu he may homely lede vs in to his blessyd brest. by his swet opyn syde and shewe vs there in party of the godhed and ye loyes of hevyn.'[95] This is precisely the language of Franciscan mysticism. The term *homli,* however, which she frequently applies to Christ, often has the sense of 'meek' or 'kind' and corresponds fairly exactly to the word *curteis* and the virtue of *mansuetudo,* as in the following sentence: 'he that is hyghest and myghtyest. noblyest and wurthyest. Is lowest and mekest. homlyest. and curtysest.'[96] An example of Julian's knack of clothing theological thoughts in pithy formulations is the way she summarizes St John's teaching on the divine indwelling with this precise and concentrated formulation: 'in vs is his homelyest home and his endlesse dwellyng.'[97] This expression, which seemed so important to Julian that she included it in both the short and the long version of her *Revelations,* has a compact precision about it which is unsurpassable. She also reveals her remarkable individuality not least in the fact that she mentions man's own attempts to experience divine intimacy as a special problem. She warns against a familiarity of man with God which is too great, too much taken for granted — and the examples already quoted show that there were grounds enough for such a warning in the Middle Ages. In mysticism there are plenty of warnings against too great a familiarity with God, which can easily become a habit and end in disappointment, but Julian has a justification for her warning which is unique in English mysticism. She demands that man must not misuse the *homelyhed* with God for unrestrained familiarity, but must keep a fitting distance, and she reminds her readers of the courtly ideal of *curtesye*: 'be we ware yat we take not so rechelously this homelyhed for to leue curtesye.'[98] This courtly motivation is reminiscent of German mysticism where it is found above all in Mechthild of Magdeburg. Mechthild describes the soul as 'wolgezogen',[99] and since this is another courtly term, the comparison with

Julian's call to *curtesye* suggests itself.

In any treatment of the theme of the intimate familiarity between man and God the related motif of the secrecy of the love relationship is always more or less clearly implied, and the mystics tend to place great emphasis on this aspect. They seem to have a special liking for the allegorical interpretation of Hosea 2:14 where Israel is compared with a woman led by God as her lover into the seclusion of solitude. In German mysticism the term *heimlicheit*, which is cognate with *homlines*, implies both the motif of familiar intimacy and also that of the sheltered secrecy in which the intimate encounter takes place. When, for instance, on one occasion Mechthild of Magdeburg speaks of the 'sunderlichú heimlicheit, das zwischent gotte und einer jeglichen sele ane underlas gat',[100] this brings both motifs together in an ideal manner. It is from the verse from Hosea quoted above that Rolle in his *Incendium Amoris* concludes that the way of life of the recluse is the only appropriate one for him, because only in this way can he escape from the noise of the world and guarantee himself a secluded spot where he can experience God.[101] Rolle's interpretation of the Old Testament imagery is particularly impressive in his *Melos Amoris*. Here he explains to his readers that God's relationship with the soul is no different from that of a lover who does not want his kisses to be a public spectacle but takes his beloved somewhere where they can be undisturbed together, 'ut . . . sola cum solo sedeat secure'.[102]

The pseudo-Dionysian influence is clear in Walter Hilton who refers to the otherness of God in the sheltered secrecy of *mirknes*. Hence the experience of secret intimacy is at first restricted to this darkness, i.e. Hilton informs the reader that he must get used to this darkness, must become familiar with it: 'vse for to wonen in þis mirknes & be often assaynge to ben homly þerin.'[103] In the second part of his *Scale*, however, where his mysticism takes on a strongly christocentric character, he, too, shows how a soul which is reformed by 'feith and feeling' can attain an intimate and personal experience of God in secret solitude. Although Hilton, too, refers to Hosea, he maintains, unlike Rolle, that the soul which has attained a 'hiȝenes of þoȝt' through accompanying Christ, is in a state of solitary seclusion even if living amongst worldly people.[104] In this solitude the soul then feels 'so grete homlynes (of) þe blissed presence of oure Lorde Iesu'[105] that here this term *homlynes* must certainly contain something of the meaning of 'secrecy'. When it is necessary to lay special emphasis on this secrecy, Hilton, like the other mystics, usually uses the terms *privy* and *privity* (more rarely *secret* and *secrecy*), which as a rule correspond to the Latin terms *arcanum* or *secretum*. For instance in the very same chapter Hilton says that the soul is led away from love of the world 'into þe pryuey chambre (into) þe siȝt of oure Lorde Iesu'[106] from whom it receives rich consolation, as the prophet has already said: 'Secretum meum mihi, secretum meum mihi' (Isa. 24:16). And in his *Incendium Amoris* Rolle speaks of the 'arcanum amancium',[107] which Misyn translates as 'þe priuete of lufars'.[108] It is interesting to note that the word *dyrne*, which is so common in secular lyric poetry in the sense of the two lovers being together in secret, is not used in mystical texts apart from the one example which we find in the fourteenth century version of the *Ancrene Wisse*.[109]

The 'commercium cum Deo'

The term *commercium*, which is frequently found in Latin mysticism, is closely related to the concept of *familiaritas*. It can imply the element of intimacy between man and God, but it often emphasizes the aspect of intercourse and exchange between the soul and God. In Classical Latin *commercium* meant, amongst other things, 'purchase of goods' and 'exchange' in both the material and spiritual senses, as well as 'intercourse' and 'traffic', and even in Classical Latin literature there are isolated instances where *commercium* meant the intercourse between gods and men.[110] In its religious meaning the term then went over from Classical Latin into patristic literature and into the Roman liturgy. There its meaning is essentially the reuniting of the soul with God through Salvation and its communion with the Mystical Body of Christ.[111] Bernard of Clairvaux uses this term to describe the ecstatic union of the soul with the *Verbum*: 'Dulce commercium, sed breve momentum et experimentum rarum!',[112] a passage which Rolle may well have had in mind when he says: 'Amari enim et amare dulce est commercium.'[113]

When the German mystics translate this Latin term into the vernacular, they often give it the meaning 'purchase' or 'exchange'. Thus, for example, in the *Paradisus anime intelligentis* we read that through his love towards God man is making 'einen seligin kauf'.[114] Mechthild of Magdeburg has the soul say to Love that, in renouncing earthly love in favour of divine love, she has 'einen seligen wehsel getân',[115] i.e. has made a good exchange. This word *wehsel* is an important term in Middle High German *minnesang* terminology, which, as Lüers suspects, was probably taken over from the spiritual sphere into the realm of secular love poetry.[116] For *websel* does not merely mean 'purchase' or 'exchange', but is the name for a particular type of poem in early *minnesang*, in which the relationship between the lover and his beloved is put into words through the intermediary of a messenger. The term *commercium* also contained an erotic element even in Classical Antiquity, since it could have the meaning 'amorous behaviour' and was frequently linked with the word *connubium*.[117]

How is the idea of *commercium* with its various shades of meaning reflected in the texts of the Middle English mystics? Richard Misyn translates the term as used by Rolle in the above-mentioned quotation quite simply with the word *chaunge*, i.e. in the sense of 'exchange': 'To be lufyd truly, & to lufe, is a swete chaunge.'[118] If no erotic overtones are discernible here, the same is not true of the term *daliaunce* which is commonly used in English mysticism and which corresponds to some extent with the idea of *commercium* in its meaning 'conversation', 'communion', 'amorous talk', 'sexual union'.[119] At the end of the second book of the *Scale* Hilton describes the intercourse of the soul with Christ with the words: 'Alle þese lufly daliaunces of priuey speche atwix Iesu & a soule'.[120] Since Jesus has been described in the preceding sentence as the *spouse* of the soul, *daliaunce* here assumes the meaning of a love dialogue or a familiar intercourse of two lovers, a meaning which is familiar from secular love poetry.[121] This motif is again supported by the passage from the prophet Hosea which we have already quoted, and also by the passage from the *Song of Songs* where the *sponsa* says of her bridegroom: 'En dilectus meus loquitur mihi' (S. of S. 2:10).

But the word *daliaunce* does not always have an erotic association in English mysticism. The earliest occurrence of the word in a mystical context — a passage in Rolle's *Meditations on the Passion* — has no erotic overtones at all: Rolle is here comparing the suffering Christ with a book written in red ink and asks if he may always study it so that Christ may be 'my meditacion, my speche, and my dalyaunce'.[122] Julian of Norwich uses *dalyance* as a synonym for *comenyng* and thus in the sense of the word *communio*, which overlaps partly in meaning with *commercium*; anyone who wants communion with his soul must seek it in God: 'if we wylle haue knowyng of oure soule and comenyng and dalyance ther with it behovyth to seke in to oure lord god.'[123]

In contrast to the main representatives of English mysticism, who in fact do not use the word *daliaunce* very much, the word assumes a central significance in Margery Kempe's autobiography. She seems to model herself on Rolle's and Julian's use of the word. Margery's use of the word *dalyen* is reminiscent of Rolle's *daliaunce*, when she employs it to describe the mystical immersion in the Passion of Christ: 'sche dalyed in þe Passyon of owyr Lord Ihesu Crist.'[124] She also applies the noun *daliaunce* to mystical contemplation and means primarily the way God communed with her in her visions when he initiated her into his mysteries: 'sche incresyd in grace . . . of hy contemplacyon & of wonderful spechys & dalyauns whech owr Lord spak and dalyid to hyr sowle.'[125] In addition she also uses the term *daliaunce* to describe mystical ecstasy as such, which so overwhelms her that she falls to the ground: 'her dalyawns was so swet . . . þat þis creatur myt not oftyn-tymes beryn it but fel down & wrestyd wyth hir body',[126] or which overcomes her in the most varied situations in life, even when she is riding on a donkey.[127] Thus we have the unique situation of Margery Kempe extending the meaning of a term which is already current in English mysticism.[128] Our survey of the use of this term in English mysticism also shows that the *MED* interprets its religious meaning too narrowly in defining it as 'spiritual conversation; communion'.

VIII

*

The experience of God as a spiritual sense perception

In the course of our inquiry it has become clear again and again how frequently even in English mysticism the experience of the mystical *unio* has been expressed in sensual terms. In this the English texts are continuing a trend which has a long tradition in Latin mysticism, which indeed goes back to Origen who developed the theological doctrine of the spiritual senses, and who seems to have held that man does not merely possess physical sense organs but spiritual ones as well.[1] It is really quite remarkable that he devised this doctrine with the help of the highly idiosyncratic system of biblical allegory which he developed, especially in connection with an exegesis of the *Song of Songs*. If the mystics now frequently use the language of earthly sense perceptions in a spiritual meaning when relating their personal experiences, then it would be wrong, as we have already indicated, to understand and assess this language simply as the use of metaphor in the normal sense of the term, for this is no mere makeshift language but rather one in which the mystical experience itself takes place. In theological terms the 'spiritual senses' are not just five powers permanently residing in the soul — by analogy with the physical senses — but are temporary spiritual acts, ultimately effected by divine grace. In these acts it seems to the soul that it is experiencing a supernatural object which reveals itself as if it were present in some concrete manner. Hence this spiritual sense perception can certainly become similar to that of the physical senses, and therefore the language which expresses such experiences is something rather different than mere metaphor. We shall now examine in detail how far these 'metaphors' of touching, feeling, hearing, smelling and seeing find their expression in English mysticism over and above the examples from different contexts which we have already mentioned.

The 'unio' as mystical enjoyment of God

The fruitio Dei

When discussing the theme of the mystical enjoyment of God we must start with Augustine's famous distinction between *frui* and *uti*: 'Frui enim est amore alicui rei inhaerere propter seipsam. Uti autem, quod in usum venerit ad id quod amas obtinendum referre, si tamen amandum est.'[2] Here of course Augustine drew on the distinction between the two terms which already existed in Latin Antiquity.[3] *Frui* is the loving enjoyment, *uti* the mere use. It is only in the *visio beatifica* that the soul, created in the image of God, attains its complete fulfilment in the enjoyment of God, the *fruitio Dei*.[4] It was primarily due to Bernard of Clairvaux that this concept became so important in Late Medieval mysticism. Bernard does not in fact use the term *frui* very often but he links it with the theme of the bridal love between God and the soul in a way which is very revealing for his affective mysticism.[5] In England this motif is found above all in Rolle's Latin works, but he does not use it to express the *fruitio* of God, of the divine countenance, but rather the enjoyable experiencing of the transcendental realm altogether. Hence the theological motif undergoes many new variations and is extended to produce poetic images. For instance on one occasion Rolle says of the blessed: 'Vivunt in gloria, invisibilis vite fruuntur melodia.'[6]

We are particularly interested here in how the motif of mystical *fruitio* is taken over into vernacular English mysticism. The Late Middle English translation of the *Imitatio Christi* uses the loan-word *fruishen*, and we read: 'I desire to fruishe þe inwardly, but I may not take þe.'[7] Since the *MED* cites the translation of the *Imitatio Christi* as the earliest occurrence of this verb, we clearly have here one of those rare instances where a word is introduced into the vernacular in England in mystical texts and is only later applied to other areas in a different meaning. The same applies to the noun *fruicioun* which also first appears in English in a spiritual meaning. It occurs for example frequently in the *Mirror of Simple Souls*, as early even as the prologue by the English commentator 'M. N.', who speaks in quite traditional terms of the 'diuine fruycion'[8] of the soul which has experienced divine grace. And later at a stylistic climax of the tract we read that divine love makes possible a 'fruycion agreable'[9] 'in a soule nou3ted'. In the *Booke of Gostlye Grace* we read rather significantly of Bernard of Clairvaux that he was so filled with divine wisdom that 'in a fulle swete fruycion ande experyeence he sauorede alle thyngges whiche he knewe be þe Holy Goste'.[10] On several occasions the *Mirror of Simple Souls* has the term *usage*, but there does not seem to be any difference in meaning between this and *fruycion*, especially in the expression 'usage of þe diuine grace of þe Trinite'.[11] We can observe the same thing in Wyclif's *Lanterne of Ly3t* where, in the description of the gifts of the Holy Ghost, we find the following explanation: 'þe fourþe [spiritual endowment] is fruycioun, or ellis þus in more pleyn speche . . . vse of þe godhed & loue of God euerlasting.'[12] The fact that *fruycioun* is here explained to the reader through the more common *use* indicates that the last vestiges of the Augustinian distinction between *frui* and *uti* have been lost.

But this does not by any means exhaust the particular linguistic peculiarities we can observe in the translation of the motif of *fruitio*. For it is noticeable that the most important works of English mysticism, the texts of Hilton, Julian and the author of the *Cloud*, do not use the term *fruicion* or the verb *fruishen* − perhaps because they felt it was too abstract and theological and hence unsuitable for their lay readers. But in that case it is strange that they do not fall back on the verb *brouken* (OE *brucan*), which is etymologically related to *frui*, but sometimes substitute the verb *usen*. Not only does Wyclif opt for it in the example quoted above, but Rolle's translator Misyn uses it as well.[13] When Wyclif in the sentence quoted above speaks of 'vse of þe godhed & loue of God', this reflects a tendency found in mystical texts too − to paraphrase *fruitio* with the word *louen* or *loue*, as is also the case with Misyn.[14] This is a clear linguistic dilution of the Latin theme; for although it is true that love does in fact lead to the actual *fruitio*, nevertheless *fruitio* is a much more intense phenomenon than could possibly be expressed by the mere word *louen* or *loue*. Nor does the author of the *Chastising of God's Children* produce an adequate translation for the motif of *fruitio* when he takes passages from Ruysbroeck's *Gheestelike Brulocht*, for he translates the formulation 'fruitiui amoris'[15] of the Latin version merely as 'wiþ a lastyng loue'.[16]

It was without any doubt Julian of Norwich who succeeded in producing the best vernacular rendering for the motif of *fruitio*. It is one of the particular characteristics of her *Revelations* that the term *enjoien* runs through them like a leitmotif, usually in the meaning 'rejoice'. Julian doubtless has in mind here St Paul's call to the Christians to rejoice in Christ at all times (Phil. 4:4). But one can occasionally deduce from the context that with her use of the verb *enjoien* she intends a precise rendering of the idea of *fruitio Dei*, as in the following quotation, where she recommends her reader to renounce 'the beholdyng of alle tempestes. that myght lett vs of true enIoyeng in hym'.[17] Misyn's way of translating also reveals an affinity of meaning between *enjoien* and *frui*, for on one occasion he translates the *frui* of Rolle's text as *deliten*,[18] whilst in another place he translates *delectare* as *enjoien*.[19] So we can say that in Julian we can already discern the common present-day meaning of the verb *to enjoy*, which the *MED* puts at the end of the Middle English period. In later mystical texts from the late sixteenth and early seventeenth centuries the verb is used unambiguously to express the idea of *fruitio Dei*, as for instance in R. Southwell who says of the man who has seen God 'your best you have enjoyde',[20] or in Crashaw's anagram poem on his own name where he expresses the hope that he 'in the end . . . may inioy his dearest Lord'.[21]

The eating and tasting of God

In European mystical texts the idea of the mystical enjoyment of God is often illustrated with the concrete image of the soul eating God, consuming God. The Mystery Cults of Antiquity are familiar with the consuming of God as an image for the mystical union,[22] and it is a common theme in the Bible, especially the New Testament.[23] The fact that this theme is so widespread in the mysticism of the High Middle Ages is, as has already been shown, doubtless linked with the medieval revival of symbolism for the Blessed Sacrament.[24] But on the other hand it is interesting to note that in the case of the English mystical authors there is frequently no direct reference to the Eucharist.[25] For them a spiritual mediation through bread and wine is not a prerequisite for the spiritual, mystical sense experience. In keeping with the medieval love for analogy, the evocation of the spiritual 'sense experience' of the soul is sometimes taken to such lengths that the soul is endowed with mouth, gums and teeth. Thus Rolle is familiar with the 'os cordis'[26] and the 'palatum cordis'.[27] One of the most expressive statements about the *unio* must surely be Mechthild of Magdeburg's assertion about the soul 'das si nút denne got essen mag'.[28]

In English mysticism we hardly ever find this image with the same immediacy and directness except in Julian of Norwich, who speaks in her *Revelations* of the soul swallowing God: 'we endlesly be alle hyd in god verely seyeng and fulsomly felyng . . . And hym hall swetly swelwyng.'[29] Since Julian modifies the word *swalowen* with the adverb *swetly*, and since later[30] the verb *to swallow* could be used purely and simply to express the sacramental eating of God, then it is clear that in this quotation the element of passion and force which is contained in the idea of swallowing recedes into the background, to be replaced by the thought of the sacramental eating. Nevertheless it is quite striking that later editors of Julian's *Revelations* deleted the word *swelwyng* and chose the less vivid expressions *smelling* and even *following*, perhaps with the intention of replacing Julian's metaphorical expression with a more restrained image.[31]

Apart from this the image of the eating of God is only rarely found in English mysticism. But Rolle's exegesis of Ps. 15:5 in his *English Psalter* must be included in this group of images. Here he promises the souls that they will drink God: 'i. and my halighis sall drynke god.'[32] Apart from this, Rolle, like the other English mystics, prefers to speak of the rather more weakened concept of being nourished by divine food. This usually serves as a description for divine love in Rolle's tract *Ego Dormio*, which contains a *Cantus Amoris* where we read: 'Intil þi lyght me lede, and in þi lufe me fede.'[33] In his *Melos Amoris* on the other hand, Rolle places the metaphors of food in a larger allegorical framework, so that the idea of consuming God is now only implicit: in a reference to the apple tree of the *Song of Songs*, which was seen in the Middle Ages as a symbol for Christ or the tree of the cross, Rolle has the souls climb their beloved tree and eat its fruit: 'ascendant ad arborem altam ad quam anhelant integre amore . . . masticantes mellifluum fructum'.[34]

Apart from the enjoying and eating of God, we also frequently meet in European mysticism the no less concrete motif of mystical tasting, where there is usually a direct reference to the famous line in the Psalms: 'Gustate, et videte quoniam suavis est Dominus' (Ps. 33:9). Mechthild of Magdeburg says for example: 'mir smekket nit wan alleine got.'[35] This range of metaphors is popular in English mysticism, too, but it is noticeable that there are few statements like the author of the *Cloud*'s comment on the 'heiʒ sauour of þe Godheed',[36] where the writers speak directly of the tasting of *God*. The English mystics, instead of speaking of the tasting of God, prefer to speak more indirectly of the taste of divine love or heavenly joy, and in this context the verbs *sauouren*, *tasten* and *felen* serve as synonyms. A good example is the definition of contemplation in the tract *A Ladder of Foure Ronges*, a version of the *Scala Claustralium* of Guigo II: 'Contemplacion is a risyng of hert into God that tastith sumdele of heuenly swettnesse & savourith.'[37] Similarly the author of the *Cloud* explains to his reader that he can 'taast of goostly felyng in God . . . by grace'.[38] In addition Rolle again provides interesting examples. He loves the image of the banquet, the idea of a feast which the soul is determined to find 'tasty' and in this way to indicate the goal of its desire.[39] And the divine sweetness is not merely tasted passively by the soul, but in response to the experience of heavenly sweetness the soul itself produces the pleasant taste of the mystical *iubilus*.[40]

The reader of these mystical texts is constantly reminded that this tasting of God also implies a spiritual *knowledge* of him. It has been pointed out for instance that in Tauler the words *smacken* and *smac* are often used, not in their original meaning but rather in the sense of 'feel' or indeed 'know', as in the formulation 'verstentnisse und smackende wisheit'.[41] Rudolf of Biberach, whose mysticism has a strong affective character, refers to Augustine, Bernard and William of St Thierry in reminding us that wisdom cannot be acquired through intellectual effort but only through the experience of the spiritual senses, for the word *sapientia* is derived from *sapere*.[42] In the eulogy which personified Wisdom sings about itself in the *Book of Wisdom* it is significant that it uses sensual images to describe its own characteristics, equating itself with 'cinnamomum et balsamum' and with 'myrrha electa' — comparisons which culminate in the sentence: 'Spiritus . . . meus super mel dulcis.'[43] And Bible passages which talk of salt are often interpreted allegorically and applied to wisdom, because wisdom, like salt, enhances taste. This is why we read in the *Ancrene Wisse*: 'Salt bitacneð wisdom. for salt ȝeueð mete smech. & wisdom ȝeueð sauur.'[44] Hilton describes the soul which lapses back into its 'fleshlied' as 'blynde & vnsauoury',[45] i.e. incapable of knowing God. He contrasts man's 'erþly felynge', his creatural perceptual ability, with the 'heuenly sauour' which man becomes capable of through his 'gostlynes'.[46] The devil hates a soul which 'fele verreili þe sauour of gostly knowyng and þe luf of God',[47] and here the expression 'sauour of gostly knowyng' is very akin to Tauler's 'verstentnisse und smackende wisheit'. Hilton's linking of *sauour* with love of God in this quotation is also very much in line with affective mysticism — we read in Grosseteste for instance: 'sapientia oritur ex amore'.[48] Hence for the mystic affective contemplation implies receiving wisdom and savouring divine love at the same time. The idea of knowledge and wisdom which are sensual and which can be savoured, was widely accepted and completely taken for granted until the seventeenth century, and is something which we today, who are so used to the idea of the 'dissociation of sensibility' — to use Eliot's famous phrase — have long since lost.

'Felen' and 'feling' as mystical terms

Just as the process of spiritual tasting is an attempt in medieval mysticism to express wisdom and knowledge in concrete terms, so too spiritual 'feeling' is often used as a synonym for the perception of transcendental reality, for spiritual knowledge. The words *felen* and *feling* occur with much the same frequency in English mysticism as the corresponding terms *sentire, sensatio, gefuelen, gefuelunge* in Latin and German mysticism. Lehmann, however, who was the first to examine the meaning of *sentire, felen, feling* in the mysticism of Richard Rolle,[49] succumbed to the fundamental error of simply equating these terms with the present-day meaning of 'feeling' with all its emotional overtones. For Rolle *felen* is first of all a synonym for *savouren*, as we can see from the fact that he describes what man can experience from the realm of the transcendental as a *savoure* which can be felt: 'For when men hase feled oght of þat savoure, þe mare þai have þe mare þai covayte.'[50] But in the context of his mysticism of the Passion *felen* also takes on the meaning 'to share the experience', 'to re-enact': the soul would like to re-live the Passion but cannot because its heart is made of stone: 'it may not of þi passyoun a lytel poynt fele'.[51] Julian of Norwich is also equally concerned with such a re-living of the Passion.[52]

The ultimate goal of Rolle's mysticism is to feel divine love, to experience it on a personal, existential level. Hence he urges his reader: '[A]ll vanitese forsake, if þou his lufe will fele.'[53] The intensity of the fire of mystical love is so great that Rolle can only compare it with his famous image of the burning finger: 'he or scho, þat es in þis degre, mai als wele fele þe fyre of lufe byrnand in þaire saule, als þou may fele þi fynger burn.'[54] Hilton takes up this thought in his (?) *Qui Habitat* when he has the soul say that it is as a result of divine love that 'i seo þe and fele þe as i seo þe sonne & fele þe hete of hit beo schynyng of þe beem'.[55] The remaining mystics agree with Rolle in emphasizing that divine reality can be felt. Thus Julian for instance describes the possession of God as a feeling of his intimate presence: 'The hyghest blesse . . . is to haue god . . . hym verely seyng hym swetly felyng.'[56] For the author of the *Cloud* as for Rolle the immediate way to this experience of God lies in the love of God, and for him *feling* can take on the meaning 'love' in the sense of *caritas*, as in the *Book of Privy Counselling*, where he translates the biblical passage 'Sciencia inflat, caritas edificat' (1 Cor. 8:1) with the words: 'In knowyng is trauaile, in feling is rest.'[57] The *Chastising of God's Children* expresses this in concrete terms, saying that the 'sharpe dartis' of divine love combine with the 'heete of charite' to produce a 'gostli felyng' in the soul which was previously capable of 'noo felyng', no spiritual sensation.[58] Since the goal of the English mystics is 'to fele in experience þe frute of his loue',[59] and since here as elsewhere in the writings of the author of the *Cloud* the term *experience* is often used as a synonym for *feling*, these texts reveal very clearly their affective character, and we are reminded of such figures as Anselm of Canterbury in whom we can already discern the significance of mystical experience,[60] but above all of Bernard of Clairvaux who speaks of the *Song of Songs* almost as a 'liber experientiae'.[61] Bernard expresses the teaching of affective mysticism — that love is the only form of experience and knowledge of God — with the words 'In tantum cognoscitur Deus in quantum amatur'.[62] And the author of the *Cloud* has a sentence which contains the same expression: 'after a trewe feling comeþ a trewe knowing in Gods scole.'[63] But in English mysticism the word *felen* does not only mean the 'feeling' love of God, but can sometimes simply have the meaning 'become aware, become conscious' — again something which can be seen particularly well in the work of the author of the *Cloud*. For in the *Cloud* the way that leads to the experience of God is sometimes described in terms of man having to strive to overcome the consciousness of his own existence: 'þat he desire . . . for to lakke þe wetyng & þe felyng of his beyng',[64] for only in this way can he become capable of 'þe hiʒe felyng of God'.[65]

When C. Pepler in his interpretation of Hilton's mysticism defines the term *feeling* as the 'type of intuitive awareness which may be either in the senses or in the mind itself',[66] this is an extremely imprecise definition. This term is so important for Hilton and is accorded such a central function in his mysticism that it merits closer examination. Hilton's description of the mystical teaching on the Three Stages sheds more light on his use of *felen* and *feling*. For Hilton the first stage of contemplation consists of the 'cnowynge of God' which is acquired through 'reson'.[67] The simple believer usually attains the second stage if he has come to sense his own 'meknes', if he immerses himself in the divine 'meknes' as it is revealed in the Passion of Christ, and if he then 'feleth feruour of loue and gostly swettnesse'.[68] The highest form of mystical contemplation for Hilton, however, consists '[in] hope, in cognicion, and in affecion, þat is for to seyen in knowyng and in perfit lufinge of God',[69] an expression which calls to mind the other English mystics. But he attaches great importance to the fact that the soul with all its powers must first be 'reformed' by God, and he distinguishes two main kinds of such reforming: first the reforming in faith, as happens with the ordinary Christian, and, second, the transformation into the original state before the Fall, which he calls *feling* and by which he means the loving surrender of affective mysticism.[70] At the same time, however, Hilton expressly stresses that this surrender implies a movement towards God of the whole soul with all its powers, the affective ones as well as the purely spiritual ones:

> For þou shalt vndirstond þat þe soule haþ two maner of felinges: one withouten [of] þe fyue bodili wittes, anoþer wiþinne of þe gostly wittes, þe which arne properly þe miʒtes of þe soule, mynde, resoun, and wille. When þese myʒtes arne þurʒ grace fulfillid in al vundirstondyng of þe wille of God and gostly wisdam, þan haþ þe soule new graciouse felynges.[71]

Thus *feling* here means the ability which man has as a gift of divine grace, to experience God through the powers of his soul. And Hilton bases this view ultimately — as he himself indicates — on a verse from St Paul, where the concept νοῦς is rendered in the Vulgate as *sensus*: 'nolite confirmari huic saeculo, sed reformamini in novitate sensus vestri.'[72] Since Hilton sees man's ability to experience God as belonging to the totality of the powers of the soul, he too, like the author of the *Cloud*, treats the terms *knowyng* and *felyng*, knowledge and love, as interchangeable synonyms, and has a predilection for the formulation 'knowyng and felyng of God'.[73]

But when Hilton on one occasion speaks of the unfathomableness of God and warns his reader that she must immerse herself in this unfathomableness in a 'gostly felyng',[74] he is here extending the term into a synonym for mystical contemplation as such, and the Latin translation then uses the word 'meditacio' as a roughly adequate term.[75] On one occasion Margery Kempe equates *felyngys* directly with *contemplacyons*.[76] And finally the phenomenon of the vision which plays such an important role especially in female mysticism, can also be expressed by the word *feling*. On one occasion Hilton describes the 'vision oþer reuelacions' as 'felinges',[77] and Julian too, like Margery Kempe, hints at this in her visions,[78] perhaps in direct imitation of Hilton. The fact that *feling* can have the meanings 'vision' and 'contemplation' is unfortunately not noted in the *MED*.

The touching of man and God

The wish of the soul to touch God, which is prefigured on numerous occasions in the Bible,[79] is closely related to the idea of mystical feeling. It is symptomatic of the strong homiletic tendencies of English mysticism that the soul is frequently connected with the woman, mentioned in the Bible,[80] who is suffering from an issue of blood, and who seeks a cure for her sickness by touching Christ, for the medieval exegete looked upon her sickness as a symbol for sin. The author of the *Cloud* draws a direct analogy between this woman and the soul when he exhorts his reader:

> fonde for to touche bi desire good gracious God as he is, þe touching of whome is eendeles helþe by witnes of þe womman in þe gospel: Si tetigero vel fimbriam vestimenti eius, salua ero. 'If I touche bot þe hemme of his cloþing, I schal be saa[f]'. Miche more schalt þou þan be maad hole of þi seeknes for þis heiȝe heuenly touching of his owne beyng, him owne dere self.[81]

This is a quite remarkable statement, for here the author refers to the example of the woman who touches Christ, but at the same time speaks only in abstract terms of God or the divine being. This is not the case with Hilton, who in his *Scale* retains a decidedly christocentric tendency. He says of the soul which has been reformed by *feeling* and which is ready for the mystical experience of God, that it 'touchiþ Iesu, & þurȝ vertue of þat vnspekable touchynge it is made hool & stable in itself',[82] for 'Þer is no lufe þat risiþ of knowynge & of special biholdynge þat may touchen so nere oure Lorde Iesu as þis lufe may.'[83] Towards the end of his meditation on the Passion, Richard Rolle is surely also referring to the New Testament story of the sick woman when he begs Christ to grant him grace 'to touche þe with criynge mercy for my synnes'.[84] The same is certainly true of Julian of Norwich when she urges so succinctly: 'touch we hym and we shalle be made cleene.'[85] These examples correspond with scholastic teaching, for we read for example in Thomas Aquinas: 'Mens humana aliquo modo tangit eum cognoscendo vel amando',[86] although the English authors stress almost exclusively the 'amando'. Common to the various English treatments of this theme is the fact that they are not prompted by the same passionateness which characterizes treatments of this theme in German mysticism. Mechthild of Magdeburg, for instance, uses a very powerful image when she explains that 'ich ruere ane underlas dise grundelosen gotheit.'[87] In comparison with this, Margery Kempe comes off very badly, for in her treatment of this motif she shows the unpleasant side of medieval female mysticism. In her book Christ thanks his 'dowtyr' for so often having bathed him in her soul,[88] and when he appeared to her in a dream she took his toes in her hand and felt them.[89] This is certainly an expression of the theme of man touching God, but the 'detour' via the idea of the incarnation of God becomes almost an end in itself for Margery. For her it is nothing short of the highest goal to be able to feel the physicalness of God *realiter*: '& to hir felyng it weryn [i.e. Christ's toes] *as it had been very flesch & bon*'.[90]

But in fact in Western mysticism it is more often God who touches man. Master Eckhart uses this idea on one occasion in an attempt to illustrate the birth of God in the soul: 'Gotes geburt in der sêle ist niht anders denne ein sunderlîchez götlîchez berüeren.'[91] In English mysticism there are no parallels to this image of Eckhart's, nor to Mechthild of Magdeburg's attempt to bring out the erotic connotations of metaphors of touching, by having God say to the soul: 'so muos ich dich ... mit miner gotlichen nature berueren als min einige küniginne.'[92] On the other hand Hilton in his *Scale* describes the way that the soul which perseveres in affective prayer is touched by divine grace in an extremely dynamic, passionate language:

> hit [grace] woundiþ þe sowle wiþ þe bliseful swerd of lufe, þat þe bodi [falliþ] doun and mai nouȝt bere hit. Þis touchinge is of so gret miȝte þat þe moste vicious or flescli man lifende in erþe ... schulde be riȝt sad and sobre a gret while after.[93]

This theme of man being touched by divine love is altogether highly characteristic of Hilton's mysticism. He discusses at great length how those contemplatives who have only recently decided on a *vita contemplativa* still reveal a 'litelnes & weiknes of here soule' and are therefore not yet in a position to 'bere a litel touchynge of God'.[94] But, Hilton goes on to say, the soul soon senses that 'þe leste touchynge of lufe & þe leste sperkle of gostly liȝt ... is so mikel & so confortable, so swete & so delitable ... þat it is ouertaken with it.'[95] Indeed the soul 'berste' with it and dissolves into weeping, sighing and other emotions.

Like Hilton, the author of the *Cloud* understands mystical contemplation itself as just such a divine touching, and this helps him to express that man cannot control it but only receives it as a gift of divine grace: 'God may, kan & wile . . . touche diuerse soules . . . sodenly with þe grace of contemplacion.'[96] And Julian, too, for whom the goal of the mystical way consists in being touched by God, understands this touching as a gracious act of God on man: 'he wylle that we redely intend to his gracious touchyng more enIoyeng in his hole loue'.[97] Sr Anna Maria Reynolds has pointed out that this use of the motif of touching as 'God's direct action on the soul' is reminiscent of the pseudo-Dionysian concept of 'ἐπαφή'.[98]

We find a more dynamic formulation in the *Mirror of Simple Souls* where it is said of the soul in the *unio* that 'a rauischinge deep liȝt toucheþ hir & peersiþ hir and fediþ hir of þe moost nyȝ'.[99] And elsewhere the English commentator explains that the mystical soul 'may not suffre þat enyþing towche hem but þe pure touchinges of loue or þing þe whiche lediþ þerto'.[100] But this range of metaphors takes on a particular significance above all in the *Treatise of Perfection of the Sons of God*, the translation of Ruysbroeck's *Vanden Blinckenden Steen*, where we notice a special predilection for the idea of divine touching and where we read, for instance, that 'the flowynge in touchynge of god makys vs in spyrryt lyevynge'.[101]

The 'unio mystica' as a smelling and hearing or speaking of God

Allegories of the sense of smell are also an essential ingredient in all accounts of the mystical union of man with God. And again it was the Bible that provided the decisive impetus, especially the *Song of Songs*, for there the lovers seem almost to drip with the scent of choice ointments and herbs,[102] and at the very beginning of the poem the sponsa asks her beloved: 'Trahe me, post te curremus / In odorem unguentorum tuorum.' Augustine cries out in his *Confessiones*: 'flagrasti, et duxi spiritum et anhelo tibi';[103] Jacopone da Todi in a *Lauda* sings the praises of the 'Odor divino',[104] and Margaretha Ebner speaks of the holy 'rauch' and the divine 'schmack',[105] to list but a few examples chosen at random from European mysticism. In English mysticism this range of metaphors is for the most part limited to Rolle's Latin writings, and he thus demonstrates once again that the breadth of his metaphorical spectrum is fully comparable with continental mysticism.

If the author of the *Cloud* speaks mostly in abstract terms of the naked existence of God, Rolle attempts to make God sensually experienceable, as in his image of the 'sapor condiens, odor redolens'.[106] Furthermore, the fragrance of God often solidifies to become a cloud overshadowing the soul: 'Anima utique obumbrata amoris odoribus,'[107] an image which reveals an almost poetic expressiveness. Walter Hilton, who is regarded as the author of the *Qui Habitat*, on one occasion declares that the contemplative souls are the model for others and he expresses their exemplariness in the image that they are 'swete odour to oþur men'.[108] He also explains in connection with a psalm verse, that the reciting of a psalm, if it proceeds from a burning heart, in other words it if is recited in mystical loving surrender, 'ȝeldiþ vp a swete smel to þe face of oure Lorde Iesu'.[109] And finally we find a beautiful use of this kind of metaphor in Julian of Norwich, who describes the act of ultimate union with God after the soul has died in love-longing, with the words: 'And we endlesly be alle hyd in god . . . hym delectably smellyng.'[110]

It is interesting to see that Julian also turns this image into the negative, when she gives an account in her *Revelations* of a vision in which the devil appeared to her and gave off an evil smell.[111] This concept was presumably familiar to her from medieval spiritual literature, for an evil-smelling devil appears, for instance, in the legend of *Seinte Marherete*. When Marherete tells this devil that she herself 'smelle of þe swote Iesu',[112] she is basically taking up the words of St Paul that the faithful are 'Christi bonus odor' (2 Cor. 2:15). There is an extension of this motif in the translation of Catherine of Siena's main work, where we find the highly effective statement that the souls which are devoted to God are a 'swete smel of oonheed, or vnyoun'[113] which the devil cannot smell. In Margery Kempe's autobiography, as is to be expected, this traditional mystical image, too, is so to speak absorbed by popular piety. The fact that Margery 'Sumtyme . . . felt swet smellys wyth hir nose'[114] should of itself be sufficient proof of the immediacy of her experience of God. But what a difference from the way the great mystics speak about the *unio*, when Margery has Christ say to her that he will carry her soul up into heaven 'wyth gret myrthe & melodye, wyth swet smellys & good odowrys'.[115]

In mystical texts God's speaking to man is often mentioned as a concrete expression of the *unio*. The biblical passages which were traditionally understood first and foremost as prefiguring the mystical *unio*, speak of an intimate conversation between God and man — beginning with Moses who meets God in the cloud and converses with him.

It is interesting that in mystical texts what is said in the conversation between God and man is not important. They are concerned solely with the fact of mystical communication between man and God. God's speaking to man is frequently interpreted as a mystical love dialogue — certainly suggested in the first place by the joyful exclamation of the beloved in the *Song of Songs*: 'En dilectus meus loquitur mihi' (S. of S. 2:10). The author of the *Ancrene Wisse* devotes a very beautiful and extended exegesis to this verse, in which he justifies why the recluses are forbidden to converse with people outside their cell by saying that the bride who hears the voice of the sponsus has no other wish than to follow him:

> ne ʒeoue ʒe to swuch mon nan inʒong to speokene . . . . Lokið
> nu hu propreliche þe leafdi i canticis godes deore spuse leareð
> ow bi hire sahe hu ʒe schule seggen. En dilectus meus loquitur
> michi . . . Ich ihere mi leof speoken. he clepoeð me ich mot gan.
> ant ʒe gan ananriht to ower deore leofmon. & meaneð ow to his
> earen þe luueliche cleopeð ow to him wið þes wordes. Surge
> propera amica mea.[116]

Since in the *Song of Songs* the lover also singles out the voice of the sponsa for special praise as one of her glories, so too the recluse, if she really wishes to be the bride of Christ, must withhold her voice from the world and dedicate it to Christ alone: 'ʒef þu wult swuch beon. ne schaw þu na mon þi wlite. ne ne leote bl<ð>eliche here þi speche. ah turn ham ba to iesu crist to þi deorewurð e spus.'[117]

The verse from Hosea 'ducam eam in solitudinem, et loquar ad cor eius' (Hos. 2:14) further contributed to the development of the love dialogue between God and the soul. There is also, as we have already mentioned, Rolle's striking treatment of this verse in his *Melos Amoris*, where he argues that a true lover does not kiss in public but takes his beloved off to a place of solitude and 'Tunc loquitur quod libet'.[118] Hilton, too, takes up this thought towards the end of the second part of his *Scale*, where he puts forward a variation on the theme of the love dialogue. This variation consists of the rather beautiful image of the loving whispering of God to his soul, an image which has the important function of summarizing in a very concise manner virtually the whole of his teaching. It is, he says, a matter of being deaf to the world in an attitude of humility, purity and virtue, so that the soul will be able to hear Christ's loving whispering, his loving murmuring:

Him bihouiþ for to han mikil klennes in soule, in meknes & in alle
oþer vertues, & to ben halfe deefe to noyse of werdly iangelynge.
þat schuld wis(e)ly perceifen þese swete gostly *rownynges*.
Þis is þe voice of Iesu.[119]

For every 'knowynge of soþfastnes' is 'a priuey rownynge of Iesu in
þe ere of a clene soule'.[120] He supplements this theme with a reference
to a verse from Job: 'Porro ad me dictum est verbum absconditum'
(Job 4:12).[121] But the 'verbum absconditum' ('hid wurde'), which Jesus
utters to the soul, is not expressed any more concretely but merely
declared to be *inspiracioun*. For Hilton it is solely the fact of mystical
communication which is decisive, and he lets the idea of the loving
whispering speak for itself.

There is a similar picture in German mysticism, which uses the verb
runen, the cognate of the English *rownen*, although here there is less
extensive reference to the Bible than in Hilton. There is an obvious
reference to the verse from Job in Tauler: 'Solt du daz vetterliche
verborgene heimliche wort in dir hoeren daz in dem heiligen gerúne
in dem innersten der selen wurt gesprochen.'[122] But the German translation of Rudolf of Biberach's main work makes a direct reference to
Job: 'Got ret ovch etwenne heimlich rúnende, als in her Jobs buoch
geschriben ist: "Ein verborgen wort wart zvo mir sprochen" '.[123]

The range of metaphors for the dialogue between God and man has
been developed still further in Franciscan mysticism. Here the wound
of Christ which he received from the lance at the crucifixion is offered
to the soul as a dwelling place, where, united with him, it can say to
his heart: 'In hem [the wounds] i wole reste me & shlepe, ete &
drynke, rede, preie & þinke & do wat i shal; þere shal I speke to his
herte & sumwhat begge of his loue.'[124] This process of 'materializing'
sensual imagery, which we can observe here in Hilton's translation of
the *Stimulus Amoris*, is again something which was taken to extremes
in texts of female mysticism. The great mystical texts are satisfied with
the implied suggestion of mystical communication, but in the texts of
the women mystics the imagination knows no such restraints. They
often speak in quite concrete terms of lengthy auditions, of very intimate conversations of the soul with God, Jesus and Mary, conversations
which are by no means limited to matters concerning salvation, but
which are meant time and time again to confirm that the writer is
specially chosen. Thus Margery Kempe claims to have received an
assurance from Christ that she will have 'a synguler grace in Hevyn'[125]
and that she may take him into her bed as her husband.[126] She describes

Doesn't connect w/
Rolle

his voice as 'melydiows . . . swettest of alle sauowrys softly sowndyng in hir sowle'.[127] In addition, in her morbidly exaggerated sensibility she frequently hears indefinable sounds and tones: on one occasion when she is picturing to herself the events of the Passion, she hears 'so hedows a melodye þat sche mygth not ber it'.[128] On another occasion she hears 'a maner of sownde as it had ben a peyr of belwys blowyng in hire ere'. She learns that this is 'þe sownd of þe Holy Gost', and a little later she feels that this sound is transformed into the voice of a dove and then into that of a robin redbreast 'þat song ful merily oftyn-tymes in hir ryght ere'.[129] These images, which stand out — especially the last one — because of their complete lack of any spiritual reference, are motivated in a very superficial manner, in that they are meant to serve as 'tokenys'[130] — as signs and pledges — of Christ's love for her.

Excursus: The significance of metaphors of music in English mysticism

Some of the most beautiful and most powerfully suggestive linguistic expressions of the mystics are the images taken from the sphere of music. Again they were able to find their models in the Bible, where there is frequent use of musical imagery, especially in the psalms. It has also been pointed out that the Fathers of the Church, presumably drawing on the Pythagorean conception of the music of the spheres, describe the world of the transcendental as a 'symphony' and as music.[131] Hrabanus Maurus gives a very comprehensive definition. According to him, music is the expression of a spiritual reality: 'Canticum significat scientiam spiritualem . . . . Canticum ad contemplationem . . . refertur. . . . Jubilatio clamor spirituali fervore expressior, sive gaudium ineffabile quod humana lingua plenius fari non valet.'[132] Absalom of Springiersbach divides music into the categories 'animalis', 'spiritualis' and 'coelestis' where spiritual music consists in growth of virtue, fear of God and love of one's neighbour, whilst heavenly music means the vision of God, the attainment of immortality of the flesh and eternity.[133]

In the English texts Margery Kempe 'in hir bodily heryng'[134] hears music which is evidently very loud so that she cannot hear anything else, whereas Julian's attempt to speak of God in musical images is by contrast far more spiritual; for she sees in a vision how he gathers the circle of his 'frendes' round him and fills them with joy 'Fulle homely and fulle curtesly with mervelous melody in endelesse loue.'[135] When we read in Mechthild of Magdeburg 'das denne der geist inwendig singet, das gat über alle irdensche stimme',[136] this seems almost like a condensed commentary on the famous experience which Rolle relates in the fifteenth chapter of his *Incendium Amoris*. Whilst reading the evening psalms he felt a 'suauitatem inuisibilis melodie' come over him, whereupon his thoughts turned into music, his meditation into a poem, and even the psalms changed into a supernatural music.[137] This detailed narration of Rolle's has important implications. In the mystical *unio* the divine word and the human answer to it became transformed for him, in keeping with the tradition, into a *iubilus* which transcends human language. Since this has already been the subject of several studies, we need only add a few remarks here.[138] Man's attempt to form concepts of God and the world beyond gives way to intuition. Thinking of God and about God is transformed into supernatural music, 'thoght turnes intil sang and intil melody'.[139] This music emanates from God because God himself is music. Rolle indeed addresses him as the medieval musical instrument 'cithara': 'O amor meus! O mel meum! O cithara mea!'[140] This metaphorical identification is extremely revealing precisely for Rolle's mysticism, although it is certainly not as original as Schulte maintains,[141] for God is already called a 'cithara auditui'[142] in Hugh of Strasbourg's *Compendium Theologicae Veritatis*, which was one of Rolle's sources.[143]

We constantly observe in Rolle how the images of music, together with those of fire, are linked with other sense experiences, and this helps to give his mystical language the greatest possible compactness and conciseness. We read for instance that the mystical souls 'dormiunt in lectulo contemplativi canoris',[144] or that the 'sonora iubilacio' of the soul shines outwards ('effulgeret'),[145] which caused the Middle English translator great difficulty.[146] And finally in his *Melos Amoris* he says of all those who are adept in mysticism 'Capimur .... ad contemplacionem sonantibus epulis';[147] the mystics are promised 'melodious food'. It would be premature if one were to assume in Rolle a conscious synaesthetic effect in the romantic sense. What makes him speak in this way is that the *ineffabile* character of his experience makes him reach for several sense concepts at the same time, in order to put across the intensity of his experience in the most effective way. It is also extremely likely that in the example quoted, Rolle wanted to draw an analogy with the secular banquet where the musical framework had an important function.[148] There is also in this last example a strong influence of biblical language. Rolle was certainly very much influenced by the psalmist's formulation which is not made very clear in the Vulgate: 'transibo in locum tabernaculi admirabilis. . . . In voce exsultationis et confessionis, *sonus epulantis.*'[149]

A further aspect of Rolle's musical imagery is seen in his *Melos Amoris* — a work hitherto singularly neglected by scholars — where the very title implies the dominance of metaphors of music. We find in this work an example which is almost unique in Middle Latin literature of the extremely exaggerated use of alliteration, where long sentences often consist exclusively or predominantly of words with the same initial consonant. This would seem to suggest that Rolle used this excessive alliteration in order to convey the transcendental music he had heard by means of a sensual linguistic analogy. And it is also precisely in his *Melos Amoris* that the theme of mystical music is treated in great detail. In Chapter 45 he indicates that passionate statements about the souls which are mystically united to God such as 'canunt . . . et odas ostendunt amantibus excelsis iperlirico in ympno. Tibiam tangunt tinnulo tenore'[150] are directly inspired by the psalm verse which calls upon man to praise God 'in sono tubae', 'in psalterio et cithara', 'in tympano et choro', 'in chordis et organo', 'in cymbalis benesonantibus' (Ps. 150:3 ff.). In line with traditional exegesis, as it is found for instance in Absalom of Springiersbach, this eightfold heavenly melody is now linked with the eight beatitudes which already refresh man in his earthly life.[151]

A comparison with the remaining English mystics reveals that, although metaphors of music are by no means as important for them as for Rolle, they nevertheless do have a role to play, especially in Hilton. When Hilton speaks of the 'harpe of þe soule' whose two strings are made of 'meknes' and 'lufe'[152] he is drawing on an old Platonic-neo-Platonic image first used in a mystical sense by John Chrysostom, in which the man who subordinates the body to the soul is called a harp.[153] There are certain connections here with continental vernacular mysticism. In his survey of mysticism in North Germany Stammler mentions Middle German 'allegorical treatises . . . in which the loving soul is said to play on its strings',[154] and in Mechthild of Magdeburg God calls the soul 'ein lire vor minen oren',[155] or a harp whose strings he knows how to pluck.[156] Finally it is significant for Hilton's metaphors of music that, as we have already mentioned, they reveal certain similarities with Rolle. His compact expression 'He þat most loueþ god, syngeþ hiȝest'[157] is very akin to Rolle's statement: 'If thou wil lufe, þan may þou syng til Cryst in melody'.[158] And , like Rolle, Hilton, too, says that prayers and hymns 'are turned as hit were in til . . . swete songe'.[159]

Another fact which is very interesting in a philological study of the imagery of English mysticism is that Rolle as well as Hilton and the author of the *Cloud* all speak at some stage directly and usually briefly of *minstralsie*. For them *minstralsie* means music which is secular and banal and which leads man astray or diverts him from his heavenly purpose. The author of the *Cloud* uses the term during his discussion of the faults of sectarians and enthusiasts. These are victims of their misguided imagination and have created for themselves a god and angels whom they parade 'with diuerse minstralsie'.[160] And in 'songe or melody or mynstralcy'[161] Walter Hilton sees the danger that the soul might be diverted from thinking of Christ and praying to him. There is a similar judgment in Rolle who feels obliged to state that in comparison with the experience of ecstatic, heavenly music 'al þe sang and al þe mynstralcy of erth' is nothing but sorrow and grief.[162] This assessment of *minstralsie* is somewhat reminiscent of the sharp criticism of the minstrels in *Piers Plowman*.[163] We are certainly not justified in deducing from this that the English mystics tended to be ill-disposed towards poetry, but it is nevertheless remarkable that they make no attempt to introduce *minstralsie* into the mystical realm by way of analogy, as Richard of St Victor does for instance, when he speaks expressly of such a mystical *minstralsy* of the heart.[164]

The 'visio Dei'

The imagery of spiritual seeing completes our survey of mystical metaphors of the senses. This imagery is very widespread in Christian mysticism, for from the beginning the mystics considered the vision of God in the *visio beatifica* to be the highest form of knowledge of God that could be experienced, and it is expressed very clearly in the central concept of *contemplatio*. There is an attempt to express the process of contemplation in visual terms on the north portal of the cathedral of Chartres, where the artist arranges several contemplative women round the portal in different stages and positions. At the highest stage the figure is no longer absorbed in a book as at the beginning, but is looking upwards, into heaven. The eye of the woman rapt in contemplation here serves to express concretely the inner eye of the soul with its ability to see spiritually. We meet the motif of spiritual seeing in the appearance of ideas in the philosophy of Plato, who explains in his *Phaidros*[165] how the beautiful which emanates from a beautiful man pours itself into the eye of the beholder and passes from there into his soul. According to Leisegang, Plato was the first to express this human perceptive ability in concrete terms using the image of the eye of the soul.[166] Oriental religions are also familiar with the idea of spiritual seeing, and we find it, too, in the Bible where St Paul introduces the concept of the 'oculus cordis' (Eph. 1:18) into Christian language. But it was really with the pseudo-Dionysius[167] and Augustine[168] that the eye of the heart became an important mystical image.

A study by G. Lüers of these metaphors of the eyes has shown that German mysticism does not only speak of the eye 'der sêle', the eye 'des herzen', the 'innerlich oge' and the 'geistlichen ogen' but also of the eye 'des gemüetes', 'der vernunft' and 'der bekanntnisse'.[169] The way the English authors specify the topos of the eye of the soul corresponds exactly to this, for apart from 'egh of þair sawls',[170] 'egh of . . . hert',[171] 'innore eiȝe'[172] and 'gostli eiȝe',[173] we also find 'eghe of oure thoght',[174] 'iȝe of . . . reson'[175] and 'eye of my vnderstanding'.[176] These vivid descriptions are meant to express that even the soul's own powers of understanding are dependent for their knowledge of God on what they are shown. Occasionally the mystics say that the soul has two eyes, but they interpret the 'seeing ability' of these two eyes differently. In Eckhart the soul has an outer eye for perceiving the sensual world and an inner eye for knowing God and eternal being.[177] The author of the *Cloud* takes up the statement of the sponsus in the *Song of Songs* who says of his beloved that she has wounded him with one of her eyes (S. of S. 4:9). It is from an allegorical exegesis of this that he develops his theory of the two eyes of the soul. According to Hodgson he also draws on Richard of St Victor and distinguishes the eyes as the eye of reason and the eye of love. With the eye of reason God's attributes can be perceived in his creation, whilst knowledge of the divine being is reserved solely for the eye of love, and he praises this love as 'a wonderful iȝe loue'.[178]

The *Tretis of Discrescyon of Spirites* chooses another approach to illustrate this theological thesis. The author starts from the verse of the psalm which states that God's dwelling place is in Zion, and explains the etymological meaning of this name as 'siȝt of pees'. By way of allegorical exegesis Zion is now taken as prefiguring the soul, and the author follows this up immediately and quite naturally by stating that the *siȝt* of the soul is identical with its *þought*.[179] The term *siȝt* also occupies a position of central importance in Middle English texts because it serves as a translation of *contemplatio*.[180] The seeing of the soul is the reception of the knowledge which is shown to it by divine grace. Hence in Middle English texts siʒt is often linked with *vnderstandyng* or *cnowyng*.[181] In this connection it is interesting to observe that on one occasion Rolle uses the term *insight* to express the necessity of self-knowledge as a precondition for knowing God: 'lene me þe liʒt of grace to haue sum insiʒt in soule',[182] and the *Orchard of Syon* speaks of the necessity of an 'inward biholdinge' of the soul 'to knowe herself'.[183]

It was incidentally the mystics who first developed the special meaning *meditatio, contemplatio, speculatio* of the verbal noun *biholding*. Thus on one occasion Rolle describes the higher part of contemplation as a 'behaldyng and ʒernyng of þe thynges of heven'.[184] The author of the *Cloud* takes over this term, which is already found in Rolle, and uses it primarily to demonstrate the problems surrounding human knowledge of God. As long as the soul is living in the body 'euermore is þe scharpnes of oure vnderstonding in beholding of alle goostly þinges, bot most specialy of God, medelid wiþ sum maner of fantasie'.[185] From this he derives the paradoxical demand which we are familiar with, that man should try to know God in 'a *blinde* beholdyng vnto þe nakid beyng of God himself only'.[186]

In this connection the important question must be asked, namely how far the English texts, which speak of a seeing knowledge of God, say anything at all about the kind of thing they are shown and the extent of it. The author of the *Cloud* does not get beyond a pure blind seeing and the impossibility of a 'cleer siʒt' of God.[187] Hilton, too, speaks in a similar vein, and on one occasion concedes that in its attempts to know the being of God human sight fails: 'I may not sen þe in þi blessed kuynde, what þou art in þi-self. Mi siʒt faleþ.'[188] And when it is said that the mystic will see divine secrets ('priuetes'),[189] this is not explained further. Instead, the authors frequently go back to the very old motif of seeing the divine countenance,[190] and they like to describe the final union in terms of the loving soul beholding its beloved.[191] Walter Hilton remarks in this context that he cannot inform the reader 'what maner be-holdyng a louere of god schal haue in god',[192] but he assures him that he will find 'þing i-nouh feir & preciouse in þe gostli cuntre, wher-wiþ-al þou schalt feden þe likyng of þi gostly eiʒe'.[193] The treatment of this motif hints at the use of a powerfully suggestive poetic language, and indeed we find genuine poetry especially in German female mysticism, where Mechthild of Magdeburg, for example, lets the eyes of the soul play in God.[194] In English mysticism it is primarily Richard Rolle who writes in a comparable manner. He constantly strives to express the transcendental realm in concrete terms by introducing isolated sensual details even though they may not be particularly relevant theologically — for instance he lets the souls see the citizens of heaven.[195] In addition there are in his writings many linguistically very convincing attempts to express the transcendental character of the vision in language — as in the beautiful image that the soul is inflamed by the fire of the vision of eternity.[196]

If we compare the Middle English mystics with one another, we find that Julian is the only one amongst them who does not limit herself to very cautiously worded hints about the vision of the here-after, but rather experiences the theological truths of salvation as a *beholding* or vision. *Beholding* in fact becomes almost a fundamental mystical attitude for her, and it is her reaction to God's *shewing*. Here we must first of all remember that from Augustine onwards the Middle Ages distinguished three different kinds of visions.[197] In the corporal vision (*visio corporalis*) man sees with his eye physical things which are, however, invisible to others. In the spiritual vision (*visio imaginativa*) the physical eye, and with it the natural perceptive faculties, is switched off, so that the vision occurs in sleep or in prayer and takes the form of man being transported to a spiritual seeing. In the third form of vision (*visio intellectualis*) man does not perceive anything physical, for this is a vision where perception is at a purely spiritual level. The tract *The Chastising of God's Children* gives its readers this detailed definition of the three kinds of vision, calling them 'corporal', 'spiritual', and 'intellectual' visions[198] and quotes as an example of the intellectual vision St Paul's being transported into the third heaven, for 'he say wiþout ony figure or ymage god in hym-silf, þat is to say in his godhede'.[199] If we now return to Julian's *Revelations* we see that she too distinguishes a threefold staging of her visions: they take place partly in 'bodly syght', partly in 'goostely syght' and partly in a vision which she describes as 'gostly in bodely lycknesse' and 'more gostly withoute bodely lycknes'.[200] 'Bodyly syght' would thus seem to correspond to the *visio corporalis* and 'goostely syght' to the *visio intellectualis*, although according to Molinari, who has made a detailed study of this terminology of Julian's,[201] the vision 'gostly in bodely lycknesse' corresponds to the *visio imaginativa* and the vision 'more gostly withoute bodely lycknes' corresponds to the lower stage of the *visio intellectualis*; 'gostly syght' then, according to Molinari, means specifically the higher stage of the *visio intellectualis*. Molinari's classification is, however, not completely satisfactory, above all be-cause Julian is not consistent in the use of her own terminology. For when she tells us on one occasion that the sensual vision disappeared but the spiritual one remained,[202] 'goostely syght' is here to be understood as the imaginative grasping of the facts of salvation mediated by the sensual vision. On another occasion she sees in a 'ghostly sight' the special relationship of the creator with his creation, which is mediated to her, again, however, partly in a sensual concrete manner, by means of a small, spherical object which is placed in her hand.[203] This means therefore that in her concept of 'goostely syght' the boundary between the *visio imaginativa* and the *visio intellectualis* is somewhat fluid. It can certainly also mean the grasping of spiritual truths, the intellectual vision, as when she is transported into heaven in such a 'goostely syght' and there sees God: 'crist shewyd me his father in no bodely lycknesse. but in hys properte and in hys wurkyng.'[204] Julian was clearly not familiar with *Chastising*, otherwise she would certainly have worked out a more precise terminology for distinguishing her visions.

But although the terminology may be unclear, it is far more important to recognize that her visions have an extremely intellectual character, which stands out as quite unusual in comparison with the many German women mystics whose spiritual life is known to us from their *vitae*. Most of the visions reported there belong in the category of the sensual vision, the *visio corporalis*, and in many cases it is a question of picturing to oneself the life and death of Christ,[205] of which in the English texts Margery Kempe provides so many examples. Even imaginative visions are comparatively rare. We read of one experienced by Jützi Schulthasin who 'schowet . . . lutterlich das tussent jar im himelrich nit sind wan als ain augenblick. Sy sach och in Got alle ding. Sy sach och und schowet das man un underlas núwe wunder in Gott sicht, und das die wunder sind ewiklich stett.'[206] And, finally, the intellectual vision is almost non-existent in the *vitae* of the German nuns. Blank again quotes Jützi Schulthasin as an example: what she sees in her vision reads almost like a catalogue, e.g. 'how the Word became flesh in Mary', 'God's intention when giving his commandments in the Old and the New Testament', 'the unity of Father and Son from all eternity' or the presence of God in all things.[207]

The 'goostely syght' — partly as an imaginative, but often as a purely intellectual vision — stands firmly in the centre of Julian's *Revelations*. Even when she has a corporal vision of the Passion of Christ this is not really an end in itself, but serves only as a starting point for some theological abstract knowledge. For example she sees Mary suffering because of the Passion of Christ, and in doing so recognizes Mary's spiritual relationship with Christ.[208] Julian often sees the abstract theological meaning of a vision as a direct divine communication, even if she perceives the meaning 'without voys and openyng of lyppes'.[209] Since the 'seeing' of this 'shewing' becomes for Julian a source of knowledge, then for her 'see and know', 'syght' and 'vnderstandyng' are synonymous terms.[210] And the extent of her knowledge surpasses that of the remaining English mystics, for whilst they, as we have seen, speak only in extremely general terms of seeing the divine *privities*, Julian can to some extent become consciously aware of the *privytes* she has seen and can therefore express them in language. An example of this is her intimation that God has looked upon her but has not chided her because of her sin, and from this she derives an understanding of how sin is judged from God's point of view.[211] This understanding leads her to say: 'And to me was shewed none harder helle than synne',[212] a highly original and bold statement for an author living in the Middle Ages, for she does not accept for herself the threat of agony and torment as punishment for sin — which was such an important concept for Christianity in the Middle Ages — but sees the sin itself as the decisive punishment. Julian thus differs appreciably from, say, Tauler, who reminds his hearers in his sermons of 'vegfúr' where the souls are 'gesotten und gebraten'.[213] In contrast to the remaining English mystics but with an astonishing similarity to Dante, Julian maintains that spiritual knowledge is mediated to man in order to awaken and strengthen his love of God.[214] Like the other English authors, Julian too desires 'to be onyd in to the syght and the beholdyng of him',[215] but at the same time she is aware that her wish cannot possibly be fulfilled under earthly conditions, for 'the more the soule seeth of good. the more she desyeryth hym by grace'.[216]

IX

*

The metaphorical complex of having God

Apart from the metaphorical descriptions for the *unio mystica* we have examined up to now, which were all taken from the area of sense perceptions, there are in the Western mystical tradition a large number of vivid expressions to illustrate the soul's desire to *have* God or the soul's joy in the possession of God. The very widespread and popular expression 'to have God' which occurs in mystical texts has been interpreted — not without some justification — as an attempt 'to speak of the *unio mystica* with completely unabashed directness'.[1] This theme dates back to primitive religious modes of thinking, as a study of its historical genesis has shown.[2] According to this study it was Philo who made the decisive attempt to connect the Old Testament idea of possessing God ('κλῆρος') with the Greek concept of the mystical possession of God ('τὸν θεὸν κλῆρον ἔχειν'), an attempt which led to this connection being established in the mystical texts of Late Judaism and in Gnosticism.[3] In the New Testament it is primarily the author of the Epistles of St John who takes up this idea,[4] for he attacks the Gnostics and is therefore obliged to speak their language.[5] And it must not be forgotten that the *Song of Songs* was not the least of the influences which inspired this motif of having God, for there the sponsa, referring to the blissful union with her beloved, says: 'Tenui eum, nec dimittam.' (S. of S. 3:4). The Fathers of the Church had a predilection for the concept of 'Deum habere'. Augustine often links it with the motif of the vision of God and equates it with the related idea of the *fruitio Dei*.[6]

A glance at the English mystics shows that precisely this theme 'having God', which is widespread in German mysticism,[7] finds immense favour in their works, which is a further proof that a dynamic element is certainly not lacking in their mystical language. If on the one hand the author of the *Cloud* demands that the mystic must completely forget himself, creation and all concrete concepts of God, he assures him on the other hand that God will allow himself to be possessed by the man who loves him and is affectively disposed towards him: 'By loue may he be getyn & holden.'[8] In connection with his exegesis of the Martha and Mary episode in Luke, the author interprets the 'Porro unum est necessarium' (Luke 10:42) with which Jesus justifies Mary's inaction as the call to man to concern himself with the possession of God: ' "For o þing is nesessarie", þe whiche is God. Him woldest þou haue.'[9] And there is certainly a close connection with the *Cloud* when Walter Hilton uses almost the identical words to express the soul's wish to have God: 'Hym wilt þou haue and noþing bute Hym',[10] a wish which for Hilton applies to the possession of Christ, and which may be fulfilled in contemplation, hence his recommendation to the soul: 'Hold Him fast whils þou may, & kepe þe in grace, & lete Him not liȝtly fro þe.'[11]

The image of the soul attaching itself to its God is also frequently found in mysticism, an idea which goes back above all to the verse from St Paul: 'Qui autem adhaeret Domino, unus spiritus est' (1 Cor. 6:17). This motif was so popular in the Middle Ages that there is a mystical tract with the title *De Adhaerendo Deo*, and Augustine in particular frequently uses the terms *haerere*, *adhaerere* and *cohaerere* when discussing the love between God and the soul.[12] The verb *cleven*, cognate with the German *kleben*, is part of the basic vocabulary of English mysticism. We find it as early as Rolle's *Meditations on the Passion*, where he asks God: 'take to þe myn hert hooly . . . so þat myn hert . . . ever cleve fast upon þe',[13] and Julian explains to her readers: 'truly oure lovyr desyereth that the soule cleue to hym with all the mygthes.'[14] Margery Kempe attempts to illustrate the idea of cleaving to God in a way which is typical of popular piety, and her drastic comparison is rather excessive when she has Christ say to her: 'Dowtyr, for þu art so buxom to my wille & cleuyst as sore on-to me as þe skyn of stokfysche cleuyth to a mannys handys whan it is sothyn.'[15] Other terms which are used for this motif are: 'hongen',[16] 'holden bi',[17] 'drawen nere',[18] and 'fastnen',[19] all of them being Germanic terms of great vividness, while the loan-word *to adhere* only became established in New English.

As is clear from the study of the theme of having God, even in Greek texts the verb ἔχειν in its mystical usage tended to take on the meaning of εἶναι, and thus the concept of possessing God became the same as 'being in God'.[20] The most impressive treatment of this idea in English mysticism is in Julian of Norwich, who manages to produce a linguistically most convincing illustration of the dialectical relationship between man and god in the process of union. For her the soul being in God means at the same time God being in the soul; just as God embraces the soul, so the soul encloses God:

> the hye goodnesse of the trynyte is our lord and in hym we be closyd and he in vs / We be closyd in the fader. And we be closyd in the son. And we are closyd in the holy gost. And the fader is beclosyd in vs. the son is beclosyd in vs. And the holy gost is beclosyd in vs.[21]

The image of the soul dwelling in God or God dwelling in the soul,[22] an image widespread in the Bible, is frequently used to express this mystical union. Thus Master Eckhart says of the soul: 'diu sêle wonet in gote mit bekentnüsse unde mit minne.'[23] In English mysticism, however, the idea of the soul dwelling in God is not very common. Instead, in the works of the author of the *Cloud* and in Hilton it is a precondition for the mystical union, that in his laborious way to God man must come to terms with living in the cloud of unknowing, of darkness, which separates God from him.[24] The Franciscan mysticism of the Passion developed the image of the soul dwelling in the wounds of Christ, an image which is very drastic and utterly foreign to our present-day taste. We find it for instance in Hilton's translation of James of Milan's *Stimulus Amoris*, where we read: 'thi sowle wolde ouȝt of þi bodi. and ai wone in cristes woundes.'[25]

In English mysticism the theme of God dwelling in man is appreciably more widespread. In the poem *A Song of the Love of Jesus*, which is probably to be ascribed to Rolle, the reader is urged to give his soul to God 'þat he þe dwell within',[26] for this is God's 'wonnyngsted'.[27] Although this example may be less vivid than many of the treatments of this motif in German mysticism, where Mechthild of Magdeburg for instance describes the omnipresence of God with the image 'Es enist kein herre mer, der zemale in allen sinen húsern wone, denne alleine er',[28] Julian has succeeded here, too, in finding a concise formulation by applying the idea of indwelling to the soul and to God at the same time. She tells us that God dwells in the soul, and consequently the soul dwells in God: 'Hyely owe we to enIoye yat god dwellyth in oure soule. And more hyly we owe to enIoye that oure soule dwellyth in god.'[29] Such an antithetical mode of expression, which is formed along the lines of the rhetorical figure of *commutatio* and which illustrates the indissolubility of the union between the soul and God, is highly characteristic of the style of her mystical language. It does not, however, detract from the individuality of her dialectically skilful style if we observe that similar linguistic formulations can occasionally be found in German mysticism, as for instance in Tauler who says of the souls: 'sú wonent in Gotte und Got wonet in in.'[30] And there cannot be really any question of an influence from German mysticism here. The parallelism would seem rather to be the result of both going back to the same source, namely the words of Christ in John 6:56, where there is already a hint of this antithesis: 'qui manducat meam carnem . . . in me manet, et ego in illo.'

In addition Julian seizes another possibility of expressing the metaphor of the mystical indwelling in more concrete terms, by introducing into her work the image of God seated, as we have already seen elsewhere. Just as God frequently appears in the Bible in a seated position, enthroned, so too Julian attaches great importance to the fact that in one of her visions she has seen him seated, and she interprets this as a symbol of divine peace: 'The syttyng of the fader betokynnyth the godhede. that is to sey. for shewyng of rest and pees. For in the godhed may be no traveyle.'[31] And again, typically, it is the dialectical aspect of this seated posture which she takes up: for on the one hand God is the seat of the soul: 'oure soule syttyth in god in very rest',[32] and on the other hand God sits in the soul which is here expressed concretely as a city: 'I vnderstode yat it [the soul] is a wurschypfulle cytte. In myddes of that cytte (sitts) oure lorde Iesu'[33] and: 'That wurschypfull cytte yat oure lorde Iesu syttyth in. it is oure sensualyte in whych he is enclosyd.'[34]

This image shows better than almost any other in Julian how deeply she is rooted in the tradition of medieval theology, in other words how great her knowledge of Latin theology must have been. Even the very unusual identification of the soul with a city has a theological background and is a very important metaphor in European mysticism, taken from the allegorical interpretation of a passage in the New Testament. For the mystics are very fond of referring to the sentence in Luke 'ipse [Jesus] intravit in quoddam castellum' (Luke 10:38), where Luke describes the entry of Jesus into Bethany. From this passage and also partly from the statement in the Book of Proverbs that the soul which is well-ordered and secure against afflictions can be compared to a city (Prov. 24:15), the mystics develop an image which is also found in non-Christian contexts, and which can be traced back to Plato's comparison of the soul with a 'πολιτεῖα'.[35] In German mysticism, Master

Eckhart in particular drew on the *castellum* of this verse from Luke and from it developed his term *bürgelin* of the soul, to illustrate that the innermost soul is the place of the *unio mystica*.[36] In the English texts we find this metaphor as early as the *Ancrene Wisse*, where we read that the devil 'asaileð ower castel & te sawle burh'.[37] It is conceivable that Julian derived her inspiration for her image of the city of the soul from the *Tretyse of þe Stodye of Wysdome*, which speaks of the 'cite of oure concyence'.[38] Margery Kempe was most likely inspired to her metaphor 'þe cite of hir sowle'[39] — which the *MED* wrongly cites as the first occurrence of the word *cite* in its mystical meaning — by the *Revelations* of Julian whom she admired so much.

The image of God sitting in the soul is also very popular in medieval mysticism, especially in the texts of the women mystics. We are reminded first of all of Suso who was closely connected with German female mysticism. We read in his biography that in a vision he 'sah, daz der lip ob sinem herzen ward als luter als ein kristalle, und sah enmiten in dem herzen ruweklich sizen die ewigen wisheit in minneklicher gestalt'.[40] Muschg tells how the mystic Anna of Ramschwag in the nunnery of Katharinental looked into her body in a vision and saw there two beautiful children embracing each other, whom she recognized as God and her soul.[41] Adelheid Langmann from the nunnery of Engelthal is ordered by God to look into her 'hertze', and what she sees there proves once again the popularity of these metaphors which are almost crying out to be expressed in a sculptural form: 'do sah si ihr sele gegen unserm herren sizzen . . . do neigt sich di sel uf unsern herren und er legt sein arm umb si.'[42]

If we return to English mysticism, we make the interesting observation that even for these metaphors the decisive impulse again comes from the allegorical interpretation of a verse from the Bible. For in his *English Psalter* Rolle interprets the verse 'Dominus in templo sancto suo: dominus, in celo sedes eius' (Ps. 10:4) to the effect that 'he is restand in vs. for in haly saules is his rest, and his sete'.[43] It is very revealing that in her account of the advice she received from Julian, which we have already mentioned, Margery Kempe also remarks that Julian told her that the Bible ('Holy Wryt') states that 'þe sowle of a rytful man is þe sete of God, & so I trust, syster, þat ȝe ben.' This clearly refers to the psalm verse we have just quoted.[44] Thus Julian herself gives us an important pointer which we must constantly bear in mind in our comparative study of mystical metaphors, namely that even the most striking parallels between English and German mysticism do not necessarily indicate any influence of the one on the other, but may well have come about because in both cases there was the same recourse to Latin mysticism and the Bible.

It is only to be expected that in her visions Margery Kempe, too, experiences the image of God sitting in her soul. Nor is it any surprise that in her case the tendency to develop the scene is taken much further, when she depicts how there are three cushions in her soul, one gold, one red and one white, for the Trinity to sit on:

> þu thynkist . . . dowtyr, as þow þu haddist a cuschyn of gold, an-oþer of red veluet, þe thryd of white sylke in thy sowle. And þu thynkist þat my Fadyr sittyth on þe cuschyn of golde, for to hym is a-propyrd myght & power. . . . Thus þu thynkist. . . þat I am worthy to syttyn on a red cuschyn in rememorawns of þe red blood þat I schad for þe. Mor-ouyr þu thinkist þat þe Holy Gost sittyth on a white cuschyn, for þu thynkist þat he is ful of lofe & clennesse.[45]

But it cannot be said in this case that her pleasure in the sensual, concrete detail makes her lose sight of the central spiritual content, for the colour of the cushions has symbolic value: the gold cushion symbolizes the omnipotence of God, the red the Passion of Christ and the white the love and purity of the Holy Spirit.

X

*

The mystical experience of God as rest, sleep, death and complete absorption of the self

In the last chapter we met the image of God sitting in the soul, and this posture of sitting is relevant in another way in English mysticism. Richard Rolle for instance insists that he can only find the rest which is absolutely vital for any experience of God if he is in a sitting position: 'For sittand am I in maste rest, and my hert maste upwarde.'[1] Hence he is only granted his ecstatic experience when he is *sitting* in a chapel. Scholars tend to look upon Rolle's predilection for the sitting position when he is sunk in contemplation as idiosyncratic,[2] but this is not quite right. We hear for example of the person to whom the *Book of Privy Counselling* is addressed that 'þou louest to be only & sit by þi-self',[3] and in an audition Margery Kempe hears Christ say to her that she should not grow tired 'to syttyn a-lone be þi-self & thynkyn of my lofe'.[4] Not the least of the reasons why the sitting position is preferred, is because an allegorical understanding of several biblical passages almost suggests it: in the *Song of Songs* the sponsa says she has sat under the shade of the tree of her beloved (S. of S. 2:3), a passage which Rolle quotes verbatim in his *Melos Amoris*.[5] In particular it was Mary's sitting at the feet of Christ (Luke 10, 39) which served as a model for the contemplative, and examples are found in the *Ancrene Wisse*[6] and later in the *Cloud*.[7] If the contemplative prefers to adopt a sitting position, this is basically a physical, concrete expression of the allegorical, spiritual understanding of the biblical passage. But this bodily posture also retains its character as a sign and symbol to indicate man's complete communion with himself, the concentration of all his senses, his thinking and his feeling, which, as we have already discussed, is an indispensable prerequisite for experiencing the mystical *unio*. It is also interesting to observe that — again purely metaphorically — this concentration of man's is occasionally expressed concretely as man sitting in himself, as in Master Eckhart who on one occasion speaks directly of the 'insiczen in sich selber'.[8] Similarly the author of the *Cloud* sees the mystic who has attained self-knowledge as someone who sits in himself, ruling like a king over all the powers of his body and soul: 'þorow þe whiche knowing he sitteþ quietly in hymself, as a king crouned in his rewme, miȝtly, wisely, and goodly gouernyng himself and alle his þouȝtes & steringes, boþe in body & soule.'[9] And of course one cannot assume here either that the anonymous author drew his inspiration for this image from Master Eckhart – rather it is apparent that the author of the *Cloud* obtained the image from the allegorical interpretation of the verse in the Book of Proverbs where we read of a king who, seated, directs his thoughts and movements with wisdom and discretion: 'Rex qui sedet in solio iudicii / Dissipat omne malum intuitu suo' (Prov. 20: 8). In a similar way to Eckhart and the author of the *Cloud*, the *Mirror of Simple Souls* uses the image of sitting to illustrate the soul's complete detachment from all creatural ties, by saying of the soul which has been freed in this way that it 'sittiþ al in fredom'.[10]

In addition Rolle extends the metaphors of sitting in several respects. Thus for instance the ultimate union of the soul with God in the next world is described vividly as the soul sitting amongst the seraphim.[11] There is a particularly interesting passage in Rolle's *Incendium Amoris*, where he once again has recourse to the *Song of Songs* and allegorizes Solomon's litter. He sees its golden backrest as a symbol for the contemplatives, for it is precisely on these, who are living in complete rest, that Christ lays his head, and the gold colour symbolizes their purity and their mystical fire: 'Reclinatorium aureum sunt uiri contemplatiui in quibus, in summa quiete existentibus, specialiter reclinat caput suum Christus. Nam et ipsi in ipso singulariter requiescunt.'[12] Whilst in English mysticism the image of man leaning on God is quite common, the converse is only found in Rolle, who thus again demonstrates his originality and his great freedom in the use of mystical figurative language.

But the mystics do not always resort to the sitting posture when, as in Rolle's example, they wish to paint a picture of the soul resting in God, but frequently make the desired or attained rest their direct theme. The reason why this motif is so popular is because it is already found in the Bible, e.g. Heb. 4: 11: 'Festinemus ergo ingredi in illam requiem', or Eph. 2: 14: 'Ipse ... est pax nostra', and there is a whole series of other biblical passages which the mystics draw on. In Latin mysticism the most famous line is Augustine's 'Inquietum cor nostrum donec requiescat in te.'[13] Rolle, the author of the *Cloud*, Hilton and

Julian all praise God as 'pese' or 'rest'.[14] The *Mirror of Simple Souls* uses a highly individualistic language when it says of the soul that 'hir þouȝt is sett in þe pesible, þat is, in þe Trinite'.[15] As is frequently the case in mysticism, the author of the *Tretis of Discrescyon of Spirites* also refers to Psalms 131 and 75, where it is said of God that his dwelling is peace and his city is in Zion, whereby, as is usual in the Middle Ages, the meaning of the word Zion is allegorized as 'siȝt of pees'.[16] With the help of very varied images Rolle attempts to express the theme of resting in God in concrete terms. In order to illustrate that God's rest embraces the whole cosmos and that the soul can attain this rest, he chooses the expressive image that the souls attain the peace of the poles of heaven, 'pergunt ad pacem polorum',[17] which in the tradition of mystical language is a strikingly original image. Another vivid treatment of this motif which is equally original and effective, is his formulation that the soul which has been refreshed by mystical peace enters into the kingdom of heaven fresh, like a rose: 'velut rosa, rosidus et recens redit ad regnum requie refectus.'[18] In the mysticism of the Cross of St Bernard and St Francis, the image of dwelling in the crucified Saviour, which we have already mentioned, is also used to express in concrete terms the attainment of complete mystical rest. The erotic component which is characteristic of the mysticism of St Bernard and St Francis, is also introduced into this motif in the tract *A Talkyng of þe Loue of God*, where the soul, contemplating the suffering Christ, says: 'euer glad mai I ben . . . & euer resten in þe to cluppen & cusse.'[19]

The idea of mystical sleep, which is akin to the motif of rest, is also erotically coloured in the author of the *Talkyng of þe Loue of God*, for the soul uses the language of a worldly lover when speaking to Christ: 'A midde þi loue I. wol me don. bi twene to þin armes. and þere wol I. slepen and waken.'[20] It was above all else the mystically interpreted 'lectulus . . . floridus' which was important for equating contemplation with sleep, but also the cry of the sponsa worried with desire for her bridegroom: 'Ego dormio, et cor meum vigilat' (S. of S. 5: 2).[21] It is, however, interesting to observe that, apart from the *Talkyng of þe Loue of God* and Rolle, the English mystics are not simply satisfied with the mere effect of the image of mystical sleep and that they do not simply speak of the sleep of the soul, but that they add a homiletic explanation about how far the soul actually falls asleep and what kind of sleep it is. Thus in the *Book of Privy Counselling* man is urged to silence the noise of the three enemies, the world, the flesh and the devil, by the sleep of the blind vision of God. In addition the author expressly justifies the fact that he compares the 'work' of mystical surrender with sleep: '& wel is þis werk licnyd to a slepe'. For just as in sleep the physical senses ceased their activity, so too in spiritual sleep the spiritual senses and powers of the intellect were so engaged and emptied of everything else that 'þe sely soule may softely sleep & rest in þe louely beholdyng of God as he is'.[22] We find a similar statement in Walter Hilton; he begins his discussion of the theme by stating in a linguistically very concise manner the paradox contained in the verse from the *Song of Songs* which we have just quoted: for him the soul sleeps the 'wakir slepe of þe spouse'.[23] But there can only be talk of sleep with reference to the physical eye, since the soul has turned away from all worldly attachment and all fleshly activity. Through this sleep the soul becomes all the more awake so that it can understand the processes in its innermost self and can comprehend divine reality: 'Þe more I slepe fro outwarde þinges, þe more waker am I in knowynge of Iesu & (of) inwarde þinges';[24] 'Þe more þat þe eiȝen are spered in þis maner slepe fro þe appetite of erþli þinge, þe scharper is þe inner siȝt in lufly beholdynge of heuenly fairhed.'[25] To this exegesis Hilton adds an allegorical interpretation of the New Testament episode of the Transfiguration of Christ: the apostles, who had accompanied Christ, had first fallen asleep, in other words had abandoned all worldly attachment. But through the fact that they then afterwards saw the transfigured Christ, they became a prefiguration of the contemplative's vision of God.[26]

But Hilton also transfers the motif of mystical sleep to God himself. Basing himself on the New Testament account of the sleeping Jesus, who is on a stormy sea with his disciples, Hilton reveals to his reader that, according to the mystical understanding of this account, it was the human soul in which Jesus lay hidden asleep. It was her task to wake him with calls of desire so that he would rush to help her.[27]

There are thus many shifts of emphasis in the use of metaphors of sleep, and the same is also true of the use of the image of death to express the union of man with God. The joining of man with God is experienced as a spiritual death and rebirth. It has even been possible to say that it is 'one of the most accepted truths about the *unio mystica* . . . that it necessitates or effects a death'.[28] For Hilton this death is a *mortificatio* of man, the abandoning of all worldly attachment,[29] for in the eyes of the world embracing contemplation seems like entering the grave.[30] Hilton's views are close to the homiletic tradition of the *ars moriendi*. The author of the *Cloud*, however, takes up the traditional allegorical exegesis of Jacob's wives and children, in interpreting the birth of Benjamin and the simultaneous death of his mother, Rachel, as the death of reason in contemplation: 'as sone as a soule is touchid wiþ verrey contemplacion . . . þan diȝeþ alle mans reson.'[31]

Undoubtedly the most impressive use made by the mystics of metaphors of death occurs when these are chosen to express concretely the intensity of mystical love-longing. Orphic mysticism, Christian mysticism and Sufi mysticism are alike in that in all of them mystical love desires death,[32] just as in the *Song of Songs* love and death are connected in the statement: 'fortis est ut mors dilectio' (S. of S. 8: 6). This is why the tract þe *tree & xii. frutes of* þe *holy goost* produces the formula: 'right as deth doth to þe body. so doth loue to þe soule.'[33] The erotic mysticism of the Passion of St Bernard and St Francis in particular is fond of identifying love and death. There the soul 'dies' from longing for the beloved or desires to be united with him in a death in love. Since Christ is praised in mysticism as the ideal lover of the soul, Augustine interprets his own death in the final analysis as the wedding with his bride,[34] and Bernard of Clairvaux expressly calls the mystical ecstasy of the bride a death.[35] In German mysticism it was chiefly Mechthild of Magdeburg who made use of this metaphor of death in love. In her *Fliessendes Licht der Gottheit* we find the sentence: 'ich sturbe gerne von minnen, möhte es mir geschehen.'[36] For Julian of Norwich physical death is the immediate consequence of love-longing: 'we shall dye in longyng for loue . . . And we endlesly be alle hyd in god.'[37] Richard Rolle too feels himself close to death as a result of the intensity of his love — 'En, morior amore',[38] he cries out on one occasion. Man's death and the experiencing of divine reality in the form of heavenly music are for him one and the same thing, for 'mors . . . mihi esset ut melos musice, quanquam iam, tanquam in paradiso positus, subsistam, sedens in solitudine.'[39] This passage is reminiscent of a formulation in Bernard of Clairvaux, who says of the death of the mystic: 'Iam cantando moritur homo, et moriendo cantat.'[40]

In the tract *A Talkyng of* þe *Loue of God* the soul turns to the crucified Christ with the words: 'Let me nou dyen in þi blisful armes.'[41] In this image, as we have already shown in a different context, the dying is conceived as a synonym for mystical ecstasy along the lines of the teaching of St Bernard and of Franciscan mysticism. The analogy with the secular motif of sexual ecstasy as a death — a motif which we find in literature certainly as early as Thomas's *Tristan* — is taken so far here, that any religious meaning can only be derived from the context.[42]

There was a grave danger that in popular piety these metaphors of death would sink into a welter of sentimentality, and again we find that Margery Kempe did not manage to avoid this danger. She sees the Passion of Christ so physically present before her that she stretches out her arms in compassion and love and cries out 'wyth lowde voys': 'I dey, I dey'.[43] In her attempt to re-live the Passion she becomes so hysterical that she turns as blue as lead, and a priest has to carry her out into the fresh air, for fear that she may die. If the intensity of Margery Kempe's experience suggests a comparison with St Francis of Assisi and his stigmatization, it is nevertheless very apparent at the same time how much Margery lacks the deep spirituality of Francis.

Metaphors for the *unio mystica* reach their climax in the images where there is an attempt — as with the images of the motif of death which we have already touched upon — to express the union of the soul with God as a complete loss of being and a dissolving into the all of God. Thus again and again in mystical texts we find the statement that the soul is consumed, devoured or absorbed by God, a very old idea which is to be linked with certain biblical themes such as St Paul's statement that 'absorbeatur quod mortale est, a vita' (2 Cor. 5: 4), for in Latin mysticism the term *absorbere* is often used to express this thought.[44] The German mystical writers also frequently took up this theme and translated it into the vernacular. Thus Tauler for instance can say of the soul that it is 'von der wunderlichen gotheit ingeslunden'.[45] An examination of the use of these metaphors in English mysticism confirms once again the tendency on the part of the English writers largely to avoid any over-bold use of imagery. As so often it is only Richard Rolle who merits special mention, for in the language of the highest passion of love he tells us that the soul is absorbed by the violence of God's kisses and is 'absortus in osculis'[46] — an image which clearly seems to be too bold to the somewhat unimaginative translator, Richard Misyn, since he renders it with the too weak idea that the soul is 'ouercomyn in kyssynge'.[47] How different this is from the Middle English translation of the *Revelations* of Birgitta of Sweden, where we are told in passionate dynamic terms of the 'swelowynge [of] the sowle in-to God'.[48] Rolle's milder statements, like the description of the mystic as someone whom 'amor Christi perfecte absorbuerit',[49] are also translated by Misyn with the help of the adequate English verb *swalowen*: 'Hym certayn . . . cristis lufe has swaloyd.'[50] We can discern here a connection with Latin models, as for instance with Anselm of Canterbury's entreaty 'ut amoris tui abysso totus absorbear'[51] — an image which, however, must yield pride of place to Ruysbroeck's marvellous description of the *unio* as an 'ontson-ckenheiden van minnen'[52] in the sea of God, which recurs in the Middle English translation (the *Treatise of Perfection of the Sons of God*) in the concise formulation 'swalowynge of loue'.[53] Ruysbroeck's famous image of the soul immersed in the sea of divine love, which occurs frequently in his mysticism, also plays an important role in German mysticism. We meet it for instance in Suso who uses the term *entsunkenheit*,[54] and who says of the true mystic: 'Er versank die wil als gar in gote.'[55] And here the linguistic skill of the English mystics lags far behind the creative abilities of the Germans. Instead of being equally ecstatic in their praise of the experience of the Absolute, the English mystics use this motif of being sunk or being immersed only in a negative context, as when the author of the *Cloud* recom-mends to his reader that, if he is to attain a state of contemplation, he should get himself into a kind of sleeping state 'al forsobbid & for-sonken in sorow', sorrow in fact 'þat he is',[56] i.e. that he exists.

The dissolving and merging of the soul into God is described even more expressively in the metaphors of drowning, and again it is Suso who brings these metaphors to a poetic climax when he says for example of the soul that it has enjoyed love-play with God 'und lag also verzogen und versofet von minnen under dez geminten gotes armen'.[57] If we compare this with the use of this motif amongst the English writers, what strikes us once again is the use of the image in a negative manner: the author of the *Cloud* warns his readers against being 'drounyd in þe lust of sensualyte'.[58] And here again the homiletic tendency of English mysticism makes itself unmistakably heard. One can almost observe an affinity of imagery with William Flete's homi-letic tract *De Remediis contra Temptationes*, where the Red Sea which the Israelites had to cross, is interpreted allegorically as the life of the Christian in the world: Christ, as the soul's guide, has come 'in to þis see of tribulacions and temptacions'.[59] Another statement of the author of the *Cloud*, however, that the soul is 'deeply drenchid in ful & in fynal forsakyng of it-self'[60] in divine love, is somewhat reminiscent of German mysticism. Otherwise the ecstatic tone of these metaphors, which is so widespread amongst the continental mystics, is scarcely found in English apart from in translations of continental works. One exception, which deserves special attention, is the *Mirror of Simple Souls*, which shows a marked preference for this kind of figurative language, so much so that it even affects the glosses of the English commentator 'M. N.'. In his prologue this commentator informs the reader that the soul hopes 'to be drenchid in þe hiȝe floode, and vnyed to God bi rauyschinge of loue'.[61] 'M. N.' thus adopts the impressive metaphorical style of this continental tract, where we read for instance that divine love 'þrowiþ' the soul 'in myddis of myddel of diuine loue, in whiche, seiþ þis soule, I am ydreynt'.[62] Apart from this we only find these metaphors, which reflect the deep emotion of the mystic, in the translation of Ruysbroeck, where we also read: 'and so we maye in euerlastynge loue drowne, and alle of oure selfe into inserchable depnesse be drown(d)e'.[63]

In Christian mysticism the process of man's becoming freed from all creatural limits in the *unio mystica* is often expressed through the idea of melting, an idea which has a long tradition and which can already be shown in Plato.[64] But the Christian mystics derived this thought mainly from the language of the psalms and in particular from allegorical treatments of the *Song of Songs*, where the sponsa summarizes the effect of her love in the words: 'anima mea liquefacta est' (S. of S. 5:6). This traditional motif of the soul melting with God is constantly adapted by the German mystics to produce highly original statements. Tauler, for example, speaks of the 'versmeltzen [of man] in dem ungeschaffenen geiste Gottes',[65] and Suso, who carves the name Jesus on his breast, addresses him with the passionate words: 'du muost hût in den grund mins herzen gesmelzet werden.'[66] If we examine the English mystics, we find that they consider these metaphors particularly suitable for expressing in language the merging of the soul and God into each other, for they make frequent use of this image. Thus 'M. N.', the commentator of the *Mirror of Simple Souls*, describes the soul which has been transported in ecstasy as being 'al molten in God for þe tyme'.[67] Richard Rolle is one of those mystics who tend to stress the eroticism in these metaphors, for he draws a conscious analogy with sexual ecstasy when he says that the soul 'in amplexus sponsi tota liquefiat',[68] which calls to mind the 'vliessende minne' of the German mystics but also the *amor liquidus* or *liquefactus* of the Latin texts.[69] The soul melts like wax from the glowing heat of divine love; in the words of the translator, Misyn, the soul appears 'all multyn in fyre of lufe'.[70] Rolle's language sometimes has a compactness about it which is almost poetic, especially in those passages where he links the images of melting with his favourite theme of music. He says, for instance, in his *Incendium Amoris* that the honey of love and the sweetness of the Song of Jesus causes man to melt: 'Spiritus melle diuini amoris et dulcedine canoris Ihesu est liquefactus.'[71]

XI

*

The image of God in the soul, mystical deification and union in the ground of the soul

The 'imago' and 'similitudo' character of the soul and its 'reformatio'

In an attempt to round off our study of the metaphors used in English mysticism to illustrate the union of man with God, we must now extend the theological background somewhat and outline as briefly as possible the essential characteristics of the doctrine of the soul's creation in the image and likeness of God, which is of decisive importance for Christian mysticism. The so-called *imago Dei* doctrine, which is 'one of the oldest and most central doctrines in the theology of the Fathers',[1] and which was taken from there into Scholastic theology, is concerned with the problem of how man who has fallen through sin, may be restored to his original state of being in the image of God. In doing so it links 'a fundamental tenet of biblical revelation with the philosophical view of antiquity of man's similarity with God and his kinship with God, especially as it is expressed by the Platonists and Neoplatonists'.[2] A word of thanks is due here to L. Scheffczyk, whose useful collection of a wide variety of scholarly contributions on this theme makes it considerably easier, even for the layman, to gain some insight into the complexity of the problems surrounding this theme.[3] Let us first outline the most important basic positions of the Fathers and of Scholasticism. The theological doctrine of man as the image of God goes back to the key passage in the Old Testament, 'Faciamus hominem ad imaginem et similitudinem nostram' (Gen 1: 26), where the Septuagint uses the Greek terms εἰκών and ὁμοίωσις. A fundamental exegetical problem is how this passage can be reconciled with a series of New Testament theses, especially 2 Cor. 4:4 and Col. 1:15 which speak of Christ as the image of God, and Rom. 8: 28-30 and 2 Cor. 3:18 which state that man is newly created in the image of God through becoming like Christ who is the image of God.[4] The question therefore is: did man in the Fall lose the property of being the image of God, if this image must be newly created by man's becoming like Christ? Catholic theology answers this question by postulating the thesis that there are different degrees of being the image of God, one natural and one supernatural. From Irenaeus onwards theologians for a long time tried to support this distinction by means of a corresponding interpretation of the terms *imago* and *similitudo*.[5] More recent studies have rejected such a distinction of the two terms as untenable, but nevertheless Catholic theology has retained the double interpretation of the image of God to the present day. It is argued that even after the Fall man retained the natural image of God through his rational soul, *anima rationalis*, which enables man to have a natural form of knowledge of God just as before, even though, as Aquinas concedes, the *anima rationalis* too suffered some loss.[6] Augustine had already expressed this idea concretely, elevating the actual, the non-sensual *anima* itself into a *trinitas creata*, with the help of the three powers of the soul, *memoria*, *intelligentia* and *voluntas*, which he discusses as an essential part of his psychology in his *De Trinitate*,[7] and by which he means the powers of the soul 'in the performance of their functions'.[8] In the same work Augustine also defines the created trinity of the soul with the terms *memoria*, *intelligentia* and *amor*,[9] and this suggested identification of *voluntas* from the first ternary and *amor* from the second ternary is one which is seized upon with particular relish in the affective mysticism of St Bernard and St Francis. According to scholastic teaching, however, man can only regain the supernatural image of God, which was lost in the Fall, through divine grace, through his association with Christ as the new Adam, through the act of being transformed back into the original divine image.

And the English mystics see their justification for talking of the soul as the image of God, in the fact that they look upon the soul as a created trinity which has to be reformed. Both the author of the *Cloud* and Hilton render the Augustinian ternary of the soul as 'minde, reson, & wille'[10] or 'mynde . . . witte . . . wille',[11] whilst the *Mirror of Simple Souls* prefers 'memoire . . . vndirstondinge . . . wille'.[12] And they define the term *wille* more precisely by using it in the sense of affective mysticism and in accordance with Augustine's second ternary as a synonym for *loue*, and by considering it to be the most important of the soul's powers. The will of the soul is also love, because as the third member of the created trinity it corresponds to the Third Person of the Holy Trinity, the Holy Spirit who is divine love: 'And þe lufe and þe wil mad clene brenninde in to God . . . and so hit haþ þe likenes of þe Holi Gost, þe whilk is blissed lufe.'[13] Thus in the same context Hilton can render the Augustinian ternary of the soul (the 'mad trinite') with the terms 'mende, siȝt, and lufe of þe vnmad Blisside Trinite',[14] and it is perhaps in imitation of this that Julian defines the 'made-trynyte'[15] of the soul as being made up of 'kynde loue of oure soule . . . clere lyȝte of oure reson . . . stedfaste mynde whych we haue of god in oure furst makyng'.[16]

It is important to be conscious of the fact that in Augustine's famous ternary of the soul the terms *intelligentia* and *voluntas* or *amor*, which are contrasted with each other, are inherently antithetical terms. A remarkable dialectical relationship between *intelligentia* or *intellectus* and *amor* can be observed in some mystical authors imitating Augustine or the pseudo-Dionysius. This is typical of Richard of St Victor in particular: mystical knowledge of God is ultimately only made possible by *amor* which opens the eyes of *intelligentia*.[17] We find the same statement in Hilton who in his *Scale of Perfection* explains that it is first God's love which opens the eye of reason, and then man is able to know and love God.[18] Furthermore Hilton draws on the Augustinian distinction between the *ratio inferior* and the *ratio superior*. Augustine teaches that the lower reason has the task of knowing and ordering earthly things and that the higher part of reason is the actual image of God, which makes it possible for man to know God.[19] And we find a correspondingly differentiating definition of *reson* in Hilton's *Scale*:

> resoun . . . is departid in two: in þe ouer party & in þe neþer party. Þe ouerer party . . . is proprely þe ymage of God for bi þat only þe soule knowiþ God & lufiþ Hym. And þe neþerer . . . liþ in knowyng & reulynge of erþly þinges for to vse hem discretly.[20]

Hilton is thus not speaking of a purely intellectual knowledge of God, but describes the activity of this *ratio* as knowing and loving at the same time. But in Christian mysticism we also find the thesis that love and knowledge are ultimately rooted in the *mens*, a term by which Augustine understands 'the essence of the soul together with all its powers'. This is usually translated into English as *mynd*, but *mynd* is also used to render one of the powers of the soul, *memoria*. In the *Cloud* it means *mens* including

all the faculties of the soul: 'boþe þe self reson, & þe þing þat it
worcheþ in, ben comprehendid & contened in þe mynde';[21] '& boþe
þe wille & þe þing þat it wilniþ þe mynde conteneþ & comprehendiþ
in it.'[22]

The teaching on the image of God gives rise to a further thesis
which is important for Christian mysticism, namely that the soul, as
Augustine, Aquinas and Bernard of Clairvaux stress, has a 'capacitas
Dei'.[23] Tauler finds a very impressive formulation for this, when he
tells his reader that the soul becomes 'Gotz griffic und empfenglich'.[24]
In English mysticism it is Richard Rolle in particular who frequently
introduces this thought into his mysticism, often paraphrasing it and
implying it in ever new images. Thus he calls the soul 'capax carminis
canori'[25] or even 'capax sonori saporis'.[26] No uniform terminology for
this motif developed in Middle English texts; Misyn sometimes manages
with the loan-word 'capacite'.[27]

The question arises as to how far the human soul's attribute of being
the image of God was impaired by the Fall. Hilton gives a clear answer
to this in the second part of his *Scale* and quotes the words of St Paul:
'Renovamini . . . spiritu mentis vestrae, et induite novum hominem.'
(Eph. 4: 23), which he explains with the words: 'ȝe schul be reformed
not in bodily felynge ne in ymaginacioun, bot in þe ouer party of your
resoun.'[28] Thus it is precisely the *resoun* which needs the act of *reformatio*. This is why Hilton adds the explanation: 'your resoun þat is
properli þe image of God þurȝ grace of þe Holi Gost shal be cloþed in
a new liȝt of soþfastnes, holynes & riȝtwisnes.'[29] Hilton does not therefore refer expressly to the theological thought of whether the image of
God is retained after the Fall, he is concerned exclusively with the
soul's need for reform after the Fall. In his *English Psalter* Rolle
actually says of man that because of his sinfulness, he is no longer able
to know in whose image he was created.[30] Julian of Norwich attaches
importance to *reson*, which for her is nothing short of the greatest gift
of God. In Chapter 80 of her *Revelations* she gives an indication of her
understanding of this *reson* when she says that God is 'wurschyppyd'
in three ways in the earthly life, namely through 'kyndly reson',
through the teaching of the Church and through the workings of the
Holy Spirit in grace.[31] This statement would seem to imply that *reson*,
which is founded in God as Julian says in the same passage, has not lost
the natural image of God, for *reson* is a gift of nature, is *kyndly*. We
shall return later to Julian's scholastic argumentation, but for our
present theme we must note that, unlike Hilton, Julian does not speak
of *reson* needing to be reformed *after* the Fall. She seems rather to be

suggesting the Dominican teaching of man's having a natural, intellectual knowledge of God. It is, however, important to see that she is nevertheless at one with Rolle, the author of the *Cloud* and Hilton, because she stresses at the same time that *reson* alone avails man nothing, unless 'we haue evynly therewith mynde and loue'.[32]

Although Julian is the only English mystic who implies that the natural image of God in man persists, she does not in her mysticism follow the theological distinction between *imago* and *similitudo*, but, like all the other English mystics, uses the corresponding English terms *image* and *likeness*[33] without implying any difference in meaning between them. Thus on the one hand the connection with Latin theology is preserved in the loan-word *image*, whilst on the other hand the Latin term is made more concrete by the addition of the Germanic term *likeness* to form a doublet; the loan-word *similitude* was not used by the mystics but was only introduced into English in Late Medieval texts.[34] In the English texts *image* can mean both the human replica of the divine *imago* and the original divine image itself, as in the *Scale* where Hilton refers to a passage from St Paul and explains that it is possible at the highest stage of contemplation, as a gift of divine grace, to be united with the original divine image: 'We ... bihalden ... heuenly ioye ful schapin and onyd to þe ymage of Oure Lord.'[35] *Likeness* corresponds exactly to the term *glichnisse*,[36] which is the usual term in German mysticism for translating the word *similitudo*. When speaking of regaining the original divine image, however, the German mystics frequently use the word *bilde*, which is in fact almost a central term in German mysticism. Thus we read in Suso: 'Und so er in daz selb bilde ... wirt gebildet, so wirt er denne als von gotes geist in die goetlichen guenlichi des himelschen herren überbildet.'[37] On the other hand the English writers make comparatively little use of the concrete term *schap* which would have been at their disposal. The natural image of God in the soul, the scholastic *imago naturae* or *imago creationis*,[38] recurs in Hilton as *kyndeli schap*,[39] which is however distorted, *forschapen*,[40] by sin (the author of the *Cloud* chooses the word *disfygurid*),[41] and which can only be restored when 'Crist haue His ful schap in vs and we in Hym'.[42] The true sons of God are those who have regained 'þe ful schape & þe liknes of His Sone Iesu'[43] (i.e. the 'imaginem et similitudinem').

In Latin theology as well as *idea, exemplar, species* and *ratio*, we frequently find the term *forma* in place of *imago*. This clearly goes back to St Paul's statement that Christ was 'in forma Dei' (Phil. 2: 6) which Hilton no doubt has in mind when he says in his comment on the

Mary Magdalen episode (John 20): 'He was in forme of man'.[44] When the *Mirror of Simple Souls* states that the soul is 'meued in him, so she haþ his uerrei fourme ytake',[45] there is an obvious parallel with a similar passage in the Middle High German *Paradisus Anime Intelligentis*, where we read: 'wan dan cumit daz gotliche licht und nimit die formen der sele und zuhit si in die formen Godis.'[46] So in German mysticism, too, we have a direct borrowing of the theological technical term. According to the *MED* the borrowed meanings 'semblance, image, likeness' of the Middle English term *forme* would seem to be limited to biblical, homiletic and mystical texts.

How is the process of the *reformatio* itself dealt with in English mysticism? Since we do not have room for an exhaustive survey, we shall restrict ourselves to the most important references. Hilton's starting point, like Augustine's, is, as we have already seen, that the soul was originally a created trinity. With its *mende*[47] it should contain God the Father without forgetting him, at its creation *reson* was 'cler and briȝt wiþouten error ore mirknesse' and therefore an image of Christ as 'endles wisdam',[48] and *wil*[49] was created as a spiritual blaze of love towards God without the lust of the flesh being aroused in any way, and hence originally the soul was distinguished by 'þe dignite, þe stat, and þe wurschip of a mannes sowle bi kende of þ first makynge'.[50] But after the Fall man had fallen from 'þat Blisside Trinite in to a foul, mirk, wrecchede trinite',[51] had lost the knowledge of God and had sunk into bestial self-love. Hilton later illustrates this process by contrasting the original divine 'ymage' with an 'ymage of sin',[52] an antithesis which is somewhat reminiscent of Amrbose's 'imago diaboli'.[53]

With obvious homiletic intention he uses rhetorical means to produce an allegory designed to drive home to his reader the reality of this 'image of sin'. The image of sin is seen as an allegorical figure, an idol, each of whose limbs symbolizes a sin. Until such time as the image, with divine help, has been completely smashed to pieces, man cannot hope to regain the original image of God. Only then is he able to perceive the image of Jesus which lies hidden under the image of sin. The decisive function here is Christ's: he is the real divine image through which man can be re-formed into God only in an act of believing and loving surrender.[54] But Hilton knows two forms of *reformatio*. One is through faith, and those who are leading an active life and are still in the early spiritual stages are capable of this. With the help of their enlightened reason and grace they strive to become like him whom they believe in but cannot see. The other kind of *reformatio* occurs in the soul of the contemplative who feels and recognizes God's presence in himself through his love which enables the soul to know and love him in the act of complete surrender.[55] It is important to observe that for Hilton *reformatio* takes place completely along the lines of traditional teaching as an act of divine grace.

If Hilton's discussion of the image of God and its restoration has a certain originality about it which is impressive, we can also observe in Julian a highly original treatment of the traditional doctrine. First of all she considers in her work not only the relationship of the individual mystical soul to God, but also the question of the fate of fallen mankind altogether. But, as we have already seen, she seems to defuse the theological problem of the Fall. She teaches in fact that God foresaw the Fall from the beginning and determined upon a salvation of all mankind, i.e. she propounds the doctrine of universal salvation, the apocatastasis, a doctrine which was already taught by Origen but which was never officially accepted by the Catholic Church[56]: 'alle kyndes that he hath made to flowe out of hym to werke his wylle, it shulde be restoryd and brought agayne in to hym by saluacion of man. throw the werkyng of grace.'[57] In her writings, too, the divine *image* appears spoiled and sullied ('defowlyd').[58] But the sullying applies only to man's sensual nature, to the sensual level of the soul: 'in oure sensualyte we feyle. Whych feylyng god wylle restore.'[59] This means that Julian's understanding of the image of God is that it embraces the whole man, including his bodiliness, a theory which has been put forward in traditional teaching, but not very frequently.[60] To restore man's spoiled *ymage* Christ took upon himself this *ymage* of Adam.[61] Thus according to Julian the human nature of Christ is an *ymage* in the sense of an image of human sinfulness: 'it was the ymage and the lyknes of our fowle blacke dede. where in oure feyer. bryght blessyd lorde hyd his godhede.'[62] But because Christ through his incarnation united in himself the spiritual and sensual nature of man, in the *reformatio* the rational soul is reunited with the sensuality. It is thus possible to speak of God taking up his dwelling in man's *sensualite*.[63] This is certainly Julian's most interesting contribution to the theme of the image of God.

One thing which is common to all the English mystics is the great emphasis which is placed on the role of divine grace, *gratia reformans*, in the process of man's being transformed back into the original divine image. In Hilton especially the original meaning of the word *reformen* as a 're-forming' can still be discerned, as the following example shows: 'He doþ al; He formiþ & reformiþ.'[64]

When divine grace begins its work of *reformatio* on man, we must strive in the way he lives to become like the original divine image, which again is something which St Paul stresses. He describes this striving of man's to become like God, specifically to become like Christ, as a 'conformes fieri imaginis Filii' (Rom. 8: 29). The terms *conformis*, *conformare* and *conformitas* play a considerable role in European mysticism. K. Ruh has pointed out that the idea of *conformitas Christi* permeates Franciscan mysticism especially, and that significantly St Francis of Assisi is described in the *Fioretti* with the words: 'fù conforme a Cristo benedetto'.[65] Amongst the English authors Rolle and Hilton usually apply the *conformitas* to Christ, and it is only the author of the *Cloud* who always insists on a conformity with the abstract divinity. Whilst German mysticism chooses the loan-translation *mitformig*[66] for *conformis*, the English texts again stay close to the Latin term with the verb *conformen*. And, according to the *MED*, it was exclusively through its use in English biblical and mystical texts that this verb acquired its borrowed meaning 'to model, make like'. Occasionally the meaning of *conformen* spills over into that of the concept of *reformen*, as when Rolle in the prologue to his *English Psalter* expresses the intention he wishes to pursue in this work with the words: 'the entent is to confourme men that ere filyd in adam til crist in newnes of lyf.'[67] Hilton, however, keeps the meanings of the two verbs quite distinct: he stresses that the *reformatio* is a prerequisite for the *conformatio* which makes man like God: 'Þis is þe conforminge of a soule to God, whilk mai nouȝt be hadde bute if he be first reformed bi fulhede of vertues turned in to affeccion.'[68]

The term *transformare* is particularly popular in Latin mysticism because it is the term best able to express the actual process of man becoming transformed into God. This term too is also derived ultimately from St Paul, who uses it in the passage from the second Letter to the Corinthians which we have already quoted (2 Cor. 3: 18), where he is speaking of man being transformed into the original divine image. For Thomas Aquinas it is love which makes such a transformation possible: 'amor nihil aliud est quam quaedam transformatio affectus in rem amatam',[69] a definition which Rolle takes over almost verbatim into his *Incendium Amoris*.[70] But in Latin theology this term is not meant to express the complete identification of the replica and the original image; but rather in the transformation into the original divine image, which is the goal of the soul, there still remains a distinction between creator and creature. An exception here is Master Eckhart's statement: 'Nos transformamur totaliter in Deum',[71] which led to his being accused of heresy. In the vernacular mysticism of the Middle

Ages the theological terms *transformatio* or *transformare* were taken over in the form of loan-words. Thus Jacopone da Todi in his *Laude* praises mystical *trasformazione*,[72] Hilton describes the 'transfourmynge of þe saule in þe godhede',[73] and even John of the Cross describes the *unio mystica* as 'Amada en el Amado transformada'.[74] The term *transformare* is also taken over directly into English mysticism.[75]

A glance at German or Dutch mysticism, however, shows a quite different picture. Whilst it is true that Tauler and Ruysbroeck speak of man's need to be *transformieret*,[76] or *ghetransformeert*,[77] it is nevertheless very exceptional for them to use the loan-word. Usually they replace the preposition *trans-* with *über-/ouer-* or *durch-*, and thus, by retaining the Latin root, they produce very graphic terms like *überformunge, überformen, durchformen*[78] or *overforminghe, overformen*.[79] The fact that the English mystics make no use whatsoever of this possibility, although it was clearly open to them to do so, is a remarkable and obviously very deliberate feature of their style.[80]

The 'deificatio' of the soul

In Western mysticism the regaining of the image of God is often expressly described as a *deificatio* of man. In Underhill's view this motif lies at the heart of all mysticism,[81] and it is already implicitly contained in biblical writings. It was easy to take the New Testament idea of God's Incarnation and, by simple inversion, derive from it man's deification.[82] Other biblical passages, particularly the doctrine of the divine sonship of the faithful,[83] lent further support to this corollary. According to M. Herz it was Irenaeus who first formulated the concept of mystical deification,[84] which was then propagated further in the writings of the Fathers of the Church. The danger of a heretical misunderstanding was of course great, and in the Late Middle Ages the heretics of Ries near Nördlingen in Bavaria amongst others, succumbed to it, as Grundmann has shown.[85] The criterion for the orthodoxy of the *deificatio* doctrine was whether divine grace was recognized as the effective cause, as is expressed very clearly in Augustine's formulation: 'Manifestum est ergo, quia homines dixit deos, ex gratia sua deificatos.'[86]

The German mystics in particular were very fond of the idea of deification and used many new words and terms in their attempts to render it into the vernacular. The terms they usually use are *vergoten, gotlich, gottig* and *gotvar*.[87] Master Eckhart, who was perhaps the first to introduce the concept of *deificatio* into vernacular mysticism,[88] proclaims it, with his usual predilection for provocative statements, with the ecstatic cry: 'vrewet iuch mit mir, ich bin got worden!'[89] There are of course not many formulations of this idea in mysticism which are quite as bold as this, and indeed one can observe for the most part a quite pronounced aversion towards putting too much emphasis on precisely this doctrine. Thus Richard of St Victor on one occasion takes some of the boldness out of this thought by putting a 'quasi' in front of it, thereby reducing it to the level of a comparison: 'Six affic quasi deificari est.'[90]

This aversion appears to be particularly pronounced precisely amongst the English mystics. True, even a Master Eckhart, when dealing with this theme, insures himself so to speak by making a direct reference to the Bible, but in contrast to him the author of the *Cloud* feels constrained, when referring to *deificatio*, to adopt the orthodox standpoint expressly and stress that man can only experience deification through divine grace: 'only bi his mercy wiþouten þi desert arte maad a God in grace.'[91] When the author of the *Cloud* goes on to point out that despite the deification there nevertheless remains an essential difference between man and God, and calls upon the Bible as a kind of security for himself, we almost get the impression that he consciously wishes to dissociate himself from Eckhart: 'þou or anoþer . . . þat feleþ þe perfeccion of þis werk may soþfastly, bi witnes of Scripture, be clepid a God – neuerþeles ȝit þou arte bineþe hym.'[92] This idea seems so important to the Carthusian, Richard Methley, that, as we have already mentioned, he brings it up expressly in a separate prologue to his Latin translation of the *Cloud*, and uses it as an argument 'contra heresim begardorum'.[93] We find a similar picture in Julian, too. On the one hand she tells us that in a vision she observed no difference between God and the human being but saw both as one divine unit ('but as it were all god'),[94] but on the other hand she still adds that 'god is god. and oure substance is a creature in god',[95] i.e. that the soul does not lose its creaturalness even in the *unio*. In his approach to the idea of deification Hilton is even more reserved than the author of the *Cloud*. Whilst it is true that his main work is wholly concerned with the question of man's being transformed back into the image of God as an act of *reformatio*, it is nevertheless misleading to argue, as Vasta does in a study of *Piers Plowman*, that the whole *Scale* is more or less based on the doctrine of *deificatio*.[96] A constant feature of the thesis of the transformation of the soul into God is that the soul as a created being is taken into the uncreated divinity, whilst in the idea of deification it is easy for this essential distinction to become blurred. It seems to me therefore significant that the term is hardly ever used in English mysticism. The most extreme linguistic formulation that Hilton risks is found in his *Scale*, where he says that what Jesus loves most about a soul is 'þat it miȝt be made godly . . . like to Him in grace',[97] i.e. the soul should indeed become god-ly, god-like, and should regain the image of God (become 'like to him') but should not itself become God.

We do however frequently meet the term *deificare* in Rolle's Latin mysticism. But when he describes the heart which has been transformed by divine love as 'quodammodo deificatum',[98] we get the impression, just as with the example from Richard of St Victor, that he wants to tone down the boldness of his statement. The one solitary example in his English writings occurs in his *English Psalter*, where, like Augustine before him, he interprets Psalm 81 allegorically in the sense of the deification of man. In his exegesis Rolle takes the first verse of this psalm: 'Deus stetit in synagoga deorum: in medio autem deos dijudicat' as meaning that Christ gathers round him the community of those whom he has made Gods: 'god ihū crist stode in the gadirynge of halymen. deifide thorgh grace';[99] but again the reference to grace effecting the deification is not omitted. It is quite remarkable that this should be the only occurrence in Middle English texts of the verb *deifien* in a mystical meaning. Apart from this, *deifien* occurs almost exclusively in the context of ancient mythology, as when Lydgate says of Castor and Pollux that 'þe goddis han hem deified.'[100]

The ground of the soul in English mysticism

In our survey of the theme of the image of God in English mysticism we have seen how important the human will, man's *voluntas*, is for the mystical *unio*. But Rhenish mysticism went much more deeply and systematically into the question of precisely where in the soul the union with God takes place, and here the idea of the ground of the soul played a decisive role. If we outline briefly the lines along which this theme was developed in German mysticism and look for anything which is comparable to it in English texts, a clear picture should emerge of the most important similarities and differences between these two forms of Late Medieval vernacular mysticism.

In German mysticism the teaching on the ground of the soul, if we define it in the most general terms, states that the *unio* of man with God takes place in the ground of the human soul, because it is there that the image of God manifests itself. For a long time scholars held that, although the image of the ground of the soul was taken from courtly literature, it was only in Middle High German mysticism that the metaphor acquired a theological meaning.[101] More recent studies have attempted to throw light on the diverse influences which led to this figurative use,[102] and have shown the extent to which this motif already occurred in one form or another in Latin mysticism. It was partly inspired by the ancient image that there is in the human soul a divine spark, the *scintilla*,[103] which bears witness to man's divine origin. Another important influence was the concept '*synteresis*' (a corruption of *syneidesis*), a term frequently used by the Scholastics, usually in connection with the authority of conscience in matters of morals.[104] The distinction we have already mentioned which Augustine drew between the *ratio inferior* and the *ratio superior* in the development of his psychology was another important influence on the development of the imagery of the ground of the soul. For the *ratio superior* bears witness to the image of God in the soul and is capable of spiritual knowledge.

The idea of the *ratio superior* as a possible place for the *unio mystica* implies a sort of 'spatial' structure of the soul, and in the course of tradition a whole series of further concepts was developed to specify the place where the union of man and God took place in the soul. One of these is the ancient image of the *apex mentis* (more rarely the *acies mentis*), which dates back to the Stoics.[105] This idea of the soul having a point which is suitable for experiencing God is extremely popular in mysticism. The fact that in his psychology Augustine also developed the concept of the abyss of the soul, which he termed the *abditum mentis*, was also very important specifically for the development of the teaching on the mystical ground of the soul.[106] But the metaphor *fundus animae* was quite common both in Augustine and in Albert the Great.[107] There were also frequent medieval allegorical interpretations of the psalm verse 'abyssus abyssum invocat' (Ps. 41:8), and further, as will become clear, we must bear in mind the theology of St Paul.

The concept of the ground of the soul as it appeared in the Eckhart School would have been quite inconceivable without all these ideas we have just outlined. The fact that the point of the soul and the ground of the soul could become synonymous, interchangeable concepts in the mysticism of Eckhart and his followers is clear when we remember that for them, as for their model the pseudo-Dionysius, in the realm of the spiritual above and below are one and the same thing. Thus Master Eckhart, although he has the *unio* take place in the ground of the soul, speaks of the soul being like God in its higher part, its *ratio superior*: 'diu sêle ist gebildet nâch gote an irme obersten teile.'[108] Hence for him the higher, intellectual part of the soul can become the place of the mystical *unio*, and this gives rise to his famous metaphor of the 'houbet' of the soul.[109] But, as studies in German literature have shown, the influence of Latin theology is not in itself sufficient to account for Eckhart's use of the metaphor *grunt*, for in his writings it acquires a very specific meaning. It means 'the place of the *unio mystica*, where the ground of the soul and the ground of God are one'[110] and the place where the soul is born in God and God in the soul. Thus we read in Master Eckhart 'daz got geborn werde in der sele und diú sêle in gote geborn werde'.[111] But of course the idea of the birth of God in the soul is also a very ancient concept which we meet for instance in Poimandres.[112]

For Eckhart the prerequisite for the birth of God in the ground of the soul is that the essential core of the soul and the ground of the divine being are of the same nature. Eckhart uses many different terms to express this essential core of the soul which is eternal and inextinguishable, and which possesses the image of God, terms like *spark of the soul*, *scintilla*, *spark of reason*, *spark of divine nature*, *bürgelin*, *houbet* etc.[113] The accusation of pantheism which was levelled against Eckhart because of this teaching was of course unfounded. For in Eckhart, as more recent research has shown, the soul and God do not completely fuse, since the divine light is merely reflected in the soul. 'God is in the soul, but only in so far as he mirrors himself into it.'[114] Thus Eckhart remains comfortably within the bounds of traditional teaching, where the idea is quite common that the soul is a mirror of God and can perceive God when it looks at itself in this mirror. We read for instance in Hilton's *Scale*: 'For þi soule is bot a mirrour in þe whilk þu schalt see God gostly.'[115]

On the other hand Eckhart certainly has a tendency to produce terse formulations which are liable to be misunderstood, as for instance when he says that in the innermost soul the ground of the soul and the ground of God are identical: 'daz gotes grunt mîn grunt und mîn grunt gotes grunt [si] .'[116] At any rate Tauler is more careful in this respect, although the image of the ground of the soul appears more often in his writings than in Eckhart. For him 'ground of the soul' seems to mean 'gemüet', the 'mens' as the human mind, but also the 'pure substance of the soul'.[117] When Tauler and Suso urge man to enter into the substance of his own soul — 'gang in dynen grunt', Suso says on one occasion[118] — because this is the only way to experience

God, they are simply taking up the Thomist thesis that it is easier for man to experience God than to experience his own soul.[119] Tauler makes quite sure that there can be no doubts about his orthodoxy by stressing that the ground of the soul is *created*,[120] and that the mystical *unio* is to be understood as a 'versincken und versmeltzen' of the *created* spirit 'in dem ungeschaffenen geiste Gottes'.[121] Incidentally Eckhart's followers use the term *grunt* to denote both the ground of the soul and also the ground of God in which the soul is absorbed, but they imply rather less than Eckhart any identity of essence between the ground of God and the ground of the soul.

How far do metaphors of ground in English mysticism compare with this? Several important differences must be noted before we can embark on such a comparison. Whilst German mysticism, according to Kunisch, borrowed the metaphor *herzen grunt* from courtly poetry,[122] the image of the *hertes grund* is found in English before the great mystics in spiritual texts — and only in these.[123] The important motif that there is in the human soul a divine spark, the *scintilla*, which bears witness to the soul's origin, occurs in English only in a very general form, as when Hilton explains to the reader of his *Mixed Life*: 'vre lord haþ sent in to þin herte a luytel sparkel of his blessed fuire þat is him-self',[124] and here he refers directly to the biblical description of the devouring fire of God (Deut. 4:24). In English texts we do not find the important term *Synderesis* except in the homiletic tract *The Charter of the Abbey of the Holy Ghost*.[125] And the really characteristic feature of the German metaphors of ground, the theme of the birth of God in the ground of the soul, is completely absent in English mysticism. Even the call to man to enter into his ground in order to experience the *unio* with God is only found in England in a modified form. Nevertheless there are still some quite remarkable parallels which cannot be overlooked and which call for a detailed examination.

It is useful to look first at Rolle's mystical writings which were composed in Latin. Although he does not seem to be familiar with the motif of the ground of the soul, he makes a great deal of use in his mysticism of the image of the root of the soul which often appears in German mysticism, too, as a synonym for the ground of the soul.[126] He sets the faithful the task of planting the root of their heart in divine love: 'radicemque cordis in clarissima charitate construant et plantent perseveranter.'[127] It is very apparent that Rolle derives this figurative expression directly from the words of St Paul: 'Christum habitare per fidem in cordibus vestris: in charitate radicati, et fundati'

(Eph. 3:17). Rolle is so impressed with this Pauline statement that he constantly strives to find new formulations to express it, and frequently even tries to invert it. Alluding to this statement and at the same time to the Old Testament motif of the root of Jesse, he defines divine love as the root of the human heart: 'Radix cordis nostri sit caritas'[128] and God himself as the 'radix cordis mei'.[129] And even when he says that the soul 'figit fundamentum' in God,[130] he applies the motif of ground to God in the meaning 'foundation', as St Paul did.[131]

The work of Julian of Norwich merits special attention in our context, for the term *grounde* is almost a leitmotif in the longer version of her *Revelations*. She puts the emphasis firmly on God himself and praises him or Christ as the ground of human life.[132] Scholasticism had a decisive influence on the way her metaphors of ground developed. For, like Eckhart and Tauler, Julian starts from the Thomist idea that man is nearer to God than to his own soul: 'God is more nerer to vs than oure owne soule. for he is grounde in whome oure soule standyth.'[133] Her use of *grounde* here corresponds to the Thomist view that God is a 'fundamentum et basis omnium aliorum entium'.[134] The meanings 'origin'[135] and 'cause'[136] which the term *grounde* sometimes assumes in Julian are also Scholastic. Furthermore, when speaking of God she also uses the Scholastic term *substantia* in the form of the loan-word *substaunce* in contrast to the accidental bodiliness: 'he . . . kepyth ye substaunce and the sensualyte to geder',[137] 'He is the grounde. He is the substaunce';[138] 'And of this substauncyall grounde we haue all oure vertuse';[139] 'I Am Substancyallye aned to hym.'[140] In addition she links the concept of *substantia* with the divine *natura* in typically Scholastic fashion when she calls God *vnmade kynde*[141] (*natura increata*) and defines him as the natural ground of the soul: 'oure kyndly grounde that we haue in god'.[142] In this 'ground of kynd'[143] man is inspired with the help of divine grace to works which will lead him to an eternal life. Julian's visions, which she makes known to us in her *Revelations*, show her the nature of the soul, the substance or ground of the soul, as being so linked with the divine nature that, as we have already mentioned, she is no longer able to perceive any distinction between the two: 'And I sawe no dyfference betwen god and oure substance but as it were all god.'[144]

Does not the boldness of Julian's argumentation here approach the terse mystical language of Eckhart? As we have already seen, there have been many attempts to postulate a relationship between Julian and Eckhart.[145] But on closer examination the similarity is not such as to prove any direct influence of Eckhart on the English mystic. For, as we mentioned in the last chapter, Julian adds after the passage we have just quoted that the soul is a *created* substance: 'god is god. and oure substance is a creature in god.'[146] Thus, in contrast to Eckhart, she guards against any misunderstandings, and allies herself rather with Tauler's teaching on the soul, which we have already outlined.

A particularly striking aspect of Julian's mysticism is the fact that, in connection with her teaching on the universal salvation of mankind which we have already mentioned, she deals with the theological problem of sin in a highly individualistic manner. In her Thirteenth Revelation (ch. 27) she is shown how from the very beginning sin was incorporated into the divine plan of salvation. She sees first that because of sin man is no longer like God, and she then asks why God with the wisdom of his foreknowledge ever allowed evil at all. Thereupon she receives an answer from Christ himself, an answer which has become very well-known since T.S. Eliot incorporated it in his *Four Quartets*: 'Synne is behouely but alle shalle be wele. And alle Shalle be wele. And alle maner thynge Shalle be wele.'[147] Sin is therefore necessary for the divine plan of salvation, but is unable to thwart the divine intention of universal salvation. But Julian understands sin — and this is theologically rather unusual — not concretely as evil, but as the absence of good: 'In yis nakyd worde synne. oure lorde brouȝte to my mynde generally alle that is nott good.'[148] She thus attributes no actual reality to sin, for it possesses 'no maner of Substaunce ne no part of beyng',[149] and it is only through its painful effects that it can be perceived at all. But through sin man is purified, is forced into self-knowledge and obliged to ask for divine grace. The further argumentation in this chapter shows that for Julian the final and real function of sin is to make divine love become even more effective. The way Julian describes sin here is somewhat reminiscent of the way Eckhart speaks of sin: for him, too, sin is a nothing against which good stands out in sharp contrast. 'Man's tendency towards sin is in fact an indispensable necessity, a precondition of human existence, for only through the victorious battle against evil . . . can man fulfil the purpose of his being.'[150] But even here there is no reason to assume that Julian was inspired by Eckhart; she is more likely to have been influenced by the argumentation of the *Mirror of Simple Souls*, which states that for a soul which humbles itself 'synne is nouȝt and lasse þan nouȝt'.[151] And finally Julian's thesis also calls to mind the traditional teaching of the *felix culpa*.

Julian's discussion of the power of the human will after the Fall is to be seen in connection with her discussion of sin. For she speaks of

man still having retained for himself a 'godly wylle'.[152] But we have
to ask ourselves precisely what she means by this. Recent translations
render this quite simply as 'godly will',[153] and this term was taken as
a further reason for feeling justified in seeing an influence of Eckhart's
mysticism, since it was assumed that Eckhart's 'spark of the soul'
corresponded with Julian's teaching of 'godly wylle'.[154] But to translate 'godly wylle' as 'godly will' is to misunderstand what Julian wants
to say. First of all she is quite clearly alluding to the power of the soul
of *voluntas*, which Augustine places higher than the other two powers
of the soul, *memoria* and *intelligentia*. She follows Augustine in
defining this *wylle* as the willing love of man towards God: 'evyr more
contynuly it wyllyth good and werkyth good in the sight of god . . .
And namely and truly that we haue all this blessyd wyll hoole and safe
in oure lorde Ihesu crist',[155] and it is only here that the true way to a
knowledge of God lies. We can already see how fundamentally misleading it is to equate Julian's 'godly wylle' with Eckhart's spark of the soul,
for Eckhart had defined man's ability to perceive by means of his higher
reason as an actual possibility for experiencing God. But even apart from
that one cannot simply translate 'godly wylle' as 'godly will' and thereby imply that something in man which is essentially divine, uncreated,
makes a union with God possible. For in a later passage in the *Revelations* Julian's puzzling term appears simply as 'goodly wylle',[156] and this
is also the only form found in the oldest manuscript, Add. 37790 from
the British Library, which dates from the mid-fifteenth century.[157]
And if we examine the immediate context in which the longer version
introduces the 'godly wylle' we see that it is very reasonable to interpret
it as 'goodly wylle'. For the 'wylle' is explained in the following words:
'whych wyll is so *good* that it may nevyr wylle evyll. but evyr more
contynuly it wyllyth *good* and werkyth *good* in the syght of god.'[158]
In addition there is no consistent orthographical distinction in this
manuscript between 'god' and 'good'. For Julian 'goodly wylle' means
that despite his Fall man has still retained a will towards good, towards
God, i.e. a 'goodly wylle', but this will has become buried in his consciousness.[159] But the love of Christ awakens the human loving will, and
hence it is precisely in love, in man's choosing good in an act of his free
will, that an *unio* takes place between man and God.[160] And thus once
again Julian is within the bounds of traditional church teaching. It is
precisely this voluntative accent in Julian, which shows through whether
one assumes a 'goodly will' or a 'godly will', which is *eo ipso* an important indication that the basic tone of her mysticism is essentially different
from that of Eckhart, who inclines towards an intellectual rather than

an affective knowledge of God.

The great student of mysticism, Evelyn Underhill, has also established remarkable similarities between Julian and the Dutch mystic Ruysbroeck and drawn attention to two important features which they have in common – God's thirsting love-longing for man and the concrete depiction of God in the form of a point.[161] These motifs are, of course, also found elsewhere in mysticism, so that there is no question of any influence. In the tract *The Treatise of Perfection of the Sons of God* we possess what is probably an early fifteenth-century translation of a Latin version of Ruysbroeck's *Vanden Blinckenden Steen*. This Middle English version tells us that the soul which has God as its 'grownde' is embedded in a 'grownde of loue'.[162] Julian too interprets the original divine ground as a ground of love: 'And inward in hym was shewed a ground of loue',[163] and elsewhere she speaks of the 'mervelous depnesse of endlesse loue';[164] 'he wylle we take hede thus. that he is ground of alle oure hoole lyfe in loue.'[165] But the fact that not only with Ruysbroeck but already with Anselm of Canterbury the soul longs to drown in the abyss of divine love,[166] demonstrates once again how far such parallels are due to the common background of Latin mysticism. This is not to deny that Julian was familiar with versions of Ruysbroeck's work, for this is indeed quite possible – what is impossible is to produce conclusive evidence that she was acquainted with the Dutch mystic.

An examination of the theme of the ground of the soul in the *Cloud* and its related tracts suggests that Julian may well have derived some of her theological knowledge from their anonymous author, for in the *Book of Privy Counselling* God is also called a *grounde* in the sense of the Scholastic terms *substantia* and *essentia*, when the author explains to his reader that when the state of mystical experience of God has been reached 'þan schal þi gostly affeccion be fillid with þe fulheed of loue & of vertuous leuyng in God, þi grounde & þi purete of spirit.'[167] The author of the *Cloud* also applies the term *grounde* to the soul when on one occasion he interprets the soul's freedom from all earthly ties and its complete concentration on God in a 'nakid entent streching into God' as its 'grounde'.[168] He too, like Julian, sometimes uses the term *substaunce* to denote the actual ground of the soul; what is original is his attempt to derive this decidedly Scholastic term directly from the Bible with the help of an allegorical exegesis. In a passage in the Book of Proverbs (Prov. 3:9f.) man is urged to honour God with all his possessions ('de tua substantia') and with the first fruits of his produce ('primiciis frugum tuorum').[169] But the author of the *Cloud* gives a new interpretation to this *substantia* which he sees as the core of the soul, its *essentia*, its 'owne self'.[170] In the exegesis of this verse the first fruits are explained as the spiritual or physical gifts of man. The first of these gifts is the most important one, and this the author calls 'þi being', and in a synonym 'þe first poynt of þi spirit'.[171] The first important thing for the mystic is to feel this, his own being, since it participates in the divine being, until gradually this feeling of his own being is transformed into feeling only God, a statement which is certainly reminiscent of the German mystics but which can also be explained from the tradition of Latin mystical writings. For to express in concrete terms the place where the complete union with God occurs, the author has recourse to the traditional image of the *apex mentis*: 'a goostly worcher in þis werk schulde euermore be in þe hiȝest & þe souereynest pointe of þe sp[i] rit'.[172] Since the author of the *Cloud*, like Master Eckhart, is influenced by the mysticism of the pseudo-Dionysius, we find in his writings, too, that in the spiritual sphere all contrastive elements are resolved into one in a *coincidentia oppositorum*, and therefore he is able to urge his reader: 'com doun into þe lowest poynte of þi witte, þe whiche sum man holdeþ by verrey preof þat it is þe hiȝest.'[173] There is then no contradiction when he explains to his reader that the *unio* must take place 'in depnes of spirit'.[174] This is surely an attempt to translate Augustine's idea of the *abditum mentis*, for he not only means the depth but also the seclusion of the spirit which is contained in the term *abditum* when he says that what is secluded in the depths of the spirit is closest to God: 'more aperte is þat þing knowyn & schewid vnto him, þe whiche is hid in depnes of spirit'.[175] Altogether there is no compelling reason to assume that the author of the *Cloud* was influenced by the Eckhart School, although on the other hand the possibility certainly exists that he had one eye on the Eckhart School when he developed his teaching, and for this reason stressed very strongly that God cannot be experienced through intellectual perception but only in ecstatic love.

If we examine the work of Walter Hilton for metaphors of the ground of the soul, we find that he, too, stays within the framework of Latin theology and Scholasticism. We have already shown that Hilton sees the *ratio superior* as the place of the union between the soul and God, but he is also familiar with the *acies mentis*,[176] as a synonym for the *apex mentis*, and when in his *Scale* he mentions the 'pryuete of herte'[177] as the place for the *unio*, we can certainly see this as a loan-translation of Augustine's *abditum mentis*. His teaching that a decisive prerequisite for the *unio mystica* is that man must attain a consciousness of the being of his own soul, is also fully in accord with Scholasticism, for only in this way can the soul as a created part of God acquire the knowledge of the 'natura Dei', the 'kynde of God'.[178] Like Julian, Hilton defines God or Jesus as the life principle of the soul, as 'vnmade kynde'[179] ('natura increata'), and, like Julian and the author of the *Cloud*, he uses the Scholastic term *substantia* when he defines God as the real substance in comparison with which man is as nothing: 'my substaunce & þe beeng of my soule is as noȝt anentes þe.'[180] In the commentary on the psalms *Qui Habitat*, which is probably to be attributed to Hilton, we read in addition that the soul receives its real *substaunce* in God, and that God is prepared to enter into the substance of the soul, indeed God lives in the human soul: 'he mai, þorw his grace, entre in-to þe substaunce of my soule.'[181] This is reminiscent of the teaching of the German mystics that God dwells in the ground of the soul, but even so it is not possible to postulate any direct influence, for the idea is kept within the framework of medieval theology, and the author also supports his statement with the words of Jesus which are so popular in mystical texts: 'regnum Dei intra vos est' (Luke 17:21). So with this idea of divine indwelling there is the same kind of reliance on the Bible as we found in Julian.

In addition, in his treatment of the theme of God's dwelling in the soul, Hilton's emphasis is quite different from that of the German mystics. Although he is the only one who occasionally uses the metaphor 'ground of the heart' *expressis verbis*, in doing so he uses the word *ground* in the sense of 'bottom'. And there is a clearly discernible homiletic intention behind his use of the metaphor: man is urged to clear this ground, in which God lives, of the mortal sins which proliferate wildly in it: 'þer is mikel pride hid in þe ground of þi herte.'[182] Hence this *ground* seems almost to be a 'ground of synne'.[183] It is the place where the *ymage* of vain self-love is found.[184] Everything depends on man blocking up the bottom of the well which is in the garden of his soul and from which the stinking water of sin flows, otherwise 'it wile corupten alle þe floures of þi gardin of þi sowle'.[185] And he must dig deep in search of God: 'Þe behouiþ for to delue depe.'[186] Here the ground of the soul coincides with the traditional image of the garden of the soul, which was developed from various biblical passages — like the New Testament parable of the treasure hidden in the field (Matt. 13:44), or a verse from the Book of Proverbs which states that whoever searches for wisdom as for hidden treasures will find the knowledge of God (Prov. 2:4), but above all the 'hortus conclusus' of the *Song of Songs* (S. of S. 4:12).[187] Nor is Master Eckhart silent on the subject of the divine element in man being choked by the weeds of sin.[188] But the important difference between him and Hilton is that Eckhart only mentions this theme in passing and lays the main emphasis on the replica in the soul and the original divine image becoming united in a mystical manner, whereas Hilton's primary concern is homiletic. If we are to compare Hilton with German mysticism, it is perhaps more appropriate to compare him with the unemotional and pastorally-minded Tauler. In Tauler the ground of the soul is also described as a 'boeser grunt', a 'viheliche grunt'[189] which is corrupted by sin, but even here this motif does not assume the same importance as in Hilton, for Tauler, a pupil of Eckhart's, places the main emphasis on the birth of God in the soul and on the mystical union of God with the ground of the soul.[190]

A comparison of the interpretations of the New Testament parable of the lost coin (Luke 15:8) in German mysticism and in Hilton's *Scale* provides a particularly good illustration of the great difference which exists between Rhenish and English mysticism. In spiritual texts the image stamped on a coin provides a ready way of illustrating the image of God in man, and both Tauler and Ruysbroeck make great use of it. The parable of the woman who loses a coin in her house, lights a lamp and sweeps the house to search for it, is applied by Tauler to the *unio mystica*. He brings out the essential elements of his allegorization at the very beginning of his exegesis: the woman who has lost the coin is the 'gotheit'; the lamp which she uses to look for it is the 'vergoettete menschheit'; the coin itself represents the soul.[191] God goes in search of the soul, which — by analogy with the image stamped on the coin — bears an image, his divine image, in its ground. By looking for this image in the ground of the soul God is, as it were, uniting himself with his own self: 'in disem bilde do mint Got, do bekent Got, do gebrucht Got sin selbes.'[192] This search is made possible by the lighting of the lamp, and it is eternal Wisdom which causes this. But, led by this lamp of divine love, not only does God seek the soul, but the soul also goes in search of God in order to unite itself with him in the ground of the soul. This is why it is precisely at this point that Tauler issues the call to his hearers 'das der mensche in gange in sinen eiginen grunt'.[193] For man this means a complete separation from all ties with the world in true mystical abandonment.[194]

The intention behind Hilton's exegesis is quite different. He indicates at the outset that he intends to interpret the parable in a purely homiletic sense, by explaining that the lost coin is Jesus who is to be sought: 'þis dragme is Ihesu whilk þou hast lost',[195] and he constantly reminds his readers of this. Hilton is not concerned with a detailed explanation of the process of the mystical *unio*, which is what Tauler used the parable of the lost coin for. But rather he gives his exegesis a clearly christocentric orientation by applying it to the relationship between the soul and its Jesus, and this then leads him to use the parable as an example of the moral necessity on the part of the soul to strive to imitate Christ. And very interestingly, by means of a reference to Ps. 118:105, the lamp now becomes the word of God which helps man in this imitation of Christ, i.e. Hilton's mysticism here proves to be, *expressis verbis*, extremely biblically orientated, and the later exegesis of the parable underlines this. For he goes on to say that man also possesses a second light, namely 'þe reson of þi sowle',[196] and he quotes several New Testament verses in support of this. Hilton now follows the story-line of the parable much more closely than Tauler, allegorizing every detail: When the lamp it lit, dirt and small specks of dust are revealed in the house. These signify the carnal lusts and fears from which the house of the soul must be freed and cleansed with the help of the broom of the fear of God and the water of tears. Then it will be possible to find the lost coin – Jesus. Although Hilton, as we have already mentioned, is not concerned with the *unio* in the ground of the soul, he, too, says that Jesus is hidden in the soul, and for this reason man must enter into himself where Jesus is to be found: 'turne þi þou3t in þin oune sowle where He is hid'.[197] Hilton here refers to the biblical motif of the hidden God: 'As þe Prophete seiþ: Vere tu es Deus absconditus' (Isa. 45:15) and also to the parable of the treasure hidden in the field (Matt. 13:44), whilst Tauler, in his one direct reference to the Bible in the course of his exegesis, recalls Luke 17:21: 'das rich Gotz das ist in úch',[198] a verse which Hilton also quotes, as we saw earlier. Hilton, however, is constantly trying to find more and more new biblical passages to support his views, for a little later he expresses the motif of the divine indwelling in man in the words: 'Ihesu slepiþ in þin herte goostli',[199] thus allegorizing in a mystical way the New Testament passage where the disciples wake Jesus from his sleep because they are afraid of the storm (Matt. 8:23 ff.). There then follow general homiletic remarks on the relationship of Christ to the soul, and here again Hilton frequently quotes directly from the Bible.

Although Hilton's exegesis may well have been inspired by Latin commentaries on this New Testament parable,[200] his own individual 'style' is nevertheless clearly discernible. This consists of a particularly pronounced and incisive biblical orientation, such as can be observed time and again amongst the other English writers too — we need only recall that the author of the *Cloud* derived the Scholastic concept of *substantia* from a verse in the Bible. And here the English mystics go appreciably further than the mystics of the Eckhart School, who are certainly orientated towards the Bible but to nothing like the same extent.[201] But on the other hand the English writers quite consciously make no attempt to produce a detailed theological mystical system, even though they are theologians who are conversant with Scholasticism or, as in Julian's case, have had some kind of Scholastic training. They orientate themselves much more than their German counterparts to the spiritual horizons and the educational level of their lay audience or readership, and are concerned with the practical problems of homiletic instruction.

CONCLUSION

*

In our study we have attempted an extensive comparison between English mysticism and that of continental Europe and have tried to continue above all the work begun by H.E. Allen. In the course of our considerations we have been able to highlight various links between English and continental mysticism. We saw, for instance, that the Dutch mystic Hadewych was acquainted with mystics and recluses of both sexes in England. We were also able to detect traces of the Brethren of the Free Spirit, the Friends of God and the *Devotio Moderna* in England, and even the possibility of Beguine-like communities of women could not be excluded. The closest links between England and the continent have, however, turned out to be in the area of female mysticism. Both Julian of Norwich and Margery Kempe correspond very closely to the pattern of continental women mystics, although of course Julian's work reveals at the same time a very profound and impressive independence. Richard Rolle, too, shows a clear affinity of spirit with female mysticism, and in this he has a remarkable counterpart on the continent in the person of Henry Suso who also has close contacts with mystically inclined women.

In the Middle Ages the texts of the mystics travelled from one country to another and especially in the fifteenth century some continental texts reached England. In the dissemination of continental works as far as England, the Low Countries played an important role, as has often been pointed out.[1] A good example is Mechthild of Hackeborn's *Book of Revelations* which reached England from North Germany via the Low Countries.[2] It can, and indeed must, also be added that English mysticism by its very nature reveals striking parallels with North German mysticism. Thus a series of the characteristics which W. Stammler lists as typical features of North German mysticism[3] is also found in England: like North German mysticism the English mystical texts, too, are intensely spiritualized and homiletic in character — and here a considerable place is given to bride-mysticism. Both forms of vernacular mysticism practise restraint in their use of speculation, and in both cases the metaphorical language is limited in the main to traditional images. Finally, both have in common a strong emphasis on the necessity of divine grace, on humility, on complete abandonment of all earthly ties, and on suffering for God's sake. Such themes lead both North German and English mystics to discuss the question of how the soul can attain a state of perfection. Symptomatic of this is the fact that Ruysbroeck's tract *Vanden Blinckenden Steen*, in which such themes are strongly emphasized, was known not only in North Germany but also in England — as a translation with the title *The Treatise of Perfection of the Sons of God*. It would be wrong to regard these similarities as the result of a mere influence, for they clearly imply an affinity. The many parallels between the metaphorical language of English and German mysticism arose from a common recourse to the tradition of Christian Latin mysticism. It may well be that Richard Rolle studied in Paris and became deeply familiar with this tradition, and this is even more likely to have been the case with Walter Hilton.

It has often been assumed that English mysticism was directly influenced by Rhenish Dominican mysticism, but our examination has been unable to confirm this unequivocally. Eckhart's ideas clearly became known to a certain extent in England through the medium of the *Mirror of Simple Souls*. Certain important themes of Eckhart's were, however, not taken over with it — like the birth of God in the soul and the possibility of a purely intellectual knowledge of God. For this reason English affective mysticism is reminiscent rather of the more sober Tauler; but we were also unable to find any proof that Tauler's works were known in England. In this connection a hitherto very neglected text has been of special interest to us, namely Rudolf of Biberach's *De Septem Itineribus Aeternitatis*, which speaks of an affective knowledge of God in a night of unknowing in a manner remarkably similar to the *Cloud*.

We were also able to observe how the imagery of English mysticism is imbued throughout with that dynamic element which manifests itself so strongly in the princiapl texts of German mysticism. For English mysticism, especially the work of Rolle, draws on the passionate language of earthly love to a much larger extent than has hitherto been admitted. And here the numerous analogies with secular love literature proved to be not borrowings from profane sources but rather elements belonging to the tradition of the spiritualized and metaphorical use of 'erotic' imagery.

We have further seen that the English authors develop Middle English prose into a perfectly suitable instrument for expressing their spiritual themes in language and that there is a considerable degree of linguistic continuity between the individual texts. This confirmed for us the linguistic affinity which scholars have frequently noted between the author of the *Cloud* and Hilton, and we also observed similarities between the *Cloud* and the *Mirror*. Linguistic similarities would also seem to suggest that Julian knew the works of the author of the *Cloud* and Walter Hilton.

We noticed, too, that in many cases the English texts chose terms which are etymologically related to the German mystical terms. The vividness of the Germanic linguistic terms explains why the English mystics preferred them and why they felt them to be particularly suitable for expressing spiritual concepts in concrete terms. The English mystics, however, proved to be not nearly as creative in their use of language as the German mystics, and their contribution to the development of their own language was small. Nevertheless even in England it was in some cases precisely the mystics who derived a new meaning from a word, and therefore it is to be regretted that the *MED* has neglected the mystics so blatantly, often not listing mystical meanings of a word or failing to note particularly interesting occurrences of the figurative meaning of a term, to say nothing of the number of times its explanation of the mystical meaning of a term is unsatisfactory or even wrong.

And finally, common to all English authors is the fact that they have much more frequent recourse to the Bible than have the Rhenish mystics. This biblical tendency in English mysticism is not only seen in a frequent imitation of the language of the Bible, but, with its strong emphasis on the need for humility and the complete absence of any rules for asceticism, English mysticism assumes a basic character which is almost Pauline, and this is helped by the fact that the church as an institution is mentioned only rarely and sporadically and is certainly far less important than the individual's personal experience of God. Hence undertaking to translate the Bible into the vernacular also met the needs of the mystically orientated laity. When, towards the end of the second part of his *Scale*, Hilton recommends to his lay readers that they should immerse themselves directly in the study of the Bible, this to a certain extent corresponds with the aims of the movement started by Wyclif, for Hilton expressly states that an understanding of the Bible is difficult and can only be achieved with the help of divine grace, but that this grace works 'as wel in lewde as in lettred men',[4] i.e. Hilton concedes the right to read the Bible not only to theologians or those with a knowledge of Latin but also to the laity, and it is therefore fair to assume that the English version of the Bible was already in existence.[5] We should also remember here that the Lollards were very interested in English mystical texts. In his study of the *Recluse*, a document of the early Lollard movement, E. Colledge has shown that the gulf between the reformers and the mystics of the fourteenth century is not nearly so great as is often assumed.[6] But these are questions which go beyond the immediate aims of our study and must be left for later investigations.

NOTES

*

Introduction

1   *On the Cabbala and its Symbolism* (New York, 1969), p. 8.

2   For the use of rhetoric in the Middle Ages see E. Faral, *Les Artes Poétiques* (Paris, 1923); C. S. Baldwin, *Medieval Rhetoric and Poetic* (Folcroft, Pa., 2nd edn, 1959); T. M. Charland, *Artes Praedicandi: Contribution à l'histoire de la rhétorique au moyen age* (Paris, 1936).

3   E. Underhill, however, takes this perhaps a little too far cf. 'The Mystic as Creative Artist' in: *The Essentials of Mysticism and Other Essays* (London, 1920), p. 70.

4   *Phaidros*, p. 246 a.

5   U. Krewitt, *Metapher und tropische Rede in der Auffassung des Mittelalters*, Supplement to *Mittellateinisches Jahrbuch*, 7 (Ratingen, 1971).

6   Ibid., p. 455.

7   Ibid.

8   Ibid.

9   See especially H. de Lubac, *Exégèse Médiévale* (Paris, 1952-64), and F. Ohly, 'Vom geistigen Sinn des Wortes im Mittelalter', *ZfdA*, 89 (1958/9), pp. 1ff.

10   E. Auerbach, *Typologische Motive in der mittelalterlichen Literatur* (Krefeld, 1953), p. 16.

11   G. Gerleman, *Ruth. Das Hohelied. Biblischer Kommentar — Altes Testament*, 18 (Neukirchen-Vluyn, 1965), p. 53 and passim.

12   See B. Smalley, *The Study of the Bible in the Middle Ages* (Oxford, 1952).

13   H. S. Denifle, *Die deutschen Mystiker des 14. Jahrhunderts. Ein Beitrag zur Deutung ihrer Lehre*, ed. O. Spiess (Fribourg, 1951).

14   Cf. Underhill, *Mysticism* (London, 12th edn, 1930).

15   See, for instance, W. A. Pantin, *The English Church in the Fourteenth Century* (Cambridge, 1955), p. 248. An excellent research report on recent works on English mysticism is E. Colledge, 'The English Mystics and their Critics', *Life of the Spirit*, 15 (1961), pp. 554ff. The importance of the English mystics for the development of English prose was first pointed out by R. W. Chambers, *On the Continuity of English Prose*, EETS, OS, 191A (1932). Critics, however, felt that Chambers saw the importance of religious prose

too exclusively (for instance N. Davis, 'Styles in English Prose of the Late Middle and Early Modern Period', *Les Congrès et colloques de l'université de Liège*, 21 (1961), pp. 165ff.) and that Chambers's claims needed first to be supported and strengthened by individual studies (R. M. Wilson, 'On the Continuity of English Prose', *Mélanges de linguistique et de philologie Fernand Mossé in memoriam* (Paris, 1959), pp. 486ff.). Such individual studies were undertaken above all by P. Hodgson in her editions of the works of the author of the *Cloud of Unknowing* (*The Cloud of Unknowing and the Book of Privy Counselling*, EETS, OS, 218 (1944, repr. 1958 and 1973) and *Deonise Hid Diuinite*, EETS, OS, 231 (1955)), further by R. M. Wilson in an important examination of the language of Rolle, Julian of Norwich and Margery Kempe: 'Three Middle English Mystics', *E&S*, n.s. 9 (1956), pp. 87ff., also by E. Zeeman, 'Continuity in Middle English Devotional Prose', *JEGP*, 55 (1956), pp. 417ff. and in addition in two works by M. M. Morgan: '*A Talkyng of the Love of God* and the Continuity of Stylistic Tradition in Middle English Prose Meditations', *RES*, n.s. 3 (1952), pp. 97ff. and 'A Treatise in Cadence', *MLR*, 47 (1952), pp. 156ff.; recently also by J. A. Alford, 'Biblical *Imitatio* in the Writings of Richard Rolle', *ELH*, 40 (1973), pp. 1ff. (The studies by A. Olmes, J. P. Schneider and E. Schnell, which are mentioned in the bibliography, are too one-sided and make no attempt to set the mystics in perspective.)

16   Cf. Underhill, *The Mystics of the Church* (London, 1925), pp. 110ff.
17   See E. Gilson, *J. Duns Scotus* (Paris, 1952).
18   *Writings Ascribed to Richard Rolle* (New York, 1927).
19   A long time ago G. E. Hodgson demonstrated fairly convincingly that Allen's attempt to eliminate the *Our Daily Work* from the Rolle canon had been wrong (*Rolle and 'Our Daily Work'* (London, 1929)).
20   Hodgson, *Our Daily Work*, pp. 108ff.
21   See Allen, *Writings Ascribed to Richard Rolle*, pp. 108, 149.
22   See, for example, J. Bazire and E. Colledge, *The Chastising of God's Children* (Oxford, 1957), p. 54.
23   Cf. Allen, *Writings*, p. 335.
24   Thus in the prologue to the *Incendium Amoris* he expressly describes the mystical fire as 'ardorem spiritualem' and then almost as a metaphor (147, pp. 2f.). This work also speaks of the 'incorporeos amplexus' into which the mystical lover throws himself (243, pp. 21f.).
25   *Richard Rolle's Comment on the Canticles*, p. 72. G. G. Wright had already warned against a literal understanding of Rolle's metaphors ('The Definition of Love in Richard Rolle of Hampole' (unpublished dissertation, Madison, 1963), pp. 206f.).
26   'sicut si digitus in igne poneretur feruorem indueret sensibilem, sic ... animus ... ardorem sentit ueracissimum' (*Incendium Amoris*, pp. 146, 1ff.). (Cuts in quotations are indicated in this book by ... without brackets.)
27   Mechthild of Magdeburg for instance speaks of burning in love (*Das Fliessende Licht der Gottheit*, pp. 201, 17f.).
28   See K. Bihlmeyer, ed., *Heinrich Seuse. Deutsche Schriften* (Stuttgart, 1907), pp. 15ff.
29   M. Noetinger, 'The Biography of Richard Rolle', *The Month* (1926), 22ff. and Allen, *Writings*, pp. 490ff.

30   'Ricardus Heremita', *Dublin Review*, 183 (1928), pp. 181f.

31   'Richard Rolle and the Sorbonne' in *The Melos Amoris of Richard Rolle of Hampole* (Oxford, 1957), pp. 210ff. (first published in the *Bulletin of the John Rylands Library*, 21 (1937)). We can only outline Arnould's arguments here briefly. Of the four manuscripts which bear witness to Rolle's stay the most important is MS.1228 of the Paris Bibliothèque de l'Arsenal, which contains a history of the Sorbonne and in which Rolle is mentioned a total of seven times. We read there of a 'Ricardus Anglici, seu Radulphi de Anglia . . . vulgo dicitur de Hampole . . . Erat Sorbonae 1326'. The manuscript quotes as an important informant a 'Liber Prioris', now thought to be lost. Without really having any solid proof Arnould believes with quite remarkable conviction that this 'Liber' is identical with MS. lat. 16574 of the Bibliothèque Nationale. Here there is merely mention of a certain 'Magistri Ricardi'. Arnould maintains that the additions in MS. 1228 can be explained in this way: whilst working on their history of the Sorbonne, the compilers came across a manuscript of Rolle's works, wrongly identified him with the Magister Ricardus mentioned in the 'Liber Prioris' and then simply took the additional biographical data straight from Pits ('Richard Rolle and the Sorbonne' in *Melos Amoris*, esp. pp. 227ff.). Several objections can be raised against such an argument. First of all, there is the possibility that MS. lat. 16574 is not identical with the 'Liber' but is merely a poor copy of it, and that the compilers used a better manuscript which has since been lost. For MS. 1228 uses the name 'Ricardus Anglici seu Radulphi de Anglia', which is not in MS. lat. 16574 and which, as Arnould admits, must derive from a different source. And it must further be borne in mind that the librarian of the Sorbonne, as Arnould himself again concedes, considers MS. 1228 to be a carefully written and reliable manuscript. But there is another objection which seems almost more important: can the compilers really have been so naive as to believe that the author of a manuscript found in the Sorbonne must necessarily also have studied there? Or what other reason could they have had for including precisely Rolle amongst the numbers of those studying at the Sorbonne? (N. Marzac, too, is not convinced by Arnould's arguments cf. *Richard Rolle de Hampole 1300-1349* (Paris 1968), pp. 24f.). Arnould clearly starts his argument with the preconceived idea that Rolle is to be understood solely from the national tradition of England and not from the 'French schools of thought' (p. 238). But it need hardly be stated that the intellectual climate of medieval Paris is not to be understood as a French school of philosophy but as the philosophical and theological centre of Europe which was also shaped by non-Frenchmen like Albert the Great and Master Eckhart.

32   We have taken account of the following works of Rolle for our study: *Incendium Amoris*, *Melum Contemplativorum* or *Melos Amoris*, the *Latin Psalter*, the *Comment on the Canticles*, the *Contra Amatores Mundi* and the *Emendatio Vitae*; in addition amongst the English works the two versions of the *Meditations on the Passion*, the letters *Ego Dormio*, the *Commandment* and *The Form of Living*, the English *Commentary on the Psalms*, Richard Misyn's fifteenth century translations of the *Incendium Amoris* and the *Emendatio Vitae* as well as a further Middle English translation of the *Emendatio* which is contained in MS. Harley 2406 of the BL, and finally Rolle's exegesis of

the famous *Oleum-Effusum* verse of the *Song of Songs* which was in circulation in the Middle Ages in the form of a tract as a translated excerpt from his Latin Commentary on the *Song of Songs* (for bibliographical details see Bibliography).

33 U. Gamba, ed., *Il Commento di Roberto Grossatesta al 'De Mystica Theologia' del Pseudo-Dionigi Areopagita*, Orbis Romanus, 14 (Milan, 1942), p. 40. With its image of the 'Cloud of Unknowing' the text seems also to be alluding to the *Consolatio Philosophiae* of Boethius — albeit in order to distance itself from it. For in Boethius it is precisely when man applies himself to the study of lower things and ceases his perceptive contemplation of eternal things that he enters into a 'nubes inscitiae' (Boethius, *The Theological Tractates. The Consolation of Philosophy*, ed. T. E. Page, *et al.*, The Loeb Classical Library, 74 (London, 1918), p. 370.)

34 See J. McCann, *The Cloud of Unknowing* (London, 6th edn. 1952), p. xii.

35 See *Book of Privy Counselling* in *Cloud of Unknowing*, p. 22, 11.

36 *Deonise HD*, p. 8, 14f.

37 *Cloud*, p. 114, 7ff.

38 *Cloud*, p. 28, 10ff.

39 *Cloud*, p. 114, 3ff.

40 *Cloud*, p. 110, 1ff.

41 See the article 'Hilton' by D. Knowles and J. Russell-Smith in *DSAM*. There is today still no certainty as to what constitutes the canon of Hilton's works. Certainly there are five Latin tracts which have not yet been edited and a series of Middle English works. These latter are a letter addressed to a lay person, which is known by the title *Mixed Life*, which discusses the question of how worldly duties which cannot be renounced can be reconciled with mystical contemplation, a further letter on the song of angels with the title *Of Angels' Song* and the principal work which is in two parts and which has the probably posthumous title *The Scale of Perfection*. In addition Hilton is probably responsible for the translation of parts of the work of a certain Franciscan Lewis de Fontibus (*Eight Chapters on Perfection*), two commentaries on the psalms (*Qui Habitat* and *Bonum Est*), a paraphrase of the *Stimulus Amoris* of the Franciscan James of Milan and possibly also for a commentary on the *Benedictus*. All these works have been considered in our study.

42 J. Russell-Smith, too, admits that the information of the colophon 'cannot be disproved', although she finds in it 'a general colour of improbability' ('Walter Hilton and a Tract in Defence of the Veneration of Images', *Dominican Studies*, 7 (1954), pp. 180ff.); see also Hussey 'Latin and English in the "Scale of Perfection" ', *MS*, 35 (1973), p. 458.

43 *Scale I*, ch. 7, p. 94, 5ff.

44 *Scale I*, ch. 26, p. 129, 13ff.

45 *Scale II*, ch. 42, p. 200, 16f.

46 See, for instance, P. Hodgson, *Three 14th-Century English Mystics* (London, 1967), p. 32.

47 *Yorkshire Writers*, *I*, 177 (MS. Thornton).

48 *Scale II*, ch. 21, pp. 70ff.

49 *Revelations* (LV), ch. 18, p. 108, 20.

50 See, for instance, D. S. H., 'Dame Julian of Norwich. By a Benedictine of Stanbrook', *Clergy Review*, n.s. 44 (1959), esp. p. 707.

51 *Revelations* (LV), ch. 68, p. 262, 13f.

52 *Revelations* (LV), ch. 51, p. 209, 19ff.

53 See the useful survey in P. Gradon, *Form and Style in Early English Literature* (London, 1971), pp. 297ff.

54 *The Book of Margery Kempe*, p. 88, 26ff.

55 Ibid., line 26.

56 Ed. J.R.R. Tolkien, *EETS*, OS, 249 (1962). Against the widespread view which Shepherd reiterates in his edition of the *Ancrene Wisse* that it is pointless to try to link this text with mysticism since it is not concerned with the experience of the *unio* of God and man, it has to be argued that the author of this text assumed that the women he was addressing were leading a contemplative life and that he certainly expected them occasionally to reach the stage of contemplative prayer. Basically what the *Ancrene Wisse* does is to create the precondition for an intimate, mystical experience of God.

57 Ed. W.M. Thompson, *EETS*, OS, 241 (1955).

58 Ed. Sr M.S. Westra (The Hague, 1950).

59 Ed. J. Bazire and E. Colledge (Oxford, 1957).

60 In *Yorkshire Writers*, I, pp. 219ff.

61 R. Woolf, *The English Religious Lyric in the Middle Ages* (Oxford, 1968); D. Gray, *Themes and Images in the Medieval English Religious Lyric* (London, 1972).

Chapter I The public for mystical literature in England

1 See, for instance, D. Knowles, *The English Mystical Tradition* (London, 1961), pp. 43ff.

2 See D. Knowles and R.N. Hadcock, *Medieval Religious Houses, England and Wales* (London, 2nd edn 1971) and D. Knowles, *The Religious Orders in England* (Cambridge, 1961-2).

3 See 'religious sister' in *Chastising*, p. 95, 1; 'sister in God', 'Remedies against Temptations. The Third English Version of William Flete', ed. E. Colledge and N. Chadwick, *Archivio Italiano per la Storia della Pietà*, 5 (Rome, 1968), p. 223.

4 See the articles by E. Colledge: ' "The Treatise of Perfection of the Sons of God": a fifteenth-century English Ruysbroek translation', *ES*, 33 (1952), pp. 49ff. and R. Lovatt, 'The Imitation of Christ in Late Medieval England', *Transactions of the Royal Historical Society*, 5th series, 18 (1968), pp. 97ff.

5 MS. Pembroke College Cambridge 221: cf. introduction to *Chastising*, p. 69.

6 *Incendium Amoris*, p. 147, 11f.

7 *Cloud*, p. 137, 6ff.

8 *Medieval English Nunneries* (Cambridge, 1922).

9 Quoted from G. Schreiber, 'Mittelalterliche Passionsmystik und Frömmigkeit', *Theologische Quartalschrift*, 122 (1941), p. 111.

10 See R.W. Chambers, *On the Continuity of English Prose*, *EETS*, OS, 191A (1932), p. xcviii.

11 *The Myroure of oure Ladye*, ed. J.H. Blunt, *EETS*, ES, 19 (1873), p. 2; cf. E. Colledge in *Chastising*, pp. 76f.

12   See Allen, *Writings*, pp. 509ff.
13   See M. Deanesly, 'Vernacular Books in England in the Fourteenth and Fifteenth Century', *MLR*, 15 (1920), pp. 340ff.
14   See *Chastising*, p. 37.
15   See *Minor Works of Walter Hilton*, ed. D. Jones (London, 1929), p. xxxiii.
16   See especially H. Gneuss, 'Englands Bibliotheken im Mittelalter und ihr Untergang', *Festschrift für Walter Hübner*, ed. D. Riesner and H. Gneuss (Berlin, 1964), p. 110.
17   N.F. Blake, 'Middle English Prose and its Audience', *Anglia*, 90 (1972), pp. 437ff.
18   Ibid., p. 446.
19   *Cloud*, pp. 1, 9f.; 3, 1ff.
20   Seventeen different texts of the *Cloud* and ten of the *Book of Privy Counselling* are to be found in various manuscripts (see Hodgson's comment in her *Cloud*-edition, p. ix).
21   *Cloud*, p. 135, 2.
22   Ibid., line 3.
23   Ibid., lines 7ff.
24   W. Flete, *Remedies against Temptations*, p. 223, 37ff.
25   Newly edited by N.F. Blake in his anthology *Middle English Religious Prose*, York Medieval Texts (London, 1972), pp. 88ff.
26   See, for instance, W. Stammler, 'Studien zur Geschichte der Mystik in Norddeutschland', in *Altdeutsche und Altniederländische Mystik*, ed. K. Ruh, Wege der Forschung, 23 (Darmstadt, 1964), p. 408. The image of the monastery of the soul is widespread in English mystical and homiletic writings: Rolle speaks of the 'claustro cordis' (*Melos Amoris*, p. 122, 16), and the *Ayenbite of Inwyt* of the 'cloystre of þe zaule' (ed. R. Morris, *EETS*, OS, 23 (1866), 2nd edn by P. Gradon (1965), p. 151, 8); when in the *Tretyse of þe Stodye of Wysdome* the reader is urged to gather his 'þouȝtes' and 'desires' and to build a 'chirche' with them, 'þerin for to loue only þis worde Ihesu', this related image is very revealing, since the author of the tract indicates that he developed it directly from Ps. 25:12 ('in ecclesiis benedicam te, domine') by way of allegorical exegesis (*Deonise HD*, pp. 45, 13ff.).
27   *Yorkshire Writers*, I, 264.
28   Butler, for instance, has pointed out that in the Middle Ages the term 'contemplative life' already had a double meaning: on the one hand it implies a life of seclusion for the exclusive purpose of mystical contemplation of God; on the other hand it could be used to apply to anyone who practised contemplation, regardless of his particular external circumstances (C. Butler, *Western Mysticism*, 3rd edn (London, 1967), p. 221).
29   *Cloud*, p. 13, 18f.
30   Ibid., p. 14, 4f.; cf. Hodgson's note 13/16, p. 182.
31   Ibid., note 14/13, p. 183.
32   Ibid., p. 14, 13.
33   Ibid., p. 71, 14.
34   This has been pointed out by Hodgson in her *Cloud*-edition, note 14/13, p. 183.
35   Ibid., p. 3, 5.

36   Ibid., p. 147, 22f.
37   Ibid., p. 147, 18ff., my italics.
38   Ibid., p. 22, 3f.
39   Ibid., p. 3, 2ff.
40   *Deonise HD*, p. 62, 2ff. The same observation can be made in the case of the
      famous *Theologia Germanica* which a Teutonic Knight, the 'Frankfurter',
      who drew heavily on Eckhart and Tauler, wrote in the late fourteenth /
      early fifteenth century and which Luther valued very highly as a lay the-
      ology. In it we read that we should resist whatever is not of God, and 'this
      is how it should be in external things, in doing and leaving, speaking and
      remaining silent, waking and sleeping, walking and standing, in short in all
      manner of things and actions which a man does on his own or in the
      company of other people'. (*Eine deutsche Theologie*, ed. and transl. J.
      Bernhart (Munich, no year), p. 256.)
41   *Deonise HD*, p. 62, 2ff., my italics.
42   Ibid., p. 71 and 76, 21ff.
43   Ibid., p. 71, 1f.
44   Ibid., p. 76, 21ff.
45   F. 58^v.
46   F. 60^r.
47   F. 59^r.
48   *Middle English Religious Prose*, p. 89, 10f.
49   For the Beguines see E.W. McDonnell, *The Beguines and Beghards in Medi-
      eval Culture with Special Emphasis on the Belgian Scene* (New Brunswick,
      1954) and O. Nübel, *Mittelalterliche Beginen- und Sozialsiedlungen in den
      Niederlanden* (Tubingen, 1970); cf. also H.E. Allen in *Book of Margery
      Kempe*, pp. liiif.
50   Ed. C. Horstmann in *Anglia*, 8 (1885), p. 102.
51   This is mentioned by Thomas of Eccleston, *Fratris Thomae vulgo dicti de
      Eccleston Tractatus de Adventu Fratrum Minorum in Angliam*, ed. A.G.
      Little (Manchester, 1951), p. 99.
52   See Allen in her book, *Writings*, p. 340.
53   J.J. Jusserand, *Piers Plowman: A Contribution to the History of English
      Mysticism* (London, 1894), p. 203.
54   On the problem of dating see R.M. Wilson, *Early Middle English Literature*,
      3rd edn (London, 1968), pp. 136ff.
55   MS. Pembroke College Cambridge 221 f. 1^v (permission to quote granted
      by the Master and Fellows of Pembroke College Cambridge).
56   *Cloud*, p. 97, 13ff.; 104, 4ff., cf. Hodgson's comment pp. 1xxvi f.
57   See Colledge in his edition of *Chastising*, p. 53.
58   R. Guarnieri, 'Il Movimento del Libero Spirito, Testi e Documenti', *Archivio
      Italiano per la Storia della Pietà*, 4 (Rome, 1965), pp. 351ff.; for William
      Thorpe see R.A. Knox, *Enthusiasm: A Chapter in the History of Religion*
      (Oxford, 1950). See also R.E. Lerner, *The Heresy of the Free Spirit in the
      Later Middle Ages* (Berkeley, 1972).
59   *Scale II*, ch. 21, p. 77, 6ff.
60   Ibid., p. 76, 21.
61   Ibid., ch. 26, p. 99, 12ff. In *8 Chapters on Perfection* there is also a warning
      against a false 'spirit of freedom' and against a wrong application of St Paul's

statement 'where þe spirit of God is, þere is fredom.' (p. 13, 196ff.)

62 The basic thoughts of the *Mirror of Simple Souls* are critically analysed by E. Colledge and R. Guarnieri in the appendix to the edition of the *Mirror* by M. Doiron, *Archivio Italiano per la Storia della Pietà*, 5 (Rome, 1968).

63 *Mirror of Simple Souls*, p. 247, 24f.

64 *Chastising*, p. 189, 13.

65 *Cloud*, p. 88, 7ff.

66 He indicates that he has already had conversations with the person the *Cloud* is addressed to (*Cloud*, p. 91, 25ff.) and that his tract *A Pistle of Discrecioun of Stirings* was conceived as an answer to questions put to him in writing by members of his circle of pupils (*Deonise HD*, p. 77, 14). These remarks cannot be explained away as mere rhetorical convention to establish a rapport with the reader at the beginning of a work, for the whole work is permeated by a very personal relationship between the author and the reader, which is true also of Hilton's writings.

67 See J.M. Clark, *The Great German Mystics: Eckhart, Tauler and Suso* (Oxford, 1949).

68 *Cloud*, pp. 13, 8; 135, 1.

69 On the idea of 'Friendship with God' in general see R. Egenter, *Die Lehre von der Gottesfreundschaft in der Scholastik des 13. und 14. Jahrhunderts* (Augsburg, 1928). M. Deanesly also suspected a certain influence of the Friends of God on spiritual literature in English (*The Lollard Bible* (Cambridge, 1920), p. 218).

70 Ed. by J. Bazire and E. Colledge in *Chastising*, pp. 229ff. The original is Ruysbroeck's *Vanden Blinckenden Steen*. The translation was made from the Latin of W. Jordaens, see Colledge, *ES*, 33 (1952). For another Ruysbroeck text known in English see A.I. Doyle, 'A Text Attributed to Ruysbroeck Circulating in England', *Dr. L. Reypens-Album*, ed. A. Ampe (Antwerp, 1964), pp. 155ff.

71 *Piers Plowman*, p. 205.

72 Ed. J.K. Ingram, *EETS*, ES, 63 (1893); see especially R. Lovatt, 'The Imitation of Christ in Late Medieval England', pp. 97ff.

73 *Die Wolke des Nichtwissens*, ed. and translated by E. Strakosch (Einsiedeln, 1958), pp. 5ff.

74 Ed. Sr M.L. Pimpl (unpublished dissertation, New York, 1963).

75 Ed. A.J. McCarthy (unpublished dissertation, New York, 1961).

76 E. Underhill, 'Medieval Mysticism' in *Cambridge Medieval History* (1932), VII, 804.

Chapter II The interrelation between continental and English mysticism

1 D. Knowles, *The English Mystical Tradition* (London, 1961), p. 76.

2 See the study of E.G. Gardner: *Dante and the Mystics: A Study of the Mystical Aspect of the Divina Commedia and its Relations with Some of its Medieval Sources* (London, 1913), especially pp. 342ff.

3 See especially F.v.Hügel, *The Mystical Element of Religion as Studied in Saint Catherine of Genoa and her Friends* (London, 1909), II, pp. 90ff.

4 See the commentary on this as yet unedited work by F. Rocho in *Kindlers*

Literatur Lexikon, ed. W. von Einsiedeln (Zurich, 1971), 6, pp. 858f.

5   *Cloud*, p. lxiv.

6   Knowles, *The English Mystical Tradition*, pp. 75ff.; see especially J. Sudbrack, *Die geistliche Theologie des Johannes von Kastl. Studien zur Frömmigkeitsgeschichte des Mittelalters* (Munster, 1966), I, p. 165.

7   An edition of the medieval German translation of Rudolf's principal work is: *Rudolf von Biberach. Die siben strassen zu got. Die hochalemannische Übertragung nach der Handschrift Einsiedeln 278*, ed. M. Schmidt, Spicilegium Bonaventurianum, 6 (Quaracchi, 1969). This edition has an excellent commentary.

8   Knowles, *The English Mystical Tradition*, pp. 75ff.

9   See Schmidt, op. cit., esp. pp. 194*ff.; When dealing with the theme of experiencing God in the darkness of unknowing, Schmidt even refers in a footnote to the *Cloud*, p. 214*, footnote 3.

10 See the recent very informative survey of Eckhart research by E. Soudek, *Meister Eckhart* (Stuttgart, 1973), pp. 34ff.

11 See Schmidt, op. cit., pp. 24*ff. See also M.G. Sargent, 'The Transmissions by the English Carthusians', *Journal of Ecclesiastical History*, 27 (1976).

12 Hodgson, amongst others, subscribes to the view that the author of the *Cloud* was a member of the Dominican order, *Cloud*, p. 202, footnote 120/6.

13 *The Essentials of Mysticism and Other Essays* (London, 1920), p. 141.

14 Ibid.

15 See the *Mirror of Simple Souls*, p. 243.

16 C. Kirchberger, ed., *The Mirror of Simple Souls. By an Unknown French Mystic of the Thirteenth Century. Translated into English by MN* (New York, 1927), p. xlvi.

17 *The Book of M. Kempe*. p. liii. Underhill maintained that Tauler was translated into Middle English but did not put forward any proof (*Cambridge Medieval History*, VII, p. 805).

18 If the texts of *Chastising* and *Gheestelike Brulocht* are placed side by side, the similarities are evident:

Chastising:

Þei holden bi þat kyndeli reste þat þei haue, and bi þat ydelnesse whiche þei haue whan þei stonden so alone vpon hemsilf, þat þei be free in spirit . . .

Also up this þei seien þat as longe as a man besieþhym to gete uertues, he is nat ʒit parfite; but to her owne feelyng þei bien in perfeccion, aboue al seyntis and aungels and aboue al mede þat any man can discerue. Perfore þei trowe þat þei may no more encreese in uertues, and þat þei mowe

Brulocht:

Overmids die natuerlijcke raste die si . . . besitten in hem selven in ledicheiden, soe houden si dit, dat si vri sijn . . .

Ende hier-omme segghen si: alsoe langhe alse de mensche na doechde steet ende hi begheert den liefsten wille Gods te doene, soe es hi noch een onvolcomen mensche . . . Maer na haren dunckene sijn si verhaven boven alle chore (der heilighen ende der inghele), ende boven alle dien loen diemen in eenigher wijs verdienen mach. Ende hier-

disserue no more mede, and þat
þei mowe no more synne, in as
moche as to her owne siȝt þei
lyuen wiþouten will ... etc.
(*Chastising*, p. 139, 11ff; p. 141,
3ff.).

omme segghen si datsi nemmer
toe-nemen en moghen in doech-
den, noch niet meer loens
verdienen, noch oec hemmer-
meer sonde doen. Want si segghen dat si leven sonder wille ...
etc. (*Brulocht*, in Ruysbroeck.
Werken, I, 233, 4ff; p. 234,
4ff.).

19   J.B. Dalgairns, *The Scale of Perfection written by Walter Hilton, with an Essay on the Spiritual Life of Mediaeval England* (London, 1870), p. xix.

20   See, for instance, Underhill, *Essentials of Mysticism*, pp. 192ff.

21   'Some Literary Influences in the *Revelations* of Julian of Norwich (c. 1342 – post-1416)', *Leeds Studies in English*, 7 (1952), pp. 26f. (following D. Knowles, *The English Mystics*, London, 1927, p. 144). Nor are the 'parallels' with Tauler and Suso which P.G. Meunier sets out in his edition of Julian sufficient to assume any direct influence (*Julienne de Norwich, mystique anglaise du XIVe siècle, révélations de l'amour de dieu, traduite par un bénédictin de Farnborough* (Paris, 1911), pp. 79, 105, 172, 189, 279).

22   Reynolds, *A Shewing of God's Love*, p. 27.

23   On this point see A. Cabassut, 'Une Dévotion médiévale peu connue: La dévotion a Iésus notre mère', *RAM*, 25 (1949), pp. 234ff.

24   See 'graces' (SV); 'giftes' (LV), ch. 1, p. 1, 6 ch. 2, p. 56, 13f.

25   Her vita was edited by C. Horstmann, *Anglia*, 8 (1885), p. 174.

26   *Revelations* (LV), ch. 3, p. 61, 13ff.

27   E. Benz, *Die Vision. Erfahrungsformen und Bilderwelt* (Stuttgart, 1969), pp. 17ff.

28   Ibid., p. 27.

29   Ibid., p. 28.

30   Quoted from W. Blank, *Die Nonnenviten des 14. Jahrhunderts* (Diss. Freiburg, 1962), p. 131.

31   Benz, op. cit., p. 33.

32   Ibid., p. 177. 33ff.

33   W. Muschg, *Die Mystik in der Schweiz 1200-1500* (Frauenfeld, 1935), p. 221; on the wound-motif in Julian see P. Molinari, *Julian of Norwich* (London, 1958), pp. 16ff.

34   *Revelations* (LV), ch. 2, p. 56, 10f.

35   *Offenbarungen der Schwester Mechthild von Magdeburg*, p. 56, 37.

36   Ibid., p. 30, 1; on the question of Mechthild's education see H. Neumann, 'Mechthild von Magdeburg und die mittelniederländische Frauenmystik', in: *Mediaeval German Studies Presented to F. Norman* (London, 1965), pp. 231f.

37   Neumann, op. cit., p. 232.

38   The possibility of such an interpretation was also considered by Sr Anna Maria Reynolds, *A Shewing of God's Love* (London, 1958), p. xvii; also by R.M. Wilson, 'Three Middle English Mystics', *E&S*, n.s. 9 (1956), p. 97.

39   See Neumann, op. cit., p. 232.

40   See Reynolds, *A Shewing of God's Love*, p. xx.

41 *Revelations* (SV), ch. 6 p. 11, 22f.
42 See A. Hübner, quoted in F.W. Wentzlaff-Eggebert, *Deutsche Mystik zwischen Mittelalter und Neuzeit* (Berlin, 1944), p. 24.
43 In *Cambridge Medieval History* (Cambridge, 1932), VII p. 807.
44 *Book of M. Kempe*, p. 148. On this point see F.P. Pickering, 'A German Mystic Miscellany of the Late Fifteenth Century in the John Rylands Library', *Bulletin of the John Rylands Library*, 22 (1938), pp. 455ff.
45 *Book of M. Kempe*, p. 4, 4.
46 Cf. Allen's footnote 4/4 in *Book of M. Kempe*, pp. 257f.
47 Ibid., p. 2, 5ff.
48 For instance in Adelheid von Rheinfelden from the convent of Unterlinden; Cf. W. Muschg, *Die Mystik in der Schweiz 1200-1500* (Frankfurt, 1935), p. 215.
49 See, for instance, *Book of M. Kempe*, note 21/12, p. 267.
50 On this point see Allen's comment in *Book of M. Kempe*, note 2/20 sq., p. 256.
51 Adelheid Langmann, for instance, hears God say to her: 'mein gotlich hertze ist mer zu dir geneiget denn zu keinem menschen', *Die Offenbarungen der Adelheid Langmann, Klosterfrau zu Engelthal*, ed. P. Strauch (Strasbourg, 1878), p. 25, 8f.
52 Ibid., p. 2; Marie d'Oignies for instance also had the gift of second sight.
53 See W. Stammler, 'Studien zur Geschichte der Mystik in Norddeutschland', ed. Ruh, p. 425.
54 *Book of M. Kempe*, for instance, pp. 95, 26; 131, 1; 154, 13.
55 *The Revelations of St. Birgitta*, ed. W. Cumming, *EETS*, OS, 178 (1928).
56 Ed. C. Horstmann, *Anglia*, 8 (1885), pp. 174ff.
57 *The Orcherd of Syon*, ed P. Hodgson and G. Liegey, *EETS*, OS, 258 (1966), I.
58 For W. Flete see B. Hackett, 'William Flete' in *Pre-Reformation English Spirituality*, ed. J. Walsh (New York, 1966), pp. 158ff.
59 T. Halligan, ed., *'The Booke of Gostlye Grace'* (unpublished dissertation New York, 1963).
60 Ibid., p. cxxxiii.
61 In her edition of the *Booke of Gostlye Grace* Halligan gives an excellent survey of the dissemination of this work in England. This shows that whenever in England there is any mention of 'Sancta Matilda', 'Seynt Mawde', 'Sent Moll' or 'Molde', this always refers to Mechthild of Hackeborn — incidentally it was suspected that Mechthild of Hackeborn was behind the 'Matelda' in the Purgatorio of Dante's *Commedia* (XXXIII, 119). It is noticeable, however, that Halligan does not deny *expressis verbis* that the name 'Matilda' could in theory refer to Mechthild of Magdeburg and her *Fliessendes Licht der Gottheit*, a Latin version of which had been in existence since the late thirteenth century. The Third Booklist of the Carthusian monastery of Witham, which is preserved in MS. Laud 154, f. 7^v, apart from mentioning the work of 'sancte Mechthildis', also mentions amongst other things the *Revelaciones Sante Elisabethe Sconaug*, the mystical experiences of Elizabeth of Schönau (cf. E.M. Thompson, *The Carthusian order in England* (London, 1930), p. 321); R.J. Dean, 'Manuscripts of St. Elizabeth of Schönau in England', *MLR* 32 (1937), pp. 62 ff. gives an

account of how widespread Elizabth's vision were in England.

62 *Book of M. Kempe*, e.g. footnote 18/12, p. 265. In addition to Allen's remark it should be pointed out that Margery's statement, to the effect that God does not take any notice of what a man was but of what he wanted to be, is also found in Mechthild (*Book of M. Kempe*, pp. 49, 20f.; 90, 14f.; *Booke of Gostlye Grace*, p. 459).

63 *Booke of M. Kempe*, p. 154, 13 and Allen's footnote, p. 324.

64 On this point cf. C. Greith, *Die deutsche Mystik im Prediger-Orden* (Freibourg, 1861, reprint Amsterdam, 1965), p. 299, and F. Vetter, ed., *Das Leben der Schwestern zu Töss, beschrieben von Elsbeth Stagel, samt der Vorrede von Johannes Meier und dem Leben der Prinzessin Elisabeth von Ungarn*, Deutsche Texte des Mittelalters, 6 (Berlin, 1906), pp. 99ff.

65 Cf. W. Muschg, *Die Mystik in der Schweiz 1200-1500*, p. 133.

66 Ed. C. Horstmann, *Anglia*, 10 (1888), pp. 323ff.

67 W. Wichgraf, 'Susos Horologium Sapientiae in England. Nach Handschriften des 15. Jahrhunderts', *Anglia*, 53 (1929), pp. 123ff, 269ff. and 345ff., esp. p. 372; *Anglia*, 54 (1930), pp. 351f.; cf. also G. Schleich, 'Auf den Spuren Susos in England', *Archiv*, 156 (1929), pp. 184ff., and also 'Über die Entstehungszeit und den Verfasser der mittelenglischen Bearbeitung von Susos Horologium', *Archiv*, 157 (1930), pp. 26ff.

68 Cf. *Chastising*, p. 85 and passim.

69 See K. Bihlmeyer, ed., *Heinrich Seuse. Deutsche Schriften* (Stuttgart, 1907), p. 3*ff.

70 On this aspect in Rolle see Allen's remarks in *Writings*, pp. 66ff. and also in 'The Mystical Lyrics of the Manuel des Pechiez', *Romanic Review*, 9 (1918), p. 187.

71 J.O. Plassmann, *Die Werke der Hadewych* (Hanover, 1923), p. 108. A good concise survey of the numerous hermits in England in the twelfth century, some of whom could have been known to Hadewych, can be found in G. Shepherd, *Ancrene Wisse: Parts Six and Seven* (London, 1959), p. xxxiii.

Chapter III The Song of Songs and metaphors for love in English mysticism

1 See the excellent study by G. Gerleman, *Ruth. Das Hohelied. Biblischer Kommentar, Altes Testament* (Neukirchen-Vluyn, 1965), pp. 43ff.

2 See G. Lüers, *Die Sprache der deutschen Mystik des Mittelalters im Werke der Mechthild von Magdeburg* (Munich, 1926), p. 87.

3 Helen Gardner, 'Walter Hilton and the Mystical Tradition in England', *E&S*, 22 (1937), p. 123.

4 This has been pointed out by H.E. Allen, 'The Mystical Lyrics of the Manuel des Pechiez', *Romanic Review*, 9 (1918), p. 188.

5 See Migne, *PL*, 184c., 370.

6 See F. Ohly, *Hohelied-Studien* (Wiesbaden, 1958), p. 205.

7 See R.E. Kaske, 'The *Canticum Canticorum* in the *Miller's Tale*', *SP*, 59 (1962), pp. 479ff.

8 For questions of style see the study by G. Gerleman, op. cit., pp. 52ff.

9 Ibid., p. 54.

10   Ibid., pp. 58f.
11   *Sancti Bernardi Opera*, II, p. 148, 13f.: 'Nam iteratio, affectionis expressio est.'
12   Ibid., p. 190, 32.
13   Gerleman, op, cit., p. 95.
14   Ibid., p. 72.
15   See Gerleman, pp. 43ff.
16   *Melos Amoris*, p. 68, 5.
17   Ibid., p. 57, 26.
18   Ibid., line 26f.
19   Ibid., p. 17, 27.
20   Ibid., p. 115, 19.
21   *Incendium Amoris*, p. 157.
22   *Melos Amoris*, p. 46, 3.
23   E.g. in *Wohunge of Ure Lauerd*, p. 20, 1.
24   E.g. in *Life of St. Katherine*, ed. E. Einenkel, *EETS*, OS, 80 (1883), p. 24, 481f.
25   E.g. *Wohunge of Ure Lauerd*, p. 22, 69.
26   In the sentence 'þou hast wounded myn hert . . . my lemman' the text *A Pistle of Discrecioun of Stirings* translates the word *sponsa* of the *Song of Songs* with *lemman* (*Deonise HD*, p. 72, 17f.)
27   *Cloud*, p. 15, 16; see also Hodgson's comment in *Cloud*, p. 184, note 15/16.
28   E.g. *Ancrene Wisse*, p. 5, 9f.; see also Hodgson's note 15/4 in *Cloud*, p. 183.
29   E.g. *Wohunge of Ure Lauerd*, p. 35, 572.
30   P. 58, 10.
31   In the prologue to his *English Psalter* he expressly defines the 'matere of this booke' as 'crist & his spouse, that is, haly kyrke, or ilk ryghtwise mannys saule' (p. 4); see also Peter Lombard's *Commentary on the Psalms*, PL, 191, 59.
32   *Cloud*, p. 15, 3.
33   E.g. *Scale I*, ch. 81, p. 229, 11f.
34   *Revelations* (LV), for instance ch. 52, p. 210, 12f.
35   *Deonise HD*, p. 56, 21f.; *Scale I*, ch. 8, p. 96, 2f.; see also Hodgson, *Deonise HD*, note 56/21, p. 137.
36   *Deonise HD*, p. 35, 15f.
37   *Book of M. Kempe*, p. 87, 18ff.
38   *English Writings*, p. 79, 218ff.
39   *Scale II*, ch. 12, p. 38, 9ff. (editor's brackets).
40   *Commentaria in hierarchiam coelestem* VI (*PL* 175, 1038).
41   Quoted from the *MED*, s.v. 'bed'.
42   *English Writings*, p. 44, 11.
43   *Melos Amoris*, p. 150, 7f.
44   *Mirror of Simple Souls*, p. 294, 3.
45   *Talkyng of þe Loue of God*, p. 34, 19f.
46   *Book of M. Kempe*, p. 90, 19f.
47   *Offenbarungen der Schwester Mechthild von Magdeburg*, p. 45.
48   *Book of M. Kempe*, p. 90, 24ff.
49   C. Horstmann, ed., 'Informacio Alredi Abbatis Monasterij De Rieualle Ad Sororem Suam Inclusam: Translata De Latino in Anglicum per Thomam N.', *Englische Studien*, 7 (1884), 327.

50 *Die Sprache der deutschen Mystik*, p. 211.
51 *Ancrene Wisse*, p. 55, 15 ff.
52 *MED*, s.v. 'cos'.
53 *Melos Amoris*, p. 8, 17ff.
54 Ibid., p. 129, 12ff.
55 Quoted from Lüers, op. cit., p. 212.
56 MS. Bodl. 16, f.68^r.
57 See M. Schmidt, op. cit., p. 151, where German examples are also listed.
58 *English Psalter*, p. 87 (following Peter Lombard's *Commentary on the Psalms, PL*, 191/253).
59 *Book of M. Kempe*, p. 14, 3f.
60 See, for instance, Anselm of Canterbury, *Meditationes, PL*, 158, 761.
61 *Talkyng of þe Loue of God*, p. 68, 15f.
62 *Revelations* (LV), ch. 71, p. 273, 21ff.
63 Ibid., ch. 60, p. 241, 13.
64 *Offenbarungen der Schwester Mechthild von Magdeburg*, p. 158. See also P.R. Banz, *Christus und die minnende Seele* (Breslau, 1908), p. 72.
65 *Political, Religious, and Love Poems*, ed. F.J. Furnivall, *EETS*, OS, 15 (1866), p. 185, 81f.
66 E. Underhill, *Mysticism*, p. 383.
67 BL MS. Harley 2254, ch. 26. f. 45^v.
68 The Middle English version has: 'þis is þe pleye of loue þe whiche I am wonte to vse in an amarose sowle' (*Anglia*, 10 (1888), p. 335, 7f.)
69 See E. Colledge, 'The "Büchlein der ewigen Weisheit" and the "Horologium Sapientiae" ', *Dominican Studies*, 6 (1953), pp. 77ff.
70 *Chastising*, p. 99, 7; see also Colledge's note 99.3 (p. 264).
71 *Chastising*, p. 98, 3.
72 There we read: 'ure lauerd hwen he þoleþ þ we beon itempted he pleieð wið us as þe moder wið hire ʒunge deorling.' (pp. 118f.); cf. also *Chastising*, p. 46 and p. 263, note 98.4.
73 *Book of Privy Counselling* in *Cloud*, p. 167, 3. Hodgson rightly draws attention to comparable Bible passages such as Mark 10: 14f. (p. 213, footnote).
74 'who-so had grace to do & fele as I sey, he schuld fele good gamesumli pley wiþ hym, as þe fadir doþ wiþ þe childe, kyissyng & clippyng, þat weel were him so.' (*Cloud*, p. 88, 2ff.). Although in this quotation the expression 'good gamesumli pley' has no real meaning, the editor, P. Hodgson, refrains from amending 'good' to 'god', since the latter is only found in one not very reliable manuscript. But since Middle English tended not to make any consistent orthographical distinction between 'good' and 'god', there can be no doubt, if the sentence is to have any meaning at all, that the author of the *Cloud* is alluding to the old mystical motif of the playing God. Thus English mysticism here confirms Lüers' view that extensive studies in the field of mysticism can yield criteria for solving problems in the area of textual criticism (pp. 116ff.).
75 See, for instance, Ps. 35:9; Ps. 103:15 and also the symbolism of wine, the vine and the last supper in the New Testament.
76 On this point see above all Underhill, *Mysticism*, pp. 235ff.
77 See Lüers, op. cit., p. 268.
78 As M. Schmidt does in her edition of *Die siben strassen zu got*, p. 159*.

79 Quoted from Lüers, op. cit., p. 268; see also Banz, *Christus und die minnende Seele* (Breslau, 1908), pp. 79f.
80 Banz, op. cit., plate IX.
81 Quoted from Lüers, op. cit., p. 268.
82 *Yorkshire Writers*, II, 18, 262f.
83 *Scale II*, ch. 26, p. 101, 8.
84 *Romaunt of the Rose*: 'In gret myschef and sorwe sonken / Ben hertis that of love arn dronken'; Gower: 'How Tristram was of love drunke' (quoted from *MED*, s.v. 'dronken').
85 *Sancti Bernardi Opera*, II, 73, 18f.
86 *Incendium Amoris*, p. 274, 18f.
87 S. of S. 2:4; my italics.
88 *Scale II*, ch. 45, p. 168, 13ff; see also ch. 79, p. 228, 17ff.
89 *Mirror of Simple Souls*, p. 276, 8f.
90 Ibid., line 18f.
91 Ibid., lines 19ff.
92 E.g. *Incendium Amoris*: 'amore langueo floris prefulgidi', p. 193.
93 *Scale II*, ch. 41, p. 193, 2f.
94 *Cloud*, p. 46, 4.
95 In *Deonise HD*, p. 111, 13f.; see also Julian, *Revelations* (LV), ch. 20, p. 112; *Book of M. Kempe*, p. 20, 10f. Richard Misyn translates Rolle's 'amore langueo floris prefulgidi' with the expression 'I longe for lufe of þe fayrest flowre' (*Fire of Love*, p. 38, 40).
96 Rolle, *English Writings*, p. 42, 29.
97 *Book of Privy Counselling* in *Cloud*, p. 148, 23f. The verbs *coveten* and *yernen* are even more seldom used.
98 *Book of M. Kempe*, p. 185, 13ff.
99 'he longyth evyr for to bryng vs to the fulhed of Ioy', *Revelations* (LV), ch. 40, p. 159, 6f.
100 *Revelations* (LV), ch. 31, p. 135, 4f.
101 *Die Predigten Taulers*, p. 56, 5ff.
102 *Political, Religious, and Love Poems*, ed. F.J. Furnivall, *EETS*, OS, 15 (1866), pp. 180ff.
103 *English Writings*, p. 70, 313.
104 *Richard de Saint-Victor: Les Quatre Degrés de la Violente Charité*, ed. G. Dumeige (Paris, 1955), p. 131, 16f.
105 'Now wax I pale and wan for luf of my lemman', *English Writings*, p. 71, 330.
106 Ibid., p. 131, 17.
107 *Yorkshire Writers*, II, 14, 149ff. (Vernon MS.).
108 *Book of M. Kempe*, p. 46, 29.
109 Ibid., p. 31, 3f. (editor's brackets); see also H.E. Allen's note on this passage (p. 271).
110 *Troilus and Criseyde*, II, 1305ff.
111 *English Writings*, p. 47, 83.
112 *Talkyng of þe Loue of God*, p. 60, 25ff.; see also *Swete Ihesu, now wil I synge*, *Yorkshire Writers*, II, 22, 390 (Vernon MS.). Margery Kempe begins to feel like a 'mad woman' when she visualizes the Passion of Christ in all its detail (*Book of M. Kempe*, p. 193, 21).

113 *Richard de Saint-Victor: Les Quatre Degrés de la Violente Charité*, p. 143.

114 R. Woolf also draws attention to the Septuagint reading, *The English Religious Lyric in the Middle Ages* (Oxford, 1968), pp. 164ff. We find the reading 'vulnerata caritate ego sum' in Rolle's *Contra Amatores Mundi*, ed. P.F. Theiner (Berkeley, 1968), p. 104, 87f.

115 *Offenbarungen der Schwester Mechthild von Magdeburg*, p. 37.

116 *English Writings*, p. 42, 13.

117 *Book of M. Kempe*, p. 98, 35.

118 *Orcherd of Syon*, p. 375, 32ff.

119 *Melos Amoris*, p. 82, 33.

120 Ibid., 83, 24ff.

121 See the account of Bonetti's work by E. Colledge, *The Mediaeval Mystics of England* (London, 1962), pp. 11ff.

122 *Ancrene Wisse*, ed. J.R.R. Tolkien, *EETS*, OS, 249 (1962), p. 151, 11ff.

123 *Political, Religious, and Love Poems*, ed. F.J. Furnivall, p. 184, 57.

124 Rolle, *Meditations (English Writings)*, p. 43, *Book of M. Kempe*, p. 70, 10ff.; see also Allen's note pp. 291f.

125 MS. Digby 58, f. 45^v.

126 *The Meditations of the Monk of Farne*, ed. by H. Farmer, Studia Anselmiana, 41 (Rome, 1957), p. 182.

127 *Talkyng of þe Loue of God*, p. 52, 24.

128 *Revelations* (LV), ch. 23, p. 122, 1ff.

129 On this point see F. Ohly, *Hohelied-Studien* (Wiesbaden, 1958), p. 17.

130 Ps. 37:3.

131 See A. Cabassut, 'Blessure d'Amour', in *DSAM*, I, col. 1727.

132 *English Psalter* (Ps. 54:24), p. 198 (following Peter Lombard's commentary on the Psalms, *PL*, 191, 516); see also especially *Melos Amoris*, pp. 42f.

133 *Mirror of Simple Souls*, p. 260, 25.

134 *Comment on the Canticles*, f.106, p. 14, 1.

135 *Melos Amoris*, p. 6, 6.

136 *Incendium Amoris*, p. 152.

137 *Scale I*, ch. 30, p. 135, 17f.

138 *English Writings*, p. 41, 6.

139 See, for instance, John Hoveden's Song of the Nightingale: *Nachtigallenlied über die Liebe unseres Erlösers und Königs Christus*, ed. C. Blume (Leipzig, 1930): 'Dum cor [Christi] sentit Amoris gladium', p. 9.

140 Banz, *Christus und die minnende Seele*, plate VII.

141 Quoted from P. Dronke, *The Medieval Lyric* (London, 1968), pp. 60f.

142 Ibid., p. 61 note.

143 *Wohunge of Ure Lauerd*, p. 35, 546ff.

144 Ibid., p. 198, 16f.

145 'Studien zur Geschichte der Mystik in Norddeutschland', Ruh, op. cit., p. 419.

146 *Anglia*, 10 (1888), p. 332, 32.

147 *Scale II*, ch. 43, p. 213, 18ff. The *Talkyng of þe Loue of God* speaks of the mystical 'love song' (p. 68, 2ff.). On the love-letter see also W. Gaffney, 'The Allegory of the Christ-Knight in Piers Plowman', *PMLA*, 46 (1931), pp. 155 ff. and Sr Marie de Lourdes le May 'The Allegory of the Christ-Knight in English Literature', (dissertation, Catholic University of America,

Washington, D.C., 1932).

148 p. 276, 6ff.; Misyn translates: 'bot weil it is sayd in play: "luf gos before & ledis þe dawns" ' (Fire of Love, p. 102, 8f.).

149 English Writings, p. 68, 235ff.

150 The English Religious Lyric in the Middle Ages (Oxford, 1968), p. 167.

151 Quoted from Banz, Christus und die minnende Seele, p. 100.

152 See the other examples which Banz cites (p. 99).

153 Chastising, p. 102, 17ff.

154 Quoted from Lüers, op. cit., p. 267 (the quotation is already in abbreviated form in Lüers).

155 Ibid.; see also DSAM, III, col. 21ff., s.v. 'danse religieuse'.

156 The Apocryphal New Testament, ed. and transl. M.R. James (Oxford, 1963), p. 253, 94ff. The well-known short quotations and references to this passage in mystical texts are, however, not sufficient to prove that these apocryphal Acts had any influence on mysticism, as Dronke also points out (The Medieval Lyric (London, 1968), p. 84).

157 See Dom H. van Cranenburgh, 'Hadewychs Zwölfte Vision and neuntes strophisches Gedicht', in Ruh, op. cit., p. 170.

158 Booke of Gostlye Grace, II, p. 355.

159 English Writings, p. 44, 16.

160 Revelations (SV), ch. 12, p. 23, 20f.; see also the Mirror of Simple Souls, p. 346.

161 Melos Amoris, p. 159, 30.

162 On this point see W. Haeckel, Das Sprichwort bei Chaucer, Erlanger Beiträge zur Englischen Philologie (Erlangen, 1890), p. 2.

163 Sancti Bernardi Opera, I, 116, 5f.; see also the hymn on the Passion by Hermann Joseph, born about 1150, where we read: 'Amore quisquis vincitur', quoted from G. Schreiber, 'Mittelalterliche Passionsmystik und Frömmigkeit', Theologische Quartalschrift, 122 (1941), p. 37.

164 Quoted from De Montmorency, Thomas à Kempis: His Age and Book (London, 1906), p. 183.

165 The Works of Geoffrey Chaucer, ed. F.N. Robinson (London, 2nd edn, 1957), Canterbury Tales, Prologue 162, p. 18.

166 See for instance, A.W. Hoffman, 'Chaucer's Prologue to Pilgrimage: The Two Voices', ELH, 21 (1954), pp. 1ff.

167 Canterbury Tales, Prologue 197, The Works of Geoffrey Chaucer, p. 19.

168 Cloud, p. 88, 17f.

169 Scale I, ch. 12, p. 103, 14f.

170 Meditations on the Life and Passion of Christ, ed. Ch. D'Evelyn, EETS, OS, 158, (1919), p. 52, 1990f.

171 E.g. Melos Amoris, pp. 108, 26f.; 165, 11ff.

172 PL 195, 531.

173 See K.E. Georges, Ausführliches Lateinisch-Deutsches Handwörterbuch, II, s.v. 'nodus'.

174 See especially M. Eliade, Ewige Bilder und Sinnbilder. Vom unvergänglichen menschlichen Seelenraum (Freiburg, 1958), p. 149.

175 Orison of the Passion in Meditations on the Life and Passion of Christ, p, 62, 85.

176 Rolle, English Writings, p. 35, 261.

177 See, for instance Chaucer's *Troilus and Criseyde*, Book III, lines 1765ff., *The Works of Geoffrey Chaucer*, ed. Robinson, p. 440.

178 'Me seið þ luue bindeð', p. 208.

179 *Meditations on the Life and Passion of Christ*, p. 48, 1825f.

180 *Offenbarungen der Schwester Mechthild von Magdeburg*, p. 161.

181 D. Mehl, *The Middle English Romances of the Thirteenth and Fourteenth Centuries* (London, 1968), p. 5.

182 *Ancrene Wisse*, p. 199. On this question see W. Gaffney, 'The Allegory of the Christ-Knight in Piers Plowman', *PMLA*, 46 (1931), pp. 155ff. and Sr Marie de Lourdes le May, 'The Allegory of the Christ-Knight in English Literature' (unpublished dissertation Washington, D.C., 1932).

183 See, for instance, the excellent survey in Shepherd, *Ancrene Wisse, Parts Six and Seven* (London, 1959), p. xlv.

184 H. Kuhn, *Rittertum und Mystik*, Münchener Universitätsreden, N.F. 33 (Munich, 1962), pp. 9ff.

185 E.g. *Talkyng of þe Loue of God*, p. 8, 20.

186 Rolle's *Ego Dormio* in *English Writings*, p. 72, 358.

187 *Wohunge of Ure Lauerd*, p. xx.

188 *European Literature and the Latin Middle Ages* (New York, 1953), p. 535.

189 See Lüers, op. cit., pp. 197ff.

190 On Dante and Francis see E.G. Gardner, *Dante and the Mystics* (London, 1913), p. 12.

191 See D. Brewer, *Chaucer in His Time* (London, 1963), p. 145.

192 *Cloud*, p. 55, 9.

193 Ibid., p. 50, 11.

194 Ibid., p. 51. 20.

195 *Deonise HD*, p. 65, 22ff.

196 *Revelations* (LV), ch. 39, p. 157, 2f.

197 Ibid., (LV), ch. 83, p. 302, 7f.

198 Ibid., (LV), ch. 77, p. 290, 2ff.

199 On this point see *MED*, s.v. 'courteis' and 'courteisie'.

200 *Scale I*, ch. 49, p. 177, 21.

201 E.g. by D. Knowles, *The English Mystics* (London, 1927), p. 73.

202 F. Comper, *The Life of Richard Rolle together with an Edition of his English Lyrics* (London, 1928), pp. 155f. In her edition of the *Mirror of Simple Souls* C. Kirchberger maintained (p. 202) that the 'þoughtes of partie', referred to on one occasion in the text (p. 335, 7), were probably a reference to the *jeux partis* of the French *cours d'amour*, and thus an an image from the courtly realm. This is, however, unfortunately not the case, since the original French text of the *Mirror* has 'pensees de devocion' for these 'þoughtes of partie' (R. Guarnieri, *Il movimento del Libero Spirito* (Rome, 1965), p. 256, 6).

203 'Weltliche Lyrik im 13. und 14. Jahrhundert', *Epochen der englischen Lyrik* (Dusseldorf, 1970), pp. 55ff.

Chapter IV Metaphors for the preparation for the unio mystica

1 See E. Underhill, *Mysticism* (London, 12th edn, 1930), pp. 298 ff.

2   See J. Bernhart, *Die Philosophische Mystik des Mittelalters* (Munich, 1922), p. 70.

3   See J. Sudbrack, *Die geistliche Theologie des Johannes von Kastl* (Munster, 1966-7), I, p. 315.

4   See ibid., I, p. 317; the Stoics were also familiar with the motif of 'God in us' — it is found, for instance, in Seneca's Letters to Lucilius (Letter 41).

5   Conf. VII, 16; see also C. Butler, *Western Mysticism* (London, 3rd edn, 1967), p. 31.

6   On this point see Sudbrack, op. cit., I, pp. 314ff.

7   *English Writings*, p. 117, 6.

8   In *Chastising*, p. 232.

9   *Mirror*, p. 270.

10 Quoted from K. Berger, *Die Ausdrücke der Unio Mystica im Mittelhachdeutschen* (Berlin, 1935), p. 36.

11 *Scale I*, ch. 40, p. 154, 25f.

12 Plato, *Phaidon, Platonis Opera*, ed. J. Burnet (Oxford, 1958), I, 67 c.

13 Butler, *Western Mysticsm*, p. 99.

14 F. Comper, ed., *The Fire of Love or Melody of Love and The Mending of Life or Rule of Living*, translated by Richard Misyn from the *'Incendium Amoris'* and the *'De Emendatione Vitae'* of Richard Rolle, Hermit of Hampole (London, 1914), p. xxi.

15 *Emendatio Vitae*, MS. Bodl. 16, f. 51^V.

16 *Mending of Life* in *Fire of Love*, p. 107, 12.

17 *English Writings*, p. 116, 11f.

18 *Mirror of Simple Souls*, p. 251, 24. Hilton occasionally uses the compound 'wiþdrawen' (*Scale II*, ch. 30, p. 123, 15).

19 *Cloud*, p. 121, 5f.

20 The mystics sometimes describe the opposite of spiritual concentration — being distracted and diverted by the creatural world — as a flowing away of the soul. For Rolle's 'Vide ne cogitationibus vanis diffluas' of his *Emendatio Vitae* (f. 10), Misyn in his translation uses the verb *flowen*: 'Se þat þou flow nott with vayn þoghtis' (*Fire of Love*, p. 115, 4f.). (Incidentally the *MED* in its entry for the verb *flowen* quotes this passage under rubric 5c) 'to swim (in wealth, pleasure, etc), be affluent', whereas it really ought to be listed under rubric 5b) 'to be unstable, fluctuate'.)

21 See E. Gilson, *L'éspirit de la philosophie médiévale*, Etudes de philosophie médiévale, 33 (Paris, 2nd edn, 1948), pp. 214ff.

22 *Sancti Bernardi Opera*, II, p. 16, 12ff.

23 *Scale I*, ch. 40, p. 154, 24ff.

24 Ibid., ch. 40, p. 155, 6.

25 Ibid., ch. 79, p. 228, 1ff. (editor's brackets).

26 Ibid., ch. 80, p. 228, 20ff. (editor's brackets).

27 J. Bernhart, op. cit., p. 82; original emphasis.

28 Ibid., p. 83; original italics.

29 *Melos Amoris*, p. 39, 4.

30 Ibid., p. 147, 8f.

31 *Emendatio Vitae*, MS. Bodl. 16, f.76^V.

32 Bernhart, *Philosophische Mystik*, p. 83.

33 Ibid.

34 *Die Predigten Taulers*, ed. F. Vetter (Berlin, 1910), p. 62, 13f.
35 *English Psalter*, p. 169.
36 *A Ladder of Foure Ronges*, in *Deonise HD*, p. 107, 16f.
37 *Scale II*, ch. 36, p. 160, 6ff.
38 *Fire of Love*, p. 9, 15f.
39 Ibid., p. 8, 18f.
40 *Mending of Life* in *Fire of Love*, p. 129, 38.
41 In *Deonise HD*, p. 75, 4f. For the religious meaning of *voiden* the *OED* lists only one quotation from Wyclif. The Middle English translation of the *Mystica Theologia* of the pseudo-Dionysius renders *vacatione* (*Deonise HD*, p. 96, 15) as *avoiding* (*Deonise HD*, p. 5).
42 He only uses *voiden* in the sense of *vacare* on one other occasion – in the *Book of Privy Counselling* (*Cloud*, p. 152, 6f.).
43 We find this image for the first time in the *Cloud*, p. 24, 3.
44 *Chastising*, p. 130, 20ff. (editors' brackets). The words 'bar', 'bareyn', 'baren', 'bareness' occur in the same mystical context instead of 'voide', 'voiden', 'voidaunce' for instance in Hilton's *Scale*, where the soul is informed that it is not truly humble unless it can 'noȝten himself, & baren him fro alle þe gode dedis' (*Scale II*, ch. 20, p. 67, 21f.).
45 *Deonise HD*, p. 76, 18.
46 *Scale II*, ch. 24, p. 90, 17f.
47 *Troilus and Criseyde*, III, lines 1405f. *The Works of Geoffrey Chaucer*, ed. F.N. Robinson (London, 2nd edn, 1957), p. 436.
48 *Piers Plowman*, B text, Prol. 57, ed. W.W. Skeat, *EETS*, OS, 38 (1869), p. 3, 57.
49 *Scale II*, ch. 24, p. 90, 19ff.
50 Quoted from Schmidt, op. cit., p. 152*.
51 Ibid., p. 142, 18f.
52 Eckhart, *Deutsche Werke*, II, 549, 29; see also Berger, op. cit., p. 44, and A. Nicklas, *Die Terminologie des Mystikers Heinrich Seuse* (dissertation, Königsberg, 1914), p. 40.
53 See Lüers, op. cit., p. 145.
54 *Cloud*, p. 136, 24ff.
55 Ibid., note 17/2, p. 185.
56 Ibid., p. 17, 2.
57 Ibid., p. 136, 2f.; see also Hodgson's note p. 205.
58 Ibid., p. 143, 10f.
59 Ibid., p. 155, 27ff.
60 *Scale I*, ch. 25, p. 128, 5ff. (editor's brackets).
61 *Chastising*, p. 242, 21f. This corresponds to the 'bloter wiseloser minnen' of Ruysbroeck's original text (*Werken*, III, 19, 29f.)
62 *Offenbarungen der Schwester Mechthild von Magdeburg*, p. 44.
63 *Die Sprache der deutschen Mystik*, p. 220.
64 Quoted from Lüers, op. cit., p. 207.
65 *Scale II*, ch. 31, p. 135, 16ff.
66 *Privy Counselling*, p. 156, 16ff.; in the *Mirror of Simple Souls*, too, the soul is 'nakid', stripped of everything material, creatural, and in this state it is 'cloþed of þe liif of glorie' (p. 303, 9ff.).
67 R. Reitzenstein, *Die hellenistischen Mysterienreligionen nach ihren Grund-*

gedanken und Wirkungen Stuttgart, 3rd edn, 1927), p. 263.

68 *Revelations* (LV), ch. 5, p. 66, 10f.
69 *Cloud*, p. 25, 10ff. (editor's brackets).
70 *Meister Eckhart: Deutsche Werke*, ed. J. Quint (Stuttgart, 1958), I, p. 152, 6ff.
71 On this point see, for instance, Bernhart, *Philosophische Mystik*, p. 82.
72 *Scale II*, ch. 27, p. 110, 9; see also Lüers, op. cit., pp. 232f.
73 See Hilton, *Scale II*, ch. 37, p. 165, 4.
74 *Mirror of Simple Souls*, p. 293, 23f.
75 See Lüers, op. cit., p. 233.
76 Quoted from C. Kirmisse, *Die Terminologie des Mystikers Johannes Tauler* (Leipzig, 1930), p. 40; see also Berger, op. cit., pp. 123f. and O. Zirker, *Die Bereicherung des deutschen Wortschatzes durch die Spätmittelalterliche Mystik* (Jena, 1923), pp. 42 and 75.
77 *Werken*, III, pp. 25, 3f.
78 *Privy Counselling*, p. 149, 13.
79 *Mirror of Simple Souls*, p. 259, 12f.
80 *Scale II*, ch. 24, p. 88, 9ff.
81 *Scale II*, ch. 27, p. 110, 6.
82 *Privy Counselling*, p. 149, 13ff.
83 *Cloud*, p. 122, 13f.
84 *Mirror of Simple Souls*, p. 315, 15f.
85 *Revelations* (LV), ch. 28, p. 131, 1.
86 *Revelations* (LV), ch. 5, p. 66, 15ff.
87 *Cloud*, p. 24, 3. Hodgson draws attention to the similar concept of the 'nebula oblivionis' in Richard of St Victor (p. lxii).
88 *Cloud*, p. 121, 13f.
89 *Cloud*, p. 122, 6f. (editor's brackets).
90 Quoted from Lüers op. cit., p. 232. E. Colledge failed to notice this exact linguistic parallel when he compared the *Cloud* with Mechthild and saw a correspondence only in her 'ze nihte werden' ('Mechthild of Magdeburg', *The Month*, N.S. 25 (1961), p. 329).
91 *Cloud*, p. 25, 13ff.; there is a great affinity here between the *Cloud* and the tract *The Chastising of God's Children*, where the aim is also that the contemplative should 'in nothynge elles . . . hafe desyre ne wille bot onely in god' (*Chastising*, p. 230, 28f.). This is reminiscent of Dante's formulation: 'E'n la sua volontade è nostra pace' (*Commedia*, Paradiso, III, 85). But it also reveals a thematic connection with the great poetry of Jacopone da Todi who defines spiritual poverty as 'nulla avere — e nulla cosa poi volere . . . en spirito de libertate.' (*Le Laude*, ed. L. Fallacara (Florence, 1955), p. 202).
92 *Deutsche Werke*, II, p. 78, 3ff.
93 Ibid., II, p. 31, 19.
94 Ibid., II, p. 493, 35f. See also E. Soudek, *Meister Eckhart* (Stuttgart, 1973), p. 42. The Frankfurter's *Theologia Germanica* also follows Eckhart in this (*Eine deutsche Theologie*, modernized by J. Bernhart (Munich, no year)), p. 147.
95 *Mirror of Simple Souls*, p. 290, 20ff.
96 Ibid., p. 297, 32.
97 *Cloud*, p. 124, 1.

Chapter V Metaphors for the way of the soul to God

1 *Scale II*, ch. 21-5, pp. 70ff.
2 *Ancrene Wisse*, p. 88.
3 *Melos Amoris*, p. 156, 11f.
4 *Privy Counselling*, p. 146, 26.
5 See, for instance, *Conf.*, X.35.
6 See J. Kaup in *Itinerarium Mentis in Deum. De Reductione Artium ad Theologiam* (Munich, 1961), p. 29.
7 Quoted from Lüers, op. cit., p. 292.
8 *Yorkshire Writers*, I, p. 244.
9 *Deonise HD*, p. 72, 20f.
10 E.g. *Cloud*, p. 14, 13; *Incendium Amoris*, p. 210; *Qui Habitat*, p. 39, 1f.; *The Myroure of Oure Ladye*, ed. J.H. Blunt, *EETS*, ES, 19 (1873), p. 206.
11 On this point see Schmidt, op. cit., p. 136*.
12 See D. Jones, *Minor Works of Walter Hilton* (London, 1929), p. 105 and Hodgson, *Cloud*, note 14, 13-14, p. 183.
13 *A Ladder of Foure Ronges*, ed. P. Hodgson in *Deonise HD*, p. 115, 23.
14 *Ancrene Wisse*, p. 69.
15 'ley þi foot of loue in holis of this tree', MS. BL. Harley 2254, f. 4^r.
16 *Cloud*, p. 26, 8ff.
17 *Melos Amoris*, p. 58, 2f.
18 *Cloud*, p. 126, 25ff.; cf. also Hodgson's comment in her introduction, p. lxxiv.
19 Mechthild of Magdeburg, for instance, tells us that the blessed 'vliegent und klimment', Ruysbroeck speaks of an 'op clymmen in dat rike Gods' and in Mechthild man has an 'ufstigende gerunge' (quoted from Lüers, op. cit., p. 275f.).
20 *Form of Living* in *English Writings*, p. 96, 1 (editor's brackets).
21 *Ancrene Wisse*, p. 59, 10f.
22 *Scale I*, ch. 5, p. 92, 1ff.
23 Quoted from Lüers, op, cit., p. 275.
24 *Privy Counselling*, p. 135, 20f.; see also *Cloud*, p. 18, 9. Hodgson points out parallels to this in Rolle's definition of love in his *Commandment*: 'lufe es a wilful stiryng of owre thoght in til god', and in the prologue of the *Mystica Theologia*: 'Extensio animae in Deum per amoris desiderium' (*Cloud*, p. 185, note 17/2).
25 *Scale II*, ch. 32, p. 141, 4ff.
26 'Trahe me post te, *curremus* / In odorem unguentorum tuorum' (S. of S. 1:3).
27 See Hugh of St Victor: 'Currebant ergo, mundum post se reliquerant, Deum ante se habebant' (*De Laude Charitatis*, *PL*, 176, 972); in the Purgatorio of Dante's *Commedia* the souls are urged: 'Correte al monte a spogliarvi lo scoglio / ch' esser non lascia a voi Dio manifesto' (*Canto* II, 122f.).
28 Quoted from Berger, op. cit., p. 40.
29 *Cloud*, p. 112, 13f. In her note 112/14, p. 201, Hodgson draws attention to similar statements in Augustine, and stresses that *ronne* is a literal translation of Latin *currere* in the mystical meaning which it has, for instance, in Hugh of St Victor.

30   *English Writings*, p. 71, 330ff.

31   *Melos Amoris*, p. 89, 4.

32   Ibid., p. 69, 32.

33   Ibid., p. 79, 35.

34   In the *Incendium Amoris*, for instance, we read that the souls 'concurrunt in canticum clari concentus' (p. 158).

35   On this point see F. Ohly, *Hohelied-Studien* (Wiesbaden, 1958), p. 139.

36   *Incendium Amoris*, p. 276, 6ff.

37   Quoted from Lüers, op. cit., p. 261.

38   Ibid.

39   *Form of Living* in *English Writings*, p. 105, 13f.

40   *A Talkyng of þe Loue of God*, p. 60, 22f.

41   Muschg mentions this in his book, *Die Mystik in der Schweiz 1200-1500* (Frauenfeld, 1935), p. 117. See also Tauler's passionate statement: 'ich suochen, ich meinen, ich iagen got' (*Die Predigten Taulers*, p. 413).

42   In *Middle English Religious Prose*, ed. N.F. Blake (London, 1972), p. 138, 149ff.; see also *Ayenbite of Inwyt*, ed. R. Morris, *EETS*, OS, 23 (1866), 2nd edn by P. Gradon (1965), I, p. 75: 'Þe holy man yernþ ase grugibd, Þet habbeþ alday hare eȝe / to heuene .... And þeruore hy uoryeteþ alle oþre guodes. ase deþ þe gentyl hond: huanne ha zyþ his praye / touore his eȝen.'

43   *Cloud*, p. 87, 20.

44   Ibid., lines 18f.

45   Ibid., lines 20ff.

46   See, for instance, Ps. 54:7; 103:3; 138:9.

47   In his Dialogue *Phaidros*, 249d.e.

48   See E.G. Gardner, *Dante and the Mystics* (London, 1913), p. 174.

49   *Ancrene Wisse*, p. 69, 22ff.

50   *Offenbarungen der Schwester Mechthild von Magdeburg*, p. 273.

51   *The Bee and the Stork* in *English Writings*, p. 55, 40ff.

52   *Melos Amoris*, p. 5, 20.

53   Ibid., p. 179, 20.

54   Ibid., p. 191, 22f.

55   *Cloud*, p. 15, 20ff.

56   Ibid., p. 34, 8ff.

57   MS. Pembroke College 221, f. 9^v.

58   Quoted from H. Graef, *The Light and the Rainbow* (London, 1959), p. 188.

59   *Cloud*, p. 126, 23f.

60   Ibid., p. 28, 19f.; see also Hilton, *Scale II*, ch. 23, p. 83.

61   *Cloud*, p. 26, 11f. In her note 26, 11-12, p. 187, Hodgson draws attention to a parallel statement in *Discrecioun of Stirings*.

62   *Cloud*, p. 38, 12ff.

63   *Discrecioun of Stirings* in *Deonise HD*, p. 72, 22f. (brackets added by the editor).

64   Ibid., lines 12f.

65   Quoted from Lüers, op. cit., p. 223.

66   *Deonise HD*, p. 72, 14ff.

67   *Eight Chapters on Perfection*, p. 6.

68   *Mirror of Simple Souls*, p. 323, 11f.

69   *Offenbarungen der Schwester Mechthild von Magdeburg*, p. 104.
70   In *English Writings*, p. 69, 257f.
71   *Meditations* (Lindquist), p. 43, 17ff.
72   *Cloud*, p. 34, 20f.
73   *Christus und die minnende Seele* (Breslau, 1908), p. 62; In addition Banz draws attention to a passage in Bonaventure: 'Illabi enim menti nulli possibile est nisi soli Deo, qui eam creavit.' (Ibid.)
74   *Incendium Amoris*, p. 152, 15ff. Misyn translates this passage with the words: 'O my god, o my lufe! in-to me scrith with þi charite þirlyd, with þi bewte wounded; sclyde doune & comforth me heuy' (*Fire of Love*, p. 7, 23ff.).

Chapter VI Metaphors for speaking about God in English Mysticism

1   J. Alfaro in *Handbuch theologischer Grundbegriffe*, ed. H. Fries, 2nd edn (Munich, 1970), II, p. 217; on the theme 'God' see also the article 'Dieu' in *DSAM*, III.
2   Alfaro in *Handbuch theologischer Grundbegriffe*, II, p. 217.
3   See Lüers, op. cit., pp. 128, 131 and 196, 206.
4   See, for instance, Rolle's *Incendium Amoris*, p. 32; *Cloud*, p. 75.
5   *Book of M. Kempe*, p. 161, 13f.
6   Quoted from Lüers, op. cit., p. 197.
7   *A Song of the Love of Jesus* in *English Writings*, p. 43, 8.
8   *Melos Amoris*, p. 83, 24f.
9   Ibid., p. 3, 10.
10   Ibid., p. 57, 20.
11   On this point see H.E. Allen, 'The Mystical Lyrics of the Manuel des Pechiez', *Romanic Review*, 9 (1918), p. 169.
12   *Melos Amoris*, p. 95, 18.
13   Ibid., p. 50, 13.
14   Ibid., p. 55, 10.
15   Ibid., p. 91, 11.
16   The interpretation of the *Glossa Ordinaria* and William of St Thierry will also have had an influence (see Schmidt, op. cit., p. 134*).
17   This has its counterpart in Germany in mystics like Tauler who like to call God or Christ a 'herre'. (See A. Vogt- Terhorst, *Der bildliche Ausdruck in den Predigten Johann Taulers* (Dissertation Marburg, 1919), p. 8.)
18   *Revelations* (LV), ch. 51, p. 190, 9ff.
19   Ibid., ch. 51, p. 196, 9f.
20   Ibid., p. 197, 15ff.
21   Ibid., p. 199, 13ff.
22   Ibid., p. 187.
23   In *Heinrich Seuse. Studien zum 600 Geburtstag*, ed. E.M. Filthaut (Cologne 1966), p. 258.
24   Huizinga, *The Waning of the Middle Ages* (Harmondsworth, 1979), p. 260.
25   See G. Heinz-Mohr, *Lexikon der Symbole* (Dusseldorf, 2nd edn. 1972), p. 101f.
26   See A. Vértes in *Heinrich Seuse*, ed. Filthaut, p. 263.

27 See Lüers, op. cit., p. 186f.
28 See *MED*, s.v. 'leche'.
29 Rolle, *Meditations (English Writings)*, p. 27, 266.
30 See R. Arbesmann, 'The Concept of "Christus Medicus" in St Augustine', *Traditio*, 10 (1954), pp. 1ff.
31 *Privy Counselling*, p. 138, 28f.
32 *Cloud*, note 138/28, p. 206.
33 Coleman, too, has already admired the originality of this image (*English Mystics of the Fourteenth Century* (London, 1938), p. 104).
34 See *MED*, s.v. 'god'.
35 J. Ratzinger in *Handbuch theologischer Grundbegriffe*, III, p. 46.
36 See Ratzinger, op. cit., pp. 49f. and also F. von Hügel, *The Mystical Element of Religion as Studied in Saint Catherine of Genoa and her Friends* (London, 1909), II, p. 93.
37 Lüers, op. cit., pp. 262ff.
38 *Scale II*, ch. 26, p. 101, 10f.
39 See, for instance, *Scale II*, ch. 26, p. 101, 11ff.
40 Ibid., p. 101, 19ff.
41 *Melos Amoris*, pp. 110, 20; 109, 26ff.
42 See especially Lüers, op. cit., pp. 213ff.
43 *Melos Amoris*, p. 80, 20.
44 Ibid., p. 69, 18.
45 *A Song of Mercy*, in *English Writings*, p. 40, 15.
46 J. Koch, 'Über die Lichtsymbolik im Bereich der Philosophie und der Mystik des Mittelalters', *Studium Generale*, 13 (1960), p. 656.
47 Quoted from Koch, 'Über die Lichtsymbolik . . . ', p. 656.
48 *Privy Counselling* in *Cloud*, p. 154, 17.
49 *Scale II*, ch. 40, p. 181, 16.
50 *Cloud*, p. 122, 11f.
51 *Scale II*, ch. 27, p. 112, 15f.
52 Ibid., ch. 32, p. 138, 16ff. On this question of knowledge of God Hodgson constructs a contrast between the author of the *Cloud* and Hilton which is not really there, 'Walter Hilton and "The Cloud of Unknowing" ', *MLR*, 50 (1955), p. 402.
53 *Revelations* (LV), ch. 82, p. 301, 2.
54 *Scale II*, ch. 27, p. 112, 3.
55 Ibid., ch. 24, p. 87, 9.
56 *Revelations* (LV), ch. 82, p. 302, 6f.
57 E.g. John 1:4; 15:9; 8:12.
58 *Revelations* (LV), ch. 82, p. 303, 10f.
59 Quoted from Koch, 'Über die Lichtsymbolik . . . ', p. 663.
60 Ibid., p. 657. On fire in pseudo-Dionysius see also F. von Hügel, *The Mystical Element of Religion*, II, p. 94 and *DSAM*, V, pp. 247ff., s.v. 'feu'.
61 *Emendatio Vitae*, MS. Bodl. 16, f. 63^r; Misyn translates as 'fyryd', *Fire of Love*, p. 118, 37.
62 *Incendium Amoris*, p. 240, 15.
63 Ibid., p. 278, 5; Misyn translates this term with the adjective 'firy' (*Fire of Love*, p. 103, 23).
64 *Incendium Amoris*, p. 156, 5f.

65 *Cloud*, p. 62, 17; Hilton, e.g. *Scale I*, ch. 75, p. 224; *Book of M. Kempe*, e.g. p. 29, 18; 70, 21f. *Mirror of Simple Souls*: 'þis soule . . . is so brent in þe fornays of þe fier of loue þat sche is bicome fier', p. 277, 17f.

66 Eph. 3:18f.: 'ut possitis comprehendere . . . quae sit latitudo, et longitudo, et sublimitas, et profundum: scire etiam supereminentem scientiae caritatem Christi'.

67 *Die Predigten Taulers*, p. 367f.

68 See, for instance, Dante's *Commedia*, Paradiso, X, 1ff., and K. Ruh, 'Die trinitarische Spekulation in deutscher Mystik und Scholastik', *ZfdPh*, 72 (1953), p. 29, note 14, where there are references to various traditional passages.

69 On this point see Lüers, op. cit., p. 157ff.

70 Quoted from Lüers, op. cit., p. 159.

71 *Revelations* (LV), ch. 11, p. 89, 1.

72 Ibid., p. 90, 3f.; see also the extensive footnote by Warrack on her edition of *Revelations of Divine Love*, 13th edn (London, 1949), p. 26, where there is a reference to Dante's use of this range of metaphors.

73 *Revelations* (LV), ch. 63, p. 249, 15f.

74 'Some Literary Influences in the Revelations of Julian of Norwich (c. 1343-post 1416)', *Leeds Studies in English*, 7 (1952), p. 24.

75 *Vanden VII Sloten* in *Werken*, III, p. 116, 19f. (editor's brackets); E. Underhill also points out the affinity of motif in *The Essentials of Mysticism* (London, 1920), p. 194.

76 *Sancti Bernardi Opera*, I, p. 110, 18f.

77 Quoted from Lüers, op. cit., p. 104.

78 Ibid., p. 225.

79 *Orchard of Syon*, p. 357, 25f.

80 *Mirror of Simple Souls*, p. 294, 5f.

81 Lüers, op. cit., p. 293.

82 Ibid., p. 294.

83 In the homiletic, mystical tract *xii. frutes of the holy goost*, for example, there is a reference to the solitude of 'contemplacioun in god' as found in Ps. 54:8, and this is described as a 'wildirnis' (*the tree & xii. frutes of the holy goost*, ed. I.I. Vaissier (Groningen, 1960), p. 100, 23f.).

84 Quoted from Lüers, op. cit., p. 293.

85 'The Mystic as Creative Artist', *The Essentials of Mysticism* (London, 1920), p. 74.

86 Schmidt, op. cit., p. 139, 20f.

87 1 Cor. 2:10.

88 See Lüers, op. cit., p. 119.

89 *PL*, 158, 760.

90 Quoted from Lüers, op. cit., p. 120.

91 Schmidt, op. cit., p. 116, 20.

92 *Comment on the Canticles*, f.112, p. 17, 22ff.

93 *Scale I*, ch. 51, p. 180, 1ff.

94 For the use of this term in German mysticism see especially H. Kunisch, *Das Wort 'Grund' in der Sprache der deutschen Mystik des 14. und 15. Jahrhunderts* (Diss. Munster, 1929), p. 4.

95 *Mirror of Simple Souls*, p. 275, 30.

96 K. Ruh, 'Die trinitarische Spekulation in der deutschen Mystik und Scholastik', *ZfdPh*, 72 (1953), pp. 33f.

97 *Cloud*, p. 32, 7; *Scale II*. ch. 32. p. 137, 10; *Revelations* (LV), ch. 42, p. 166, 10.

98 *Privy Counselling*, p. 143, 19ff; cf. the *Mirror of Simple Souls*, where we read: 'He is þat is' (p. 335, 9).

99 *Cloud*, p. 207.

100 *Deutsche Werke*, II, p. 372, 3: 'Under allen namen enist kein eigner den "der dâ ist" '.

101 Schmidt, *Die siben strassen zu got*, p. 134, 4ff.

102 Ibid. Apart from the term *essentia* or *esse* the concepts *natura* and *substantia* are frequently used in Latin theology for expressing the divine essence, whereby *substantia*, as Ruh has shown (op. cit., p. 35), is occasionally defined more precisely using the words *subsistentia* and *hypostasis*. Whilst the translation terms used in the Middle High German retain this precision of definition (see Ruh, p. 35f.), there is no comparable distinction in English mysticism. There are, however, the beginnings of such a distinction in Julian's use of *substance* and *grounde*, which we shall examine in a different context later (see pp. 156f.)

103 *Incendium Amoris*, p. 162 ('Sufficit ergo tibi ut cognoscas quod Deus est, et oberit tibi si scire uelis quid Deus est').

104 *Cloud*, p. 32, 7.

105 *Scale II*, ch. 32, p. 137, 10ff.

106 *English Writings*, p. 43, 5.

107 Ibid., p. 79, 222f.

108 *Cloud*, p. 46, 22f.

109 Ibid., p. 113, 8f.

110 *Incendium Amoris*, p. 162ff.

111 *Yorkshire Writers*, II, p. 334, 7.

112 Eckhart, *Deutsche Werke*, II, p. 180, 5ff.

113 *Latin Psalter*, f. 1ᵛ.

114 *De Fide Trinitatis et De Incarnatione Verbi*, ch. 8, *PL*, 158, 280.

115 In his article on trinitary speculation which we have already quoted, *ZfdPh*, 72 (1953), pp. 24ff.

116 *English Psalter*, p. 400 (cf. the commentary on the psalms by Peter Lombard, *PL*, 191, 1021).

117 E.g. *Incendium Amoris*, p. 215: 'Deus infundit ipsam ineffabilem iubilationem'.

118 *Revelations* (LV), ch. 62, p. 248, 9f.

119 Ibid., ch. 12, p. 93, 19ff; for Catherine of Siena see H. Graef, *The Light and the Rainbow* (London, 1959), pp. 252-4.

120 *Revelations* (LV), ch. 59, p. 237, 2ff.; on this motif see A. Cabassut, 'Une dévotion, médiévale peu connue: La dévotion à Iésus notre mère', *RAM*, 25 (1949), pp. 234ff. There is also an article by E. McLaughlin, ' "Christ my Mother" ' (*Nashotah Review*, 15 (1975), pp. 229ff.; summary in the *14th Century English Mystics. Newsletter*, 2 (1976)).

121 'Sola enim Trinitas Deus propter se amanda est' (*Incendium Amoris*, p. 155).

122 *Revelations* (LV), ch. 4, p. 64, 3ff.

123 Ibid., lines 9ff.

124 F. Wulf in *Handbuch theologischer Grundbegriffe*, III, p. 195.

Chapter VII Technical terms for the mystical union and for ecstasy

1 Especially in the extensive article compiled by several authors, 'Extase' in *DSAM*, IV, pp. 2045ff. and in the article 'Ekstase' in *Reallexikon für Antike und Christentum*, ed. T. Klauser (Stuttgart, 1950ff.), IV, col. 944ff. The term 'contemplacio' will be discussed in chapter VIII, 6.

2 *Orcherd of Syon*, e.g. p. 343, 21.

3 *Booke of Gostlye Grace*, p. 94, 10.

4 *Mirror of Simple Souls*, e.g. p. 258, 31.

5 B. Schmoldt, *Die deutsche Begriffssprache Meister Eckharts. Studien zur philosophischen Terminologie des Mittelhochdeutschen* (Heidelberg, 1954), p. 41.

6 *Privy Counselling*, p. 163, 24ff.; Hodgson draws attention to the abundant use of words in '-ing' in the works of the author of the *Cloud* generally (*Deonise HD*, p. lvii).

7 *Revelations* (LV), ch. 58, p. 233, 7f.

8 *Scale I*, ch. 8, p. 96, 2f.

9 See especially Berger, op. cit., pp. 96ff. The *Mirror* is alone in using the term 'uniaunce' (p. 276, 15).

10 Nom. 1, 2, quoted from Schmoldt, *Begriffssprache*, p. 34.

11 S.th.III,2,9c; quoted from Schmoldt, *Begriffssprache*, p. 34, note.

12 Ibid.

13 *Orcherd of Syon*, p. 343, 21f.

14 In *Chastising*, p. 231, 28ff.

15 *Werken*, III, 6, 12f.

16 *Chastising*, note 231, 31, p. 313.

17 *Privy Counselling*, p. 147, 29; see also Hilton, *Of Angels' Song, Yorkshire Writers*, I, p. 172; for *unitas* in Latin mysticism see e.g. *DSAM*, IV, col. 2132.

18 *Privy Counselling*, p. 169, 11ff.

19 In *Chastising*, p. 233, 18.

20 Ms. Pembroke College 221, f.25^v.

21 *Revelations* (LV), ch. 31, p. 134, 17 and ch. 59, p. 237, 16f.

22 *Mirror of Simple Souls*, p. 335, 26.

23 *Privy Counselling*, p. 136, 14f.

24 Ibid., p. 157, 20ff.

25 *Revelations* (LV), ch. 53, p. 218, 13ff.

26 Ibid., ch. 53, p. 219, 10f.

27 Ibid., ch. 5, p. 67, 12.

28 Ibid., ch. 43, p. 168, 18f.

29 Ibid., ch. 44, p. 171, 2f.

30 Ibid., ch. 49, p. 185, 1ff.

31 In Rolle, for instance, we read: 'My lyfe es in langyng, þat byndes me, nyght and day' (*English Writings*, p. 42, 22); the *Cloud* speaks of God having kindled in the soul of the mystic a desire for him and of having secured the soul to him with a cord of desire: '& fastnid bi it a lyame of longing' (*Cloud*, p. 14, 3f.); those adept in mysticism receive the advice: 'Knyt þee þerfore bi him [God] by loue & by beleue' (*Cloud*, p. 21, 14f.); Rolle explains to his reader that as long as she still loves what is earthly 'þou may not per

fitely be coupuld with God' (*English Writings*, p. 61, 16); and in his *English Psalter*, he says the elect 'ere ioynyd til crist in luf' (Ps. 140:7, p. 470).

32 On this point see V. Warnach, 'Liebe', in *Handbuch theologischer Grundbegriffe*, II, p. 64.
33 See *DSAM*, IV, s.v. 'Extase', esp. col. 2113ff.
34 Quoted from *DSAM*, IV, col. 2113.
35 MS. Bodl. 16. f. 75^r.
36 *Mending of Life* in *Fire of Love*, p. 128, 23f.
37 See *DSAM*, IV, col. 2114.
38 '*The Doctrine of the Hert*', ed. M. Candon (unpublished dissertation, New York, 1963), p. 146, 7ff.
39 See Butler, *Western Mysticism*, (London, 3rd edn, 1967), p. 115.
40 *DSAM*, IV, col. 2116ff.
41 *Cloud*, note 150/10, p. 211.
42 *Privy Counselling*, p. 150, 19ff. (editor's brackets).
43 *Cloud*, p. 150, 15.
44 See e.g. Schmidt, op. cit., p. 231*f.
45 *Deonise HD*, p. 3, 12f.
46 *English Psalter*, p. 236 (in Bramley's edition it is Ps. 67:29).
47 *Fire of Love*, p. 30, 38f.
48 *Incendium Amoris*, p. 200.
49 *English Psalter*, p. 15.
50 Ibid., p. 154.
51 *Fire of Love*, p. 44, 23.
52 *Booke of Gostlye Grace*, p. 466.
53 *Orcherd of Syon*, p. 339, 5f.
54 *De Imitatione Christi*, ed. J.K. Ingram, *EETS*, ES, 63 (1893), p. 71, 17.
55 See *DSAM*, IV, col. 2127.
56 Ibid., col. 2124.
57 *Cloud*, p. 47, 17ff.
58 See *DSAM*, IV, col, 2124.
59 Ibid., col. 2127.
60 See, for instance, Hilton, *Scale I*, ch. 46, p. 173, 3f.
61 Ibid., *I*, ch. 8, p. 95, 4ff.
62 See *DSAM*, *IV*, col. 2123.
63 MS. Bodl. 16, f. 71^r.
64 *Incendium Amoris*, p. 271, 28f.
65 *English Writings*, p. 44, 16.
66 See *DSAM*, IV, col. 2127.
67 Quoted from ibid.
68 He discusses this in detail in the fifteenth chapter of his *Incendium Amoris*. On 'raptus' and 'ecstasy' in Rolle see above all Allen, *Writings*, esp. p. 109, and *English Writings*, p. xxviii.
69 *Incendium Amoris*, p. 151, 17f.
70 Ibid., p. 152, 27ff.; 'rauyst' occurs once in Rolle's English works (*English Writings*, p. 119, 68). The *OED* lists only one example for the mystical meaning of the verb 'to ravish', and this is taken from a passage in *Arthur and Merlin*. It has already been pointed out by Gilmour that the *OED* had overlooked this passage in Rolle as the first occurrence for the mystical

meaning of 'to ravish'. ('Notes on the Vocabulary of Richard Rolle', *N&Q*, 201 (1956), pp. 94f.).

71 *Chastising*, p. 170, 24.

72 *Book of M. Kempe*, p. 241. 9f.

73 Ibid., p. 16, 30ff.

74 Ibid., p. 200, 24f.

75 Ibid., p. 11, 23ff.; Allen has already drawn attention to this term and rightly linked it with the mystical *trahere* (*Book of M. Kempe*, note 223/37, p. 342).

76 See Lüers, op. cit., p. 308.

77 *Cloud*, p. 14, 18f.

78 *Booke of Gostlye Grace*, p. 463, 18f. See Rolle's splendid description of the mystical *tractus* in his *Comment on the Canticles* (f. 185, p. 58, 8ff.). Much more rarely the term *draw3t* means the mystical love-potion, as, for instance, in the *Mirror of Simple Souls*, where we read that the souls 'haue taasted of þe swete drawtes of heuenli fluences' (p. 258, 25); see also Allen's note in the *Book of M. Kempe*, p. 342, 223/37 sq.

79 See, for instance, *PL*, 79, 135; on the concept of *familiaritas* in general see especially *DSAM*, V, col. 47ff., s.v. 'familiarité avec Dieu'.

80 Huizinga, *The Waning of the Middle Ages*, (Harmondsworth, 1979), p. 151.

81 Ibid., p. 147.

82 See, for example, *Chastising*, p. 198, 10, where it is explained through the more usual equivalent: 'to moche famuliarite, as for to be to homly'. The same is true of the words *privy* and *privity*, which only occasionally have the meaning *familiaris* and *familiaritas* as in *Ancrene Wisse*, p. 98, 6ff.

83 One of the rare examples is found in the tract *Form of Living*, where Rolle, speaking of God's intimacy with souls, says: 'he es hamlyer to þam þan brother or syster' (*English Writings*, p. 102, 199).

84 Quoted from *MED*, s.v. 'homlines'.

85 *Scale I*, ch. 47, p. 174, 12f.

86 *Cloud*, p. 126, 11f.

87 *8 Chapters on Perfection*, p. 23, 365ff.

88 *Deonise HD*, p. 20, 8ff.

89 *Book of M. Kempe*, p. 90, 10ff.

90 Ibid., p. 79, 8ff.

91 *The tree & xii. frutes of the holy goost*, p. 157, 21ff. The tract is here drawing on Jacobus de Voragine's *Legenda Aurea*.

92 *Meditations on the Supper of Our Lord, and the Hours of the Passion*, ed. J.M. Cowper, *EETS*, OS, 60 (1875), p. 9, 275f. The visual arts, too, have portrayed the intimacy between man and God very impressively in the motif of John resting on Christ's breast, see *Die Christus-Johannes-Gruppen des XIV. Jahrhunderts*, introduction by H. Wentzel (Stuttgart, 1960).

93 *Meditations on the Life and Passion of Christ*, ed. C. D'Evelyn, *EETS*, OS, 158 (1919), p. 2, 29f.

94 *Book of M. Kempe*, p. 44, 26ff.

95 *Revelations* (LV), ch. 60, p. 241, 13ff.

96 Ibid., ch. 7, p. 76, 15ff.; the *MED* points out that Wyclif once uses the noun *homelynesse* as a direct translation term for *mansuetudo*.

97 *Revelations* (LV), ch. 68, p. 263, 9; (SV), ch. 22, p. 45, 11; on this meaning

of *homli* in Julian see P. Molinari, *Julian of Norwich* (London, 1958), p. 149ff. and J. Walsh, 'God's Homely Loving. St. John and Julian of Norwich on the Divine Indwelling', *The Month*, n.s. 19 (1958), pp. 164ff.

98 *Revelations* (LV), ch. 77, p. 290, 2ff.; Hilton, too, uses the word *homli* in the sense of 'belonging to God's court' when he speaks on one occasion of those souls 'wilk arn specialy His seruaunz and more homli of His court . . .' (*Scale I*, ch. 60, p. 195, 4ff.).

99 *Offenbarungen der Schwester Mechthild von Magdeburg*, p. 7.

100 Quoted from Berger, op. cit., p. 88.

101 *Incendium Amoris*, p. 180, 12f.

102 *Melos Amoris*, p. 149, 26ff.

103 *Scale II*, ch. 25, p. 94, 7f.

104 Ibid., ch. 40, p. 185, 22ff.

105 Ibid., ch. 40, p. 186, 8f. (editor's brackets).

106 Ibid., ch. 40, p. 187, 10ff. (editor's brackets).

107 *Incendium Amoris*, p. 248.

108 *Fire of Love*, p. 80, 30.

109 J. Påhlsson, ed., *The Recluse. A Fourteenth Century Version of the Ancrene Riwle*, Lunds Universitets Årsskrift, N.F. 1, vol. 6, 1 (Lund, 1911), p. 39.

110 The same conclusion is reached in the extensive study by M. Herz, *Sacrum Commercium*, Münchener theologische Studien, 15 (Munich, 1958), p. 13f.

111 Ibid., p. 24ff.

112 *Sancti Bernardi Opera*, II, 316, 8.

113 *Incendium Amoris*, p. 214.

114 Quoted from Lüers, op. cit., p. 160.

115 Ibid.

116 Ibid., p. 159.

117 See Herz, op. cit., p. 8.

118 *Fire of Love*, p. 55, 26f.

119 See *MED*, s.v. 'daliaunce'.

120 *Scale II*, ch. 46, p. 226, 3f.

121 On one occasion Hilton speaks of 'curteys dalyaunce' (*Scale II*, ch. 44, p. 217, 20).

122 *Meditations* (Lindquist), p. 44, 22f.

123 *Revelations* (LV), ch. 56, p. 226, 8f.

124 *Book of M. Kempe*, p. 39, 5f.

125 Ibid., p. 2, 30ff.

126 Ibid., p. 40, 1ff.

127 Ibid., p. 67, 23ff.

128 Allen maintains that this term is not found amongst the English mystics except in the last chapter of the *Scale* (*Book of M. Kempe*, p. 256, note 2/32). She also fails to grasp the full meaning of the word when she says that it expresses the 'colloquies reported as from the Divinity' (ibid.).

Chapter VIII The experience of God as a spiritual sense perception

1 On Origen see esp. K. Rahner, 'Le début d'une doctrine des cinq sens spirituels chez Origène', *RAM*, 13 (1932), pp. 113ff. See also the article 'Goût

spirituel' in *DSAM*, VI, col 626ff., to which our study is indebted.

2 Quoted from *DSAM*, V. col. 1548, s.v. 'Fruitio Dei'.

3 See *DSAM*, V, col 1547.

4 See ibid., V, col. 1550.

5 See the comment in ibid., V, col. 1553.

6 *Melos Amoris*, p. 7, 14f.

7 *Thomas à Kempis, De Imitatione Christi*, ed, J.K. Ingram, *EETS*, ES, 63 (1893), p. 126, 12f.

8 *Mirror of Simple Souls*, p. 248, 7f.

9 Ibid., p. 335, 28f.

10 *Booke of Gostlye Grace*, p. 257, 17ff.

11 *Mirror of Simple Souls*, p. 270, 9.

12 Quoted from the *MED*, s.v. 'fruycion'.

13 E.g. *Fire of Love*, p. 13, 15.

14 E.g. *Mending of Life* in *Fire of Love*, p. 124, 24; *Emendatio Vitae*, MS. Bodl. 16, f. 70^r.

15 See *Chastising*, p. 273, note 132/9. On *Chastising* see also De Soer, 'The Relationship of the Latin Versions of Ruysbroeck's "Die Geestelike Brulocht" to "The Chastising of God's Children" ' *MS*, 21 (1959).

16 Ibid., p. 132, 9. In the *Treatise of Perfection of the Sons of God*, the translation of Ruysbroeck's *Vanden Blinckenden Steen*, 'ghebrukelijcke eenicheit gods' is rendered as 'vsable oned of god' (p. 245, 30 and p. 329 note); *ghebruken* is rendered as *vsen* (p. 257, 24) and by the word *fruycioun* (p. 250, 2).

17 *Revelations* (LV), ch. 32, p. 139, 6ff.

18 *Fire of Love*, p. 9, 25.

19 Rolle's text has 'uelociter euanuit omne in quo delectabantur' (*Incendium Amoris*, p. 275, 18), which Misyn translates as 'swyftly vanyschyd all þai inioyd' (*Fire of Love*, p. 101, 24).

20 *The Poems of Robert Southwell*, S.J., ed. J.H. McDonald and N.P. Brown (Oxford, 1967), p. 9.

21 *The Poems English, Latin and Greek of Richard Crashaw*, ed. L.C. Martin (Oxford, 2nd edn, 1957), p. 234.

22 See, for instance, Lüers, op. cit., p. 178.

23 One need only think of the institution of the Eucharist or of Christ's words 'Ego sum panis vitae: qui venit ad me, non esuriet' (John, 6:35).

24 See, for instance, Lüers, p. 178, and Berger, op. cit., pp. 61ff.

25 Underhill already noted that there was an 'almost total absence of Eucharistic references' ('Medieval Mysticism', *Cambridge Medieval History* (1932), VII, p. 805).

26 *Latin Psalter*, F. 48.

27 Ibid., F. 18; on the occurrence of this range of metaphors in German mysticism, see Schmidt, pp. 155*ff.

28 Quoted from Lüers, op. cit., p. 178; see also *Die Predigten Taulers*, p. 294, 21ff.

29 *Revelations* (LV), ch. 43, p. 171, 12ff.

30 In the sixteenth century at the latest, according to the *OED*.

31 See the note by G. Warrack in her edition of the *Revelations*, 13th edn (London, 1949), p. 92.

32   *English Psalter*, p. 53.

33   *English Writings*, p. 70, 316.

34   *Melos Amoris*, p. 129, 24ff.

35   Quoted from Lüers, op. cit., p. 257.

36   *Privy Counselling*, p. 144, 26.

37   In *Deonise HD*, p. 101, 20f.

38   *Privy Counselling*, p. 171, 24f.

39   In the *Melos Amoris* the soul flies to God 'ut fruar in fine festo futuro' (p. 179, 20f.).

40   Thus in Rolle's *Latin Psalter* the soul is described as 'eructans dulcedinem qua intus abundo' — and that through its 'iubilus' (f. 33^V).

41   Quoted from A. Vogt-Terhorst, *Der bildliche Ausdruck in den Predigten Johann Taulers* (Dissertation, Marburg, 1919), p. 90.

42   'Want wisheit ist . . . genemt von gesmake vnd von suzzekeit. . . ' (Schmidt, op. cit., p. 53, 5f.); 'Dirre gesmak lit an einer bekorunge. Aber dis bekorung vnd vnphintnissi mag nieman ze . . . wort bringen . . . . Er mag wol sprechen, daz in dem .salter geschriben ist: "Bekorund vnd enphindent, wie senft vnd wie svesse got ist" ' (op. cit., p. 149, 12ff.); see Schmidt, op. cit., p. 242*.

43   *Book of Wisdom*, 24; 17ff.

44   *Ancrene Wisse*, p. 73, 26ff.

45   *Scale II*, ch. 41, p. 191, 14f.

46   Ibid., ch. 34, p. 153, 11f.

47   *Scale I*, ch. 11, p. 101, 7ff.

48   Quoted from Schmidt, op. cit., p. 242*.

49   *Untersuchungen zur mystischen Terminologie Richard Rolles* (Dissertation, Jena, 1936), p. 10.

50   *English Writings*, p. 114, 217f.

51   *Meditations (English Writings)*, p. 26, 239f.

52   'my body was fulfyllyd of felyng and mynd of cristes passion' (*Revelations* (LV), ch. 55, p. 224, 19f.).

53   *English Writings*, p. 49, 1 (editor's brackets).

54   Ibid., p. 105, 38ff.

55   *Qui Habitat*, p. 5, 4ff.

56   *Revelations* (LV), ch. 71, p. 272, 17ff. The tract *A Talkyng of þe Loue of God* especially seems to have a predilection for the term *felyng* to express its mysticism of Christ in language.

57   *Privy Counselling*, p. 172, 2f.

58   *Chastising*, p. 146, 17ff.

59   *Cloud*, p. 35, 2.

60   See J. Bernhart, *Die philosophische Mystik des Mittelalters von ihren antiken Ursprüngen bis zur Renaissance* (Munich, 1922), p. 96.

61   In his third sermon on the *Song of Songs, Sancti Bernardi Opera*, I, 14, 7.

62   Quoted from Bernhart, *Philosophische Mystik*, p. 99.

63   *Cloud*, p. 86, 18f.

64   Ibid., p. 85, 1f.

65   *Privy Counselling*, p. 156, 7.

66   'Objective Spirituality', *The Life of the Spirit*, 4 (1950), pp. 555ff.

67   *Scale I*, ch. 4, p. 89, 2ff.

68　Ibid., ch. 5, p. 91, 15f.

69　Ibid., ch. 8, p. 95, 2ff. (editor's brackets)

70　*Scale II*, esp. ch. 17, p. 55ff.

71　Ibid., ch. 31, p. 134, 17ff. (editor's brackets); on this point see A.C. Hughes, *Walter Hilton's Direction to Contemplatives* (Dissertation, Rome, 1962), esp. p. 107.

72　Rom. 12:2.

73　*Scale I*, ch. 16, p. 110, 2f.; Quite logically the Latin translation of the *Scale* (MS. Magdalen College Oxford, 141) often uses the terms *amor* and *dilectio* to translate *feling* (e.g. f. 97^v; f. 91^v); other translation terms which also occur several times are *apprehensio* (e.g. f. 90^r), *experientia* (e.g. f. 92^v) and *gustus* (e.g. f. 90^v).

74　*Scale I*, ch. 13, p. 105, 1.

75　MS. Magdalen College, Oxford, 141, f. 91^r.

76　*Book of M. Kempe*, p. 25, 25.

77　*Scale I*, ch. 10, pp. 98, 14; 99, 4.

78　Julian, for instance, speaks of 'swete gostly syghtes and felynges' (*Revelations* (LV), ch. 43, p. 171, 7), and we read in Margery Kempe: 'sche schuld . . . makyn a booke of hyr felyngys & hir reuelacyons' (*Book of M. Kempe*, p. 3, 24f.). The tract *The Chastising of God's Children*, which distinguishes between genuine and false visions, explains to the reader that it is a sign of the genuineness of visions if in them he 'feeliþ in his soule a sodeyne goostli þing spryngyng wiþ an inwarde feelyng, and a knowyng of sooþfastnesse, what it meeneþ and bitokeneþ . . . ' (p. 179, 4ff.). It is clear from the probable source for this passage, the *Epistola Solitarii ad Reges* of Alphonse of Pecha that this 'inwarde feelyng' implies an inner illumination, for Alphonse says of the soul that it 'sentit influxum intellectualis supernaturalis luminis intelligibilis veritatis (quoted from *Chastising*, p. 290, note 179.3).

79　See esp. Matt. 9:20 and John 20:11-17.

80　Matt. 9:20.

81　*Privy Counselling*, p. 139, 1ff.

82　*Scale II*, ch. 44, p. 216, 18.

83　Ibid., ch. 46, p. 225, 8ff.

84　*Meditations (English Writings)*, p. 36, 279ff.

85　*Revelations* (LV), ch. 77, p. 289, 19.

86　Quoted from Lüers, op. cit., p. 243.

87　Ibid., p. 244.

88　*Book of M. Kempe*, p. 214, 1f.

89　Ibid., p. 208, 21ff.

90　Ibid., line 23f.

91　Quoted from Berger, op. cit., p. 60; on this motif see also Lüers, op. cit., p. 243f. and Zirker, *Die Bereicherung des deutschen Wortschatzes durch die spätmittelalterliche Mystik* (Jena, 1923), p. 23.

92　*Das fliessende Licht der Gottheit*, p. 76.

93　*Scale I*, ch. 30, p. 135, 17ff. (editor's brackets).

94　Ibid *II*, ch. 29, p. 119, 12f.

95　Ibid., lines 15ff.

96　*Privy Counselling*, p. 151, 7ff.; see also *Scale II*, 193, 3.

97 *Revelations* (LV), ch. 81, p. 298, 17f.
98 'Some Literary Influences in the Revelations of Julian of Norwich (c. 1342-post-1416)', *Leeds Studies in English*, 7 (1952), 23.
99 *Mirror of Simple Souls*, p. 304, 2f.
100 Ibid., p. 279, 15f.
101 *Chastising*,p. 255, 26f.
102 See S. of S. 1:2; 1:3; 1:11; 2:13; 3:6; 4:10; 6:1.
103 *Confessiones* X: 27.
104 *Le Laude*, ed. L. Fallacara (Florence, 1955), p. 356.
105 Quoted from Lüers, op. cit., p. 258.
106 *Emendatio Vitae*, MS. Bodl. 16, f. 73^v.
107 *Melos Amoris*, p. 83, 24f.; see also *Melos Amoris*, p. 49, 37; 100, 3; 119, 25f.
108 *Qui Habitat*, p. 85, 7.
109 *Scale II*, ch. 42, p. 201, 15ff.; see also Rolle's *Latin Psalter*: 'fumus aromatum est orationes sanctorum' (f. 79).
110 *Revelations* (LV), ch. 43, p. 171, 12ff.
111 Ibid., ch. 67, p. 261, 18ff.
112 *Seinte Marherete. Pe Meiden and Martyre*, ed. F.M. Mack, *EETS, OS*, 193 (1933), p. 27, 2ff.
113 *Orcherd of Syon*, p. 199, 27.
114 *Book of M. Kempe*, p. 87, 31.
115 Ibid., p. 51, 32f.
116 *Ancrene Wisse*, p. 52, 10ff.
117 Ibid., p. 53, 7ff.
118 *Melos Amoris*, p. 149, 26ff.
119 *Scale II*, ch. 46, p. 226, 16ff. (editor's brackets).
120 Ibid., lines 12ff.; on this point see also A.C. Hughes, *Walter Hilton's Direction to Contemplatives* (Dissertation, Rome, 1962), pp. 128ff.
121 *Scale II*, ch. 46, p. 226. 5f.
122 Quoted from Berger, op. cit., p. 71.
123 Schmidt, op. cit., p. 35, 18f. Schmidt suggests as further starting points for this range of metaphors Hos. 2:14; S. of S. 2:8 and Gregory the Great's exegesis on 1 John 2:27; John 14:16 (p. 161*).
124 Hilton's translation of the *Stimulus Amoris*, MS. Harley, 2254, f. 3^r.
125 *Book of M. Kempe*, p. 50, 33.
126 Ibid., p. 90, 10ff.
127 Ibid., p. 98, 25f.
128 Ibid., p. 39, 6f.
129 Ibid., p. 90, 35ff.
130 Ibid., p. 91, 6ff.
131 On this point see Lüers, op. cit., p. 229.
132 *De rerum naturis et verborum proprietatibus et de mystica rerum significatione*, quoted from R. Assunto, *Die Theorie des Schönen im Mittelalter* (Cologne, 1963), p. 141.
133 See Assunto, *Die Theorie des Schönen*, p. 166f.
134 *Book of M. Kempe*, p. 90, 34f.
135 *Revelations* (LV), ch. 14, p. 97, 18f.
136 Quoted from Lüers, op. cit., p. 230; Butler points out that Augustine also

describes the mystical experience as music (*Western Mysticism*, 3rd edn (London, 1967), p. 25).

137 *Incendium Amoris*, p. 189, 7ff.

138 See, for instance, the works of F. Schulte, *Das musikalische Element in der Mystik Richard Rolles von Hampole* (Dissertation, Bonn, 1951) and S.J. Womack, *The Jubilus Theme in the Later Writings of Richard Rolle of Hampole* (unpublished dissertation, Durham, N.C., 1961).

139 *Form of Living* in *English Writings*, p. 106, 46.

140 *Incendium Amoris*, p. 245, 26.

141 *Das musikalische Element in der Mystik Richard Rolles von Hampole*, p. 66.

142 Quoted from Lüers, op. cit., p. 229. Lüers, however, wrongly attributes the *Compendium* to Hugh of St Victor. To indicate that this experience depends on divine initiative, Rolle compares himself with a flute which is pouring out music (*Incendium Amoris*, p. 277, 16ff.).

143 See A. Hahn, *Quellenuntersuchungen zu Richard Rolles englischen Schriften* (dissertation, Halle, 1900), p. 8.

144 *Melos Amoris*, p. 140, 20f.

145 *Incendium Amoris*, p. 244, 22f.

146 Misyn translates: 'a soundly Ioy to me suld schyne', *Fire of Love*, p. 77, 29.

147 *Melos Amoris*, p. 20, 21f.

148 On this point see, for instance, D. Brewer, *Chaucer in his Time* (London, 1963), p. 179f.

149 Ps 41:5. Bernard of Clairvaux, for instance, also refers to this verse in his famous fifteenth sermon on the *Song of Songs*, in which he calls upon the world to rejoice at the name of Jesus 'et unus ubique resonet in voce exsultationis et confessionis sonus epulantis: OLEUM EFFUSUM NOMEN TUUM' (*Sancti Bernardi Opera*, I, pp. 84ff.).

150 *Melos Amoris*, p. 138, 3ff.

151 Ibid., p. 139, 3ff.

152 *Scale II*, ch. 21, p. 73, 3ff.

153 On this point see W. Stammler, 'Studien zur Geschichte der Mystik in Norddeutschland', Ruh, op. cit., p. 409.

154 'Studien zur Geschichte der Mystik in Norddeutschland', p. 409.

155 *Offenbarungen der Schwester Mechthild von Magdeburg*, p. 62.

156 See Lüers, op. cit., p. 230; see also Hilton's *8 Chapters on Perfection*, p. 16, 238 and *The Myroure of Oure Ladye*, ed. J.H. Blunt, *EETS*, ES, 19 (1873), p. 42: 'moche more oughte we to make redy the harpe of oure herte, whan we shall synge or say the melody of oure lordes praysynge.'

157 *Bonum Est* in *Qui Habitat*, p. 59, 3; see also *Of Angels' Song*, *Yorkshire Writers*, I, pp. 175ff.

158 *English Writings*, p. 46, 67.

159 *Scale I*, ch. 7, p. 94, 5ff.; see Rolle 'þi prayers turnes intil joyful sange', *Ego Dormio* in *English Writings*, p. 69, 284f.

160 *Cloud*, p. 105, 15.

161 *Scale II*, ch. 39, p. 179, 16.

162 *English Writings*, p. 106, 77.

163 *Piers Plowman* (B-text), Passus X, 30ff.; ed, Skeat, *EETS*, OS, 38 (1869), p. 144.

164 *Benjamin Major*, Book V, ch. 18; C. Kirchberger, ed. *Richard of St. Victor*

(London, 1957), p. 210; see, however, the adpatation of Suso's *Horologium Sapientiae*, where we read of a 'gostly minstralsie' (ed. Horstmann, *Anglia*, 10 (1888)), p. 378, 35.

165 *Phaidros*, 251b.
166 Quoted from W. Gewehr, 'Der Topos "Augen des Herzens" – Versuch einer Deutung durch die scholastische Erkenntnistheorie', *DVJ*, 46 (1972), p. 629.
167 See, for instance, Lüers, op. cit., p. 129.
168 See J. Bernhart, *Philosophische Mystik*, p. 259, note 140.
169 Lüers, op. cit., p. 130.
170 Rolle, *English Writings*, p. 119, 64.
171 Ibid., p. 69, 261f.
172 *Qui Habitat*, p. 26 8f.
173 *Scale I*, ch. 9, p. 97, 23; Rolle, *English Writings*, p. 119, 69.
174 Rolle, *English Psalter*, p. 415 (see the commentary on the Psalter by Peter Lombard, *PL*, 191, 1062).
175 *Deonise HD*, p. 72, 12.
176 *Revelations* (LV), ch. 5, p. 66, 18; the *Orcherd of Syon* has 'iȝe of intellecte' (p. 201, 34) as well as 'iȝe of vndirstondyng' (p. 119, 17).
177 On this point see E. Soudek, *Meister Eckhart* (Stuttgart, 1973), p. 37.
178 *Deonise HD*, p. 72, 23; see also Hodgson's note 72/19, p. 140.
179 Ibid., p. 84, 19ff.
180 E.g. *Deonise HD*, p. 45, 10.
181 E.g. *Scale I*, ch. 3, p. 88, 2f.; *Revelations* (LV), ch. 51, p. 195, 5.
182 *Meditations* (Lindquist), p. 51, 11f.; see also *Chastising*, p. 170, 1.
183 *Orcherd of Syon*, p. 18, 20.
184 *Form of Living* in *English Writings*, p. 118, 40ff.
185 *Cloud*, p. 33, 12f.
186 Ibid., p. 32, 7f.
187 Ibid., p. 34, 17.
188 *Bonum Est* in *Qui Habitat*, p. 63, 3.
189 *Qui Habitat*, p. 14.
190 Rolle, *English Writings*, p. 72, 352. The motif is found in the Old Testament, e.g. Job 19:27. This theme is given extensive treatment in F. Nötscher, *'Das Angesicht Gottes schauen' nach biblischer und babylonishcer Auffassung* (Wurzburg, 1924).
191 Rolle, *English Writings*, p. 47, 81.
192 *Qui Habitat*, p. 27, 8f.
193 Ibid., p. 28, 7ff.
194 Quoted from Berger, op. cit., p. 65.
195 *Incendium Amoris*, p. 180, 32f.
196 Ibid., p. 226, 15.
197 *De Genesi ad Litteram*, book XII, ch. VI-XI and XXXII.
198 *Chastising*, p. 170, 8ff.
199 Ibid., p. 170, 4f.
200 *Revelations* (LV), ch. 9, p. 82, 7ff.; *Revelations* (LV), ch. 51, p. 190, 14f.
201 P. Molinari, *Julian of Norwich, The Teaching of a 14th Century English Mystic* (London, 1958), pp. 32ff.
202 *Revelations* (LV), ch. 8, p. 79, 5f.
203 Ibid., ch. 5, p. 66, 15ff.

204 Ibid., ch. 22, p. 116, 10ff.

205 On this point see especially W. Blank, *Die Nonnenviten des 14. Jahrhunderts* (Diss. Freiburg, 1962), pp. 139ff.

206 Quoted from Blank, *Die Nonnenviten des 14. Jahrhunderts* p. 143.

207 See Blank, *Die Nonnenviten des 14. Jahrhunderts*, p. 200.

208 *Revelations* (LV), ch. 18, p. 107, 11ff.

209 Ibid., ch. 13, p. 94, 13f.

210 Ibid., ch. 14, p. 99, 11 and ch. 8, p. 79, 2 and 6.

211 Ibid., ch. 27, p. 129, 8.

212 *Die Predigten Taulers*, p. 337, 24.

213 Ibid., p. 337, 24.

214 *Revelations* (LV), ch. 36, p. 148, 21.

215 Ibid., ch. 43, p. 170, 2.

216 Ibid., ch. 43, p. 170, 6f. On the concept of beholding in Julian see also Molinari, *Julian of Norwich* (London, 1958), pp. xxxf.; xxxiv.

Chapter IX The metaphorical complex of having God

1 Berger, op. cit., p. 92.

2 H. Hanse, *'Gott haben' in der Antike und im frühen Christentum. Eine religions- und begriffsgeschichtliche Untersuchung*, Religionsgeschichtliche Versuche und Arbeiten, 27 (Berlin, 1939).

3 Hanse, op. cit., p. 99ff.

4 1 John 2:23; 1 John 4:15f.

5 Hanse, op. cit., p. 104.

6 Ibid., p. 115.

7 Here we find such characteristic expressions as the following: 'Du pist mir in daz herze gegraben, Ich muz und muz dich haben.', quoted from Berger, op. cit., p. 92.

8 *Cloud*, p. 26, 4. In the *Mirror of Simple Souls* the soul begs Love 'graunteþ me myn holdynge þat I haue of þe Trinite' (p. 284, 6f.).

9 *Pistle of Discrecioun of Stirings* in *Deonise HD*, p. 73, 16f.

10 *Scale I*, ch. 46, p. 172, 15.

11 *Scale II*, ch. 42, p. 205, 21ff.

12 See the study by N.J. Perella, *The Kiss Sacred and Profane* (Berkeley, 1969), p. 90; see also, for instance, Bernard of Clairvaux's Seventh Sermon on the *Song of Songs*, *Sancti Bernardi Opera*, I, p. 35, 6ff.

13 *Meditations* (*English Writings*), p. 30, 93ff.

14 *Revelations* (LV), ch. 6, p. 72, 10f.

15 *Book of M. Kempe*, p. 91, 15.

16 See, for instance, *Qui Habitat*, p. 29, 15f.

17 See *Deonise HD*, p. 73, 17f.

18 Ibid., p. 56, 16ff.; The editors of *Chastising* seem not to have known the translation *drawen to* for the Latin *adhaerere*, since they attempt to explain the English formulation 'A taryynge drawynge to', which is a perfectly normal rendering of the Latin *adhaesio* and the Dutch *aencleuen*, by assuming that 'The English here seems to derive from a corrupt Latin text, in which, perhaps, 'adhesio' had become an adjective' (*Chastising*, p. 339, note

256, 18).

19 *Scale I*, ch. 8, p. 95, 18ff.; the *MED* does not indicate that *fastnen* can also mean *adhaerere*; it does mention the meaning 'to unite . . . in mystic union', but does not quote any examples from the mystics.

20 Cf. Hanse, op. cit., p. 118.

21 *Revelations* (LV), ch. 54, p. 221, 1ff.

22 See Lüers, op. cit., p. 298f.

23 Ibid., p. 300.

24 'ʒif euer þou schalt come to þis cloude & wone & worche þer-in' (*Cloud*, p. 24, 1); 'vse for to wonen in þis mirknes' (*Scale II*, ch. 25, p. 94, 7).

25 MS. BL Harley 2254, f. 4^v.

26 *English Writings*, p. 45, 38.

27 Ibid., p. 78, 155.

28 Quoted from Lüers, op. cit., p. 299.

29 *Revelations* (LV), ch. 54, p. 220, 6ff.; see also J. Walsh, 'God's Homely Loving. St. John and Julian of Norwich on the Divine Indwelling', *The Month*, 205 n.s. 19 (1958), pp. 164ff.

30 Quoted from Lüers, op. cit., p. 300.

31 *Revelations* (LV), ch. 51, p. 206, 18ff.

32 Ibid., ch. 56, p. 226, 5f.

33 Ibid., ch. 68, p. 262, 16f. (The word *sitts* was added in brackets by the editor.)

34 Ibid., ch. 56, p. 226, 15ff.

35 *Politeia*, 435 b, c.

36 See *Deutsche Werke*, I, 21ff.

37 P. 125; on this image see also R. Cornelius, *Figurative Castle* (Dissertation, Bryn Mawr, 1930).

38 *Deonise HD*, p. 29, 5.

39 *Book of M. Kempe*, p. 68, 16.

40 *Heinrich Seuse. Deutsche Schriften*, ed. K. Bihlmeyer (Stuttgart, 1907), p. 20, 16ff.

41 W. Muschg, *Die Mystik in der Schweiz 1200-1500* (Frauenfeld, 1935), p. 229.

42 *Die Offenbarungen der Adelheid Langmann, Klosterfrau zu Engelthal*, ed. Ph. Strauch (Strasbourg, 1878), p. 16, 5ff.

43 *English Psalter*, p. 41.

44 *Book of M. Kempe*, p. 43, 11f.; see also note 43/11-12, p. 279 and 3/2, p. 257.

45 Ibid., p. 210, 32ff.; Allen lists other interesting parallels, n. 210/4, p. 338f.

Chapter X The mystical experience of God as rest, sleep, death and complete absorption of the self

1 *Form of Living* in *English Writings*, p. 116, 264f.

2 See, for instance, Allen, *English Writings*, pp. xvii, xliii.

3 *Privy Counselling*, p. 167, 3f.

4 *Book of M. Kempe*, p. 161, 2ff.

5 *Melos Amoris*, p. 126, 7f.

6   *Ancrene Wisse*, p. 212, 12.

7   *Cloud*, p. 47, 3ff.

8   Quoted from B. Schmoldt, *Die deutsche Begriffssprache Meister Eckharts* (Heidelberg, 1954), p. 63.

9   *Pistle of Discrecioun of Stirings* in *Deonise HD*, p. 64, 20f.

10   *Mirror of Simple Souls*, p. 325, 34.

11   *Incendium Amoris*, p. 159, 9ff.

12   Ibid., p. 206, 8ff.

13   *Confessiones* I, 1.

14   Rolle, *English Prose Treatises*, p. 3, 14; *Deonise HD*, p. 85, 10; *Scale II*, ch. 27, p. 112, 7; *Revelations* (LV), ch 5, p. 68, 4.

15   *Mirror of Simple Souls*, p. 270, 15.

16   *Deonise HD*, p. 85, 4.

17   *Melos Amoris*, p. 141, 1f.

18   *Melos Amoris*, p. 46, 6f.

19   *A Talkyng of þe Loue of God*, p. 36, 23f.

20   Ibid., p. 68, 2f.

21   In Bernard of Clairvaux there is, for example, the beautiful statement: 'Dormiens in contemplatione somniat Deum' (*Sancti Bernardi Opera*, I, 107).

22   *Privy Counselling*, p. 152, 3ff.

23   *Scale II*, ch. 40, p. 189, 11. On this motif in Bernard see Butler, *Western Mysticism*, 3rd edn (London, 1967), p. 106.

24   *Scale II*, ch. 40, p. 189, 17f. (editor's brackets).

25   Ibid., p. 190, 9ff.

26   On one occasion Margery Kempe describes the state in which she received an ecstatic vision as a 'maner of sleep' (*Book of M. Kempe*, p. 208, 20).

27   *Scale I*, ch. 49, p. 178, 22ff.

28   N.J. Perella, *The Kiss Sacred and Profane* (Berkeley, 1969), p. 64.

29   He speaks of 'gostly mortifyinge', *Scale II*, ch. 29, p. 119, 14f.

30   'þou schalt . . . entre þi graue, þat is þe reste in contemplacion' (*Scale I*, ch. 15, p. 108, 12ff.).

31   *Privy Counselling*, p. 150, 13ff.; see *Deonise HD*, p. 45, 9.

32   See Perella, *The Kiss Sacred and Profane*, p. 64.

33   *the tree & xii. frutes of þe holy goost*, p. 46, 18f.

34   See Perella, op. cit., p. 66.

35   See Bernard's fifty second sermon on the *Song of Songs*. And Paul's desire 'to depart' ('dissolvi cupio', Phil. 1:23) is one which is adopted by many mystics in the same linguistic form.

36   Quoted from Lüers, op. cit., p. 265.

37   *Revelations* (LV), ch. 43, p. 171, 9ff.

38   *Incendium Amoris*, p. 176, 12.

39   Ibid., p. 193, 11ff.

40   *Sancti Bernardi Opera*, I, p. 178.

41   *Talkyng of þe Loue of God*, p. 52, 24.

42   On the motif of death in general see Perella, *The Kiss Sacred and Profane*, p. 139.

43   *Book of M. Kempe*, p. 140, 5ff.

44   E.g. by Richard of St Victor, *PL*, p. 196, 450.

45 *Die Predigten Taulers*, p. 46, 3.
46 *Emendatio Vitae*, MS Bodl. 16, f. 72^V.
47 *Mending of Life* in *Fire of Love*, p. 125, 34.
48 *Revelations of St. Birgitta*, ed. W.P. Cumming, *EETS*, OS, 178 (1928), p. 60, 13f.
49 *Incendium Amoris*, p. 223, 11.
50 *Fire of Love*, p. 62, 5f.
51 *PL*, 158, 760.
52 *Werken*, III, p. 30, 30.
53 *Chastising*, p. 249, 37ff. Another passage in this tract reads: 'neythere we may swalowe hym, ne ȝit synke hym into vs; bot he hymselfe schalle swallowe vs into hym' (p. 253, 29ff.).
54 *Heinrich Seuse. Deutsche Schriften*, ed. K. Bihlmeyer (Stuttgart, 1907), p. 182, 26ff.
55 Ibid., p. 173, 20; see also Lüers, op. cit., p. 290f. and Berger, op. cit., p. 52f.
56 *Cloud*, p. 83, 17ff.
57 *Heinrich Seuse. Deutsche Schriften*, p. 20, 21ff.
58 *Tretyse of þe Stodye of Wysdome* in *Deonise HD*, p. 28, 10.
59 ' "Remedies against Temptations". The Third English Version of William Flete', ed. E. Colledge and N. Chadwick, *Archivio Italiano per la Storia della Pietà*, 5 (Rome, 1968), 226, 2f.
60 *Privy Counselling*, p. 149, 14f.
61 *Mirror of Simple Souls*, p. 248, 15.
62 Ibid., p. 314, 35f.
63 *Chastising*, p. 233, 22ff.
64 N.J. Perella refers to this in *The Kiss Sacred and Profane*, p. 34.
65 Quoted from Lüers, op. cit., p. 256; see also Berger, op. cit., p. 59, and Vogt-Terhorst, *Der bildliche Ausdruck in den Predigten Taulers* (dissertation, Marburg, 1919), p. 83f.
66 *Heinrich Seuse. Deutsche Schriften*, p. 16, 8.
67 *Mirror of Simple Souls*, p. 313, 35.
68 *Melos Amoris*, p. 175, 3.
69 On this point see especially L. Seppänen, *Zur Liebesterminologie in mittelhochdeutschen geistlichen Texten* (Tampere, 1967), pp. 106ff.
70 *Mending of Life* in *Fire of Love*, p. 125, 35.
71 *Incendium Amoris*, p. 227, 18f.

Chapter XI The image of God in the soul, mystical deification and union in the ground of the soul

1 On this point see, for instance, P. Wyser, 'Der Seelengrund in Taulers Predigten', *Lebendiges Mittelalter. Festgabe für Wolfgang Stammler* (Fribourg, 1958), p. 283.
2 Ibid.
3 L. Scheffczyk, ed., *Der Mensch als Bild Gottes*, Wege der Forschung, 124 (Darmstadt, 1969).
4 See especially G. Söhngen, 'Die biblische Lehre von der Gottebenbildlichkeit des Menschen', *Der Mensch als Bild Gottes*, pp. 364ff.

5 See W. Hess, 'Imago Dei (Gn 1, 26)', *Der Mensch als Bild Gottes*, p. 431.

6 On Thomas Aquinas's concept of man as the image of God see especially A. Hoffmann, 'Zur Lehre von der Gottebenbildlichkeit des Menschen in der Neueren Protestantischen Theologie und bei Thomas von Aquin', *Der Mensch als Bild Gottes*, pp. 292ff.

7 *Sancti Aurelii Augustini De Trinitate Libri XV*, Corpus Christianorum, Series Latina, L (Aurelii Augustini Opera, Pars XVI, 1 and 2, ed. W.J. Mountain (Turnhout, 1968)).

8 P. Künzle, *Das Verhältnis der Seele zu ihren Potenzen. Problemgeschichtliche Untersuchungen von Augustin bis und mit Thomas von Aquin* (Fribourg, 1956), p. 20.

9 *De Trinitate*, Xxi, 17-xii, 19. See also Books XI and XIV.

10 *Cloud*, p. 115, 1; *Scale II*, ch. 31, p. 134, 21.

11 *Deonise HD*, p. 53, 13f.; in the *Tretyse of þe Stodye of Wysdome* we find 'miȝt, kunnyng, . . . wylle' (*Deonise HD*, p. 21, 10).

12 *Mirror of Simple Souls*, p. 335, 29ff.

13 *Scale I*, ch. 43, p. 161, 10ff.

14 Ibid., p. 161, 14.

15 *Revelations* (LV), ch. 55, p. 224, 4.

16 Ibid., ch. 55, p. 222, 16ff.

17 On this point see especially Schmidt, op. cit., pp. 228*ff.

18 *Scale II*, esp. ch. 33-6. For Hilton's teaching on the soul see the detailed study by A.C. Hughes, *Walter Hilton's Direction to Contemplatives* (Dissertation, Rome, 1962), pp. 39ff.

19 *De Trinitate* XII, 3.

20 *Scale II*, ch. 13, p. 43, 15ff.

21 *Cloud*, p. 116, 15f.

22 Ibid., p. 117, 4f.

23 On this point see Wyser, 'Der "Seelengrund" in Taulers Predigten', p. 284.

24 Ibid.

25 *Melos Amoris*, p. 46, 9f.

26 Ibid., p. 105, 8f.

27 *Fire of Love*, p. 44, 27.

28 *Scale II*, ch. 31, p. 135, 3ff.

29 Ibid., lines 9ff.; see also Hughes, op. cit., p. 39ff.

30 *English Psalter*, p. 17 (see the Commentary on the Psalms by Peter Lombard, *PL*, 191, 88).

31 *Revelations* (LV), ch. 80, p. 295, 15ff.

32 Ibid., ch. 56, p. 228, 8f.

33 E.g. ibid., ch. 10, p. 85, 13f.

34 On this point see the *OED*, s.v. 'similitude'.

35 *Scale I*, ch. 9, p. 97, 21ff.

36 See, for instance, L. Seppänen, *Studien zur Terminologie des 'Paradisus Anime Intelligentis'* (Helsinki, 1964), pp. 234ff.

37 Quoted from Berger, op. cit., p. 110.

38 See L. Seppänen, *Studien zur Terminologie des 'Paradisus Anime Intelligentis'*, p. 249.

39 *Scale I*, ch. 84, p. 235, 22f.

40 Ibid., ch. 84, p. 235, 9; based on the Scholastic term *deformis*.

41 *Deonise HD*, p. 44, 10.
42 *Scale I*, ch. 92, p. 245, 24f.
43 Ibid. *II*, ch. 28, p. 114, 9f.
44 Ibid. *II*, ch. 30, p. 130, 2. The *Ancrene Wisse* speaks of 'ure deoreworðe gast godes ahne furme' (p. 73, 10).
45 *Mirror of Simple Souls*, p. 293, 20f.
46 Quoted from Berger, op. cit., p. 108, see also Lüers, op. cit., pp. 184ff.
47 *Scale I*, ch. 43, p. 161, 3ff.
48 Ibid., ch. 43, p. 161, 7ff.
49 Ibid., ch. 43, p. 161, 10ff.
50 Ibid., ch. 43, p. 161, 17f.
51 Ibid., ch. 43, p. 162, 2f.
52 Ibid., ch. 55ff., pp. 186ff.
53 See W. Hess, 'Imago Dei (Gn 1, 26)', *Der Mensch als Bild Gottes*, p. 429.
54 *Scale I*, ch. 86, p. 237, 23ff.
55 See Knowles, *The English Mystical Tradition* (London, 1961), p. 106.
56 On this point see, for instance, Buchberger, Höfer, Rahner, ed., *Lexikon für Theologie und Kirche* (Freiburg, 2nd edn 1957), I, col. 708ff. and Galling, ed., *Die Religion in Geschichte und Gegenwart* (Tubingen, 3rd edn, 1962), VI, col. 1693ff.
57 *Revelations* (LV), ch. 62, p. 248, 9ff.
58 Ibid., ch. 39, p. 155, 18.
59 Ibid., ch. 57, p. 229, 10f.
60 For example by Justin and Tertullian, see W. Hess, 'Imago Dei (Gn 1, 26)', op. cit., pp. 416ff.
61 *Revelations* (LV)., ch. 51, p. 203, 12ff.
62 Ibid., ch. 10, p. 86, 6ff.
63 Ibid., ch. 57, p. 230, 1ff.; 231, 10ff.; ch. 56, p. 226, 15ff.
64 *Scale II*, ch. 28, p. 113, 13.
65 K. Ruh, 'Zur Grundlegung einer Geschichte der franziskanischen Mystik', op. cit., p. 243.
66 See Berger, op. cit., p. 109.
67 *English Psalter*, p. 4.
68 *Scale I*, ch. 14, p. 106, 2ff. (editor's brackets).
69 III Sent. d. 27, q. 1, a.1.
70 'Quid enim est amor nisi transformacio affectus in rem amatam?' (p. 195, 11f.); on this point see also C. Butler, *Western Mysticism* (London, 3rd edn, 1967), p. 109.
71 Quoted from Lüers, op. cit., p. 185.
72 *Le Laude*, ed. L. Fallacara (Florence, 1955), p. 328.
73 *Yorkshire Writers*, I, p. 176, 42f.
74 *St. John of the Cross, Poems*, ed. R. Campbell (Harmondsworth, 1968), p. 26.
75 For instance in Hilton's *Of Angels' Song*, *Yorkshire Writers*, I, p. 176, 42ff.
76 See Wyser, 'Der Seelengrund in Taulers Predigten', p. 279.
77 *Werken*, I, 247, 15.
78 See, for instance, Berger, op. cit., p. 108.
79 See Ruysbroeck, *Werken*, I, p. 100, 7; III, p. 8, 11.
80 There are also no parallels in English to the numerous Middle High German

word formations with the stem 'form-' such as *informunge, einformig, durchformig, mitformig, gotformig, kristformig*, and *einformikeit* (see Berger, op. cit., pp. 108f.).

81 *Mysticism*, p. 419.

82 Ibid.

83 See e.g. Matt. 5:9: 'Beati pacifici: quoniam filii Dei vocabuntur'.

84 Adv. haer. 3, 19, 1 (see M. Herz, *Sacrum Commercium*, p. 46).

85 H. Grundmann, *Religiöse Bewegungen im Mittelalter* (Berlin, 1935), p. 416.

86 *Enarratio in Psalmum* xlix, *Corpus Christianorum*, 10, 1.

87 On this point see especially Berger, op. cit., pp. 117ff.

88 Ibid.

89 Ibid., p. 118.

90 *Tractatus de Gradibus Charitatis, PL* 196, 1198.

91 *Cloud*, p. 120, 16f.

92 Ibid., p. 120, 11f.

93 MS. Pembroke College Cambridge 221, f. 1ᵛ. His commentary is printed in the introduction to *Chastising*, p. 52. On the relationship between God and the soul in deification Methley says very clearly that 'vtrumque manet in sua substancia' (ibid.).

94 *Revelations* (LV), ch. 54, p. 220, 15f.

95 Ibid., ch. 54, p. 220, 17f.

96 E. Vasta, *The Spiritual Basis of Piers Plowman* (London, 1965), p. 70.

97 *Scale II*, ch. 42, p. 205, 15ff.

98 *Comment on the Canticles*, f. 205, p. 69, 20; see also *Melos Amoris*, p. 43, 22f.

99 *English Psalter*, p. 301 (see also the commentary on the Psalms by Peter Lombard, *PL*, 191, 777).

100 *Troy Book*, 2. 4485 (quoted after the *MED*, s.v. 'deifien'). The adjective *deiformis* which is very popular in European mysticism is only found in England in the Monk of Farne where we read on one occasion of the soul: 'fit anima deiformis et similis Deo inter filios Dei' (*Analecta Monastica* 4 (1957), Studia Anselmiana, 41, p. 187).

101 Typical of this view is above all the work of H. Kunisch, *Das Wort 'Grund' in der Sprache der deutschen Mystik des 14. und 15. Jahrhunderts* (dissertation, Munster, 1929).

102 Especially the study of P. Wyser, 'Der Seelengrund in Taulers Predigten', *Lebendiges Mittelalter* (Fribourg, 1958), pp. 208ff.

103 See, for instance, J. Bernhart, *Die philosophische Mystik des Mittelalters* (Munich, 1922), p. 153.

104 On this point see e.g. J. Bernhart, *Philosophische Mystik*, p. 71.

105 See the important article by E. von Ivánka, 'Der Apex Mentis', *Zeitschrift für Katholische Theologie*, 72 (1950), pp. 147ff.

106 See P. Wyser, 'Der Seelengrund in Taulers Predigten', p. 227.

107 Augustine, *Confessiones* X, 8, 15; on Albert the Great and on the theme treated here generally see *DSAM*, s.v. 'fond de l'âme', V, col. 650ff.

108 Eckhart, *Deutsche Werke*, I, p. 54, 4.

109 See, for instance, Schmoldt, *Die deutsche Begriffssprache Meister Eckharts* (Heidelberg, 1954), p. 91.

110 Ibid., p. 54.

111 Eckhart, *Deutsche Werke*, II, p. 227, 8f.

112 R. Reitzenstein, *Poimandres* (Leipzig, 1904), e.g. p. 228; on the idea of the birth of God in Eckhart see M. Pahnke, 'Ein Grundgedanke der deutschen Predigt Meister Eckharts', *Zeitschrift für Kirchengeschichte*, 34 (1913), pp. 58ff. and H. Rahner, 'Die Gottesgeburt. Die Lehre der Kirchenväter von der Geburt Christi im Herzen der Gläubigen', *Zeitschrift für Katholische Theologie*, 59 (1935), pp. 333ff.

113 On this point see especially B. Dietsche, 'Der Seelengrund nach den deutschen und lateinischen Predigten', in *Meister Eckhart der Prediger*, ed. U. Nix and R. Öchslin (Freiburg, 1960), p. 218.

114 See Soudek, *Meister Eckhart* (Stuttgart, 1973), p. 39.

115 *Scale II*, ch. 30, p. 124, 19f.

116 Eckhart, *Deutsche Werke*, I, p. 90, 8.

117 Wyser, 'Der Seelengrund in Taulers Predigten', pp. 232ff.; see also A. Walz, ' "Grund" und "Gemüt" bei Tauler. Erwägungen zur geistlichen und predigerischen Ausdrucksweise eines Rufers zur Innerlichkeit', *Angelicum*, 40 (1963), pp. 328ff.

118 Quoted from Lüers, op. cit., p. 189.

119 See Seppänen, *Paradisus Anime Intelligentis*, p. 51.

120 See Wyser, 'Der Seelengrund in Taulers Predigten', p. 276.

121 Wyser, 'Der Seelengrund in Taulers Predigten', p. 277.

122 H. Kunisch, *Das Wort 'Grund' in der Sprache der deutschen Mystik des 14. und 15. Jahrhunderts*, p. 4.

123 As, for instance, in the *Ormulum*, where we find the sentence: 'Crist sahh all hiss herrtes grund, þat itt was god & clene'. (Quoted from the *MED*, s.v. 'grounde', which lists further examples.)

124 *Yorkshire Writers*, I, p. 278, 15f.; quoted from the Vernon MS.

125 Ibid., I, p. 339, 4.

126 See H. Kunisch, *Das Wort 'Grund' in der Sprache der deutschen Mystik*, p. 24.

127 *Melos Amoris*, p. 169, 13f.

128 *Comment on the Canticles*, p. 55.

129 *Incendium Amoris*, p. 245, 28.

130 *Melos Amoris*, p. 36, 25f.

131 See, for instance, 1 Cor. 3:11: 'Fundamentum enim aliud nemo potest ponere praeter id quod positum est Christus Iesus.'

132 *Revelations* (LV), ch. 28, p. 131, 8.

133 Ibid., ch. 56, p. 226, 2f.

134 3. Sent. 23. 2.1. ad 1.

135 See, for instance, *Revelations* (LV), ch. 78, p. 290, 19f.

136 See, for instance, ibid., ch. 42, p. 165, 20.

137 Ibid., ch. 56, p. 226, 4.

138 Ibid., ch. 34, p. 144, 7.

139 Ibid., ch. 59, p. 237, 15f.

140 *Revelations* (SV), ch. 4, p. 7, 7.

141 *Revelations* (LV), ch. 63, p. 250, 2.

142 Ibid., ch. 56, p. 228, 10.

143 Ibid., ch. 55, p. 223, 20.

144 Ibid., ch. 54, p. 220, 15f.

145 See, e.g. Underhill, *The Essentials of Mysticism* (London, 1920), p. 193.
146 *Revelations* (LV), ch. 54, p. 220, 17f.
147 Ibid., ch. 27, p. 127, 15ff.
148 Ibid., lines 17ff.
149 Ibid., ch. 27, p. 128, 14f.
150 Soudek, *Meister Eckhart*, p. 43f.
151 *Mirror of Simple Souls*, p. 261, 15f.
152 *Revelations* (LV), ch. 53, p. 216, 13f.
153 G. Warrack, *Revelations of Divine Love* (London, 13th edn, 1958), p. 127;
     J. Walsh, *The Revelations of Divine Love* (London, 1961), p. 148; C.
     Wolters, *Revelations of Divine Love* (Harmondsworth, 1966), p. 155.
154 See above all D. Knowles, *The English Mystics* (London, 1928), p. 144 and
     following him Sr Anna Maria Reynolds, 'Some Literary Influences in the
     Revelations of Julian of Norwich', *Leeds Studies in English*, 7 (1952), p. 27.
155 *Revelations* (LV), ch. 53, p. 216, 15ff.
156 Ibid., ch. 59, p. 238, 19.
157 *Revelations* (SV), ch. 17, p. 33, 14ff.
158 *Revelations* (LV), ch. 53, p. 216, 14ff.
159 Ibid., ch. 51, p. 196, 19ff.
160 Ibid., ch. 42, p. 165, 7f.
161 *The Essentials of Mysticism*, p. 194.
162 *Chastising*, p. 247, 6.
163 *Revelations* (LV), ch. 51, p. 200, 16f.
164 Ibid., ch. 51, p. 202, 17.
165 Ibid., ch. 39, p. 157, 13ff.
166 *PL*, 158, 760.
167 *Privy Counselling*, p. 144, 18f.; here incidentally 'purete of spirit' is a ver-
     nacular translation of the Thomist 'munditia cordis', which Master Eckhart
     renders into German as 'reinicheit des herzen' (see B. Schmoldt, *Die
     deutsche Begriffssprache Meister Eckharts* (Heidelberg, 1954), p. 144).
168 *Privy Counselling*, p. 135, 20f.
169 Ibid., p. 140, 11f.; in another context the author of the *Cloud* uses the word
     substaunce as a specifically Scholastic term with *accydentes* as its opposite
     (*Cloud*, p. 92, 21ff.; see Hodgson's note, p. 199).
170 *Privy Counselling*, p. 140, 20.
171 Ibid., p. 141, 5; p. 140, 6f.
172 *Cloud*, p. 74, 11ff. (editor's brackets).
173 *Privy Counselling*, p. 138, 4f.
174 *Cloud*, p. 88, 20.
175 Ibid., p. 89, 2f.
176 See also A.C. Hughes, *Walter Hilton's Direction to Contemplatives* (disserta-
     tion, Rome, 1962), e.g. p. 46.
177 *Scale II*, ch. 40, p. 181, 19.
178 Ibid., ch. 30, p. 124, 19.
179 Ibid., ch. 33, p. 143, 16.
180 Ibid., ch. 37, p. 165, 7f.
181 *Qui Habitat*, p. 31, 6f.
182 *Scale I*, ch. 69, p. 201, 3f.
183 Ibid., ch. 69, p. 209, 18f.

184 Ibid., ch. 42, p. 158, 15f.

185 Ibid., ch. 55, p. 187, 23f.

186 Ibid., ch. 48, p. 175, 7ff.

187 An early example in English mysticism of the soul being termed a garden occurs in the *Incendium Amoris*, where Rolle describes the soul as blooming with virtues such that it can be called a garden of Christ: 'Anima ortus Christi potest dici; quia a uiciis purgata, virtutibus floret, et suauitate cantus iubilei, quasi concentu auium gaudet.' (*Incendium Amoris*, p. 227). In the prologue to his *Commentary on the Psalms* he describes the whole book as 'crist & his spouse, that is, haly kyrke, or ylk ryghtwise mannys saule' (p. 14). Thus in the prologue he already declares the work to be of a purely mystical nature. The author of the *Cloud* uses the metaphor of the garden in *A Pistle of Preier*, drawing at the same time on the traditional allegory of the tree. Here the author places a tree in the garden of the reader's soul, and, as is usual in devotional literature, the highest fruit of this tree is love (*Deonise HD*, p. 52, 23), whilst the roots are made of 'drede' but the trunk and the branches signify 'hope'. Just as the best tasting fruit is that which is separated from the tree and no longer green, so, too, the fruit of love must be offered to the King of Heaven pure and freed from the thought of 'drede' and 'hope', i.e. one must love God for his own sake. But the most extensive use of the allegory of the garden is found in the *Ayenbite of Inwyt*, which we ought to discuss briefly. The trees in the garden are the virtues, and in their midst stands Christ as the tree of life. In contrast to Hilton's well of sin we find here the usual fount of grace, but, as in Hilton, the soul reaches for the spade of penance in order to dig in its ground and so remove everything that prevents it from seeing God. In this context there is then developed one of the greatest tree-metaphors of the English Middle Ages (*Ayenbite of Inwyt*, 2nd edn by P. Gradon, *EETS*, OS (1965), p. 94, 27ff.). God the Father appears as a gardener: since Mary Magdalen mistook Christ for a gardener, this image has been very popular in homiletic and mystical texts. In *Our Daily Work* God is called the 'gardener . . . in mannis soule' (*Rolle and Our Daily Work*, ed. G.E. Hodgson (London, 1929), p. 148.). Julian makes the identification of Christ with the gardener a part of her 'Lord-Servant' allegory: the servant is required to be 'a gardener deluyng and dykyng and swetyng' (*Revelations* (LV), ch. 51, p. 202, 2), so that in the wilderness of the earth he might save the treasure, i.e. the fallen Adam. (On the widespread use of the allegory of the garden in the Middle Ages see especially the important article by D.W. Robertson, Jr, 'The Doctrine of Charity in Mediaeval Literary Gardens: a Topical Approach through Symbolism and Allegory', *Speculum*, 26 (1951), pp. 24ff.)

188 *Meister Eckharts Buch der göttlichen Tröstung und Von dem edlen Menschen*, ed. J. Quint (Berlin, 1952), p. 72, 14ff.

189 Quoted from A. Vogt-Terhorst, *Der bildliche Ausdruck in den Predigten Johann Taulers* (dissertation, Marburg, 1919), p. 29.

190 See Wyser, 'Der Seelengrund in Taulers Predigten', pp. 247f. Hughes maintains that both Tauler and Suso had some influence (*Walter Hilton's Direction to Contemplatives*, p. 30).

191 *Die Predigten Taulers*, p. 142, 27ff.

192 Ibid., p. 146, 19f.

193 Ibid., p. 144, 1f.

194 For a similar interpretation of the coin-image in Ruysbroeck see P.L. Rey-
     pens, 'Der "Goldene Pfennig" bei Tauler und Ruusbroec', in Ruh, op. cit.,
     pp. 353ff.

195 *Scale I*, ch. 48, p. 175, 24f.

196 Ibid., p. 176, 5f.

197 Ibid., ch. 49, p. 178, 12f.

198 *Die Predigten Taulers*, p. 144, 3f.

199 *Scale I*, ch. 49, p. 178, 22f.

200 Especially, for instance, Bernard of Clairvaux's *De Gratia et Libero Arbitrio*,
     where we can already read of the soul sweeping its house free from vices
     and then finding the image of God (the coin of the parable) which previ-
     ously had been hidden in the dust of sin: 'si non evangelica illa mulier lucer-
     nam accenderet . . . everteret domum . . . drachmam suam requireret . . .
     hoc est, imaginem suam', *Sancti Bernardi Opera*, III, p. 188, 23ff.

201 See H. Kuhn *Rittertum und Mystik*, Münchener Universitätsreden, N.F.,
     33 (Munich, 1962), p. 10.

Conclusion

1 See especially E. Colledge, '*The Treatise of Perfection of the Sons of God*:
   a fifteenth-century English Ruysbroek translation', *English Studies*, 33
   (1952), p. 55 and R. Lovatt, 'The Imitation of Christ in Late Medieval
   England', *Transactions of the Royal Historical Society*, 5th ser., 18 (1968),
   pp. 97ff.

2 See especially T.A. Halligan in the introduction to her edition of the *Booke
   of Gostlye Grace*, pp. cxxixff.

3 'Studien zur Geschichte der Mystik in Norddeutschland', in Ruh, op. cit.,
   pp. 386ff.

4 *Scale II*, ch. 43, p. 211, 23f.

5 In her book *The Lollard Bible* (Cambridge, 1920) M. Deanesly also discusses Hilton's attitude to Bible reading. Strangely, however, she only
   considers his tract *Epistle on Mixed Life* and thus comes to the wrong
   conclusion that, in contrast to the German Friend of God, Otto of Passau,
   Hilton had not expressed a clear opinion in favour of Bible reading (pp.
   217ff.).

6 'The Recluse: A Lollard Interpolated Version of the *Ancrene Riwle*', *RES*,
   15 (1939), pp. 1ff. and 129ff. It is interesting to observe that Martin Luther
   valued the mystical work *Theologia Germanica*, which was heavily influenced
   by Eckhart and Tauler, so highly that he decided to publish it as a concise
   theology for the laity.

SELECT BIBLIOGRAPHY

*

Books on medieval mysticism

Beierwaltes, W., ed., *Platonismus in der Philosophie des Mittelalters*, Wissenschaftliche Buchgesellschaft, Darmstadt, 1969

Bernhart, J., *Die philosophische Mystik des Mittelalters von ihren antiken Ursprüngen bis zur Renaissance*, Reinhardt, Munich, 1922.

Butler, C., *Western Mysticism: The Teaching of Augustine, Gregory and Bernard on Contemplation and the Contemplative Life*, Constable, London, 3rd edn, 1967.

Cohn, N., *The Pursuit of the Millennium: A History of Popular Religious and Social Movements in Europe, from the Eleventh to the Sixteenth Century*, Secker & Warburg, London, 1957.

Deanesly, M., *A History of the Mediaeval Church 590-1500*, Methuen, London, 8th edn, 1954.

Daniélou, J., *Platonisme et théologie mystique*, Edition Montaigne, Paris, 1944.

Ewer, M.A., *A Survey of Mystical Symbolism*, SPCK, London, 1933.

Fairweather, W., *Among the Mystics*, T. & T. Clark, Edinburgh, 2nd edn, 1968.

Garrigou-Lagrange, R.M., *The Three Ways of the Spiritual Life*, Burns & Oates, London, 1938.

Gilson, E., *L'Esprit de la philosophie médiévale*, Etudes de philosophie médiévale, 33, Paris, 2nd edn, 1948.

Graef, H., *The Light and the Rainbow*, Longman, London, 1959.

Happold, F.C., *Mysticism*, Penguin, Harmondsworth, 1963.

Hort, G., *Sense and Thought: A Study in Mysticism*, Allen & Unwin, London, 1936.

v. Hügel, F., *The Mystical Element of Religion as Studied in Saint Catherine of Genoa and her Friends*, Dent, London, 1909, 2 vols.

Huizinga, J., *The Waning of the Middle Ages*, Penguin, Harmondsworth, 1979.

Inge, W.R., *Christian Mysticism*, Methuen, London, 7th edn, 1933.

Inge, W.R., *Mysticism in Religion*, Hutchinson's University Library, London, 1947.

James, W., *The Varieties of Religious Experience: A Study in Human Nature*, Longmans, London, 1902, repr. 1960.

Jones, R.M., *Studies in Mystical Religion*, Macmillan, London, 1909.

Jones, R.M., *The Flowering of Mysticism: The Friends of God in the Fourteenth Century*, Macmillan, New York, 1939.

Knowles, D., *What is Mysticism?*, Burns & Oates, London, 1967.

Knox, R.A., *Enthusiasm: A Chapter in the History of Religion, with Special Reference to the XVIIth and XVIIIth Century*, Clarendon Press, 1950.

Lubac, H. de, *Exégèse médiévale*, Edition Montaigne, Paris, 1952-64.

Ohly, F., *Hohelied-Studien. Grundzüge einer Geschichte der Hoheliedauslegung des Abendlandes bis um 1200*, Steiner, Wiesbaden, 1958.

Petry, R.C., *Late Medieval Mysticism*, SCM Press, London, 1957.

Pourrat, P., *La Spiritualité chrétienne*, J. Gabalda, Paris, 1918.

Powicke, F.M., *Christian Life in the Middle Ages*, Clarendon Press, 1935.

Smalley, B., *The Study of the Bible in the Middle Ages*, Clarendon Press, 1952.

Southern, R.W., *The Making of the Middle Ages*, Hutchinson's University Library, London, 1953.

Southern, R.W., *Western Society and the Church in the Middle Ages*, Penguin, Harmondsworth, 1970.

Thurston, H. (ed. J.H. Crehan), *The Physical Phenomena of Mysticism*, Burns & Oates, London, 1952.

Underhill, E., *The Mystics of the Church*, J.M. Watkins, London, 1925.

Underhill, E., *Mysticism: A Study in the Nature and Development of Man's Spiritual Consciousness*, Methuen, London, 12th edn, 1930.

Wilmart, A., *Auteurs spirituels et textes dévots du moyen age latin*, Blond et Gay, Paris, 1932.

Important texts of Christian theology and mysticism

Aelred of Rievaulx, *Speculum caritatis* and *De spirituali amicitia*, PL 195, 505ff. and 659ff.

Anselm of Canterbury, PL 158 and *S. Anselmi Cantuariensis Archiepiscopi Opera Omnia*, ed. F.S. Schmitt, Seckau, 1938-61, vol. 3.

Augustinus, *Confessiones, Bibliotheca Scriptorum Graecorum et Romanorum Teubneriana*, ed. M. Skutella, corr. edn by H. Inergensen and W. Schaub, Stuttgart, 1969.

Augustinus, *Enarratio in Psalmos* and *De Trinitate* in *Corpus Christianorum*, 10, 1-3 and 16, 1-2.

Bernard of Clairvaux, *Sermones Super Cantica Canticorum, Liber de Diligendo Deo* and *Liber de Gratia et Libero Arbitrio* in: *Sancti Bernardi Opera*, ed. J. Leclercq, C.H. Talbot, H.M. Rochais, Rome, 1957, 1958, 1963, vols 1-3.

Bonaventura, *Itinerarium Mentis in Deum. Pilgerbuch der Seele zu Gott. Lateinisch und Deutsch*, ed. J. Kaup, Munich, 1961; *De triplici via, Lignum vitae, Vitis mystica, De sex alis Seraphim* in: *Doctoris Seraphici S. Bonaventurae. . . Opera Omnia*, Quaracchi, 1882-1902.

pseudo-Dionysius Areopagita, *Mystica Theologia, De divinis nominibus, De caelesti hierarchia* in: *Dionysiaca*, ed. P. Chevallier, Paris, 1937.

Robert Grosseteste, *Commentary on the Mystica Theologia of the psuedo-Dionysius*, ed. U. Gamba, *Il Commento di Roberto Grossatesta al 'De Mystica Theologia' del Pseudo-Dionigi Areopagita*, Orbis Romanus, 14 Milan, 1942.

Petrus Lombardus, *Commentarius in Psalmos Davidicos*, PL 191, 61ff.

Hugh of St Victor, *De arrha animae, De Laude caritatis, PL* 176.

Richard of St Victor, *Benjamin Minor, Benjamin Maior, Explicatio in Cantica Canticorum, PL* 196, 1ff.; 63ff.; 405ff. *De quattuor gradibus violentae charitatis*, ed. G. Dumeige, *Richard de Saint-Victor: Les quatre degrés de la violente charité*, Textes Philosophiques du Moyen Age, 3, Paris, 1955.

Thomas Aquinas, *Summa Theologica ad modum commentarii in Aquinatis Summam Praesentis aevi studiis aptatam*, ed. L. Janssens, STD, 6 vols, Freiburg/Br., 1900.

Thomas Gallus, 'Commentary on the Mystica Theologia of the pseudo-Dionysius' in: *Thomas Gallus. Grand Commentaire sur la Théologie mystique*, ed. P.G. Théry, Paris, 1934. 'Commentaries on the Song of Songs' in: *Thomas Gallus, Commentaires du cantique*, ed. J. Barbet, Textes philosophiques du moyen age, 14, Paris, 1967.

William of St Thierry, *De contemplando Deo* and *De natura et dignitate amoris, PL* 184, 365ff.; 379ff.

Books and articles on late medieval English spirituality

Allen, H.E., 'The Mystical Lyrics of the Manuel des Pechiez', *Romanic Review*, 9 (1918), 154-93.

Bateson, M., *Catalogue of the Library of Syon Monastery*, Cambridge UP, 1898.

Blake, N.F., *Middle English Religious Prose*, E. Arnold, London, 1972.

Blake, N.F., 'Middle English Prose and its Audience', *Anglia*, 90 (1972), 437-55.

Blake, N.F., 'Varieties of Middle English Religious Prose', in *Chaucer and Middle English Studies in Honour of Rossell Hope Robbins*, ed. B. Rowland, Allen & Unwin, London, 1974, pp. 348-56.

Bloomfield, M.W., *The Seven Deadly Sins. An Introduction to the History of a Religious Concept, with Special Reference to Medieval English Literature*, Michigan State UP, 1952.

Bullett, G.W., *English Mystics*, Michael Joseph, London, 1950.

Capes, W.W., *The English Church in the Fourteenth and Fifteenth Centuries*, Macmillan, London, 1900.

Chambers, R.W., *On the Continuity of English Prose*, EETS, OS, 191 A, 1932.

Clay, R.M., *The Hermits and Anchorites of England*, Methuen, London, 1914.

Clay, R.M., 'Further Studies on Medieval Recluses', *Journal of the British Archaeological Association*, 3rd ser., 16 (1953).

Coleman, T.W., *English Mystics of the Fourteenth Century*, Epworth Press, London, 1938.

Colledge, E., 'The Recluse: A Lollard Interpolated Version of the "Ancren Riwle" ', *RES*, 15 (1939), 1-15 and 129-145.

Colledge, E., 'The Treatise of Perfection of the Sons of God: a fifteenth-century English Ruysbroek translation', *English Studies*, 33 (1952), 49-66.

Colledge, E., *The Mediaeval Mystics of England*, Murray, London, 1962.

Colledge, E. and Chadwick, N., 'Remedies against Temptations. The Third English Version of William Flete', *Archivio Italiano per la Storia della Pietà*, 5, Edizione di Storia e Letteratura, Rome, 1968.

Cumming, W.P., ed., *The Revelations of St. Birgitta*, EETS, OS, 178, 1929.

Darwin, F.D.S., *The English Medieval Recluse*, SPCK, London, 1944.

Davis, C., ed., *English Spiritual Writers*, Burns & Oates, London, 1961.

Deanesly, M., 'Vernacular Books in England in the Fourteenth and Fifteenth Centuries', *MLR*, 15 (1920), 349-58.

Deanesly, M., *The Lollard Bible and Other Medieval Biblical Versions*, Cambridge UP, 1920.

Deanesly, M., *The Significance of the Lollard Bible*, The Ethel M. Wood Lecture delivered before the University of London 13th March 1951, Athlone Press, London, 1951.

Dickinson, J.L., *Monastic Life in Medieval England*, Black, London, 1961.

Doiron, M., ed., 'Margarete Porete, The Mirror of Simple Souls, A Middle English Translation; with an Appendix: The Glosses by 'M.N.' and Richard Methley to "The Mirror of Simple Souls" by E. Colledge and R. Guarnieri', *Archivio Italiano per la Storia della Pietá*, 5, Edizione di Storia e Letteratura, Rome, 1968. The French original of *The Mirror of Simple Souls* has been edited by R. Guarnieri, 'Il Movimento del Libero Spirito Dalle Origini al Secolo XVI. Testi e Documenti', *Archivio Italiano per la Storia della Pietà*, 4, Rome, 1965.

Fisher, J.H., ed. *The Treatise of Loue*, EETS, OS, 223, 1951.

Glunz, H.H. *History of the Vulgate in England from Alcuin to Roger Bacon*, Cambridge UP, 1933.

Gradon, P. *Form and Style in Early English Literature*, Methuen, London, 1971.

Gwynn, A., *The English Austin Friars in the Time of Wyclif*, Oxford UP, 1940.

Halligan, T.A., ed. *The Booke of Gostlye Grace* (unpublished dissertation, New York, 1963).

Halligan, T.A., 'The Revelations of St. Matilda in English: The Booke of Gostlye Grace', *N&Q*, 21 (1974), 443-6.

Hodgson, G.E., *English Mystics*, Mowbray, London, 1922.

Hodgson, P., '*A Ladder of Foure Ronges by the which Men Mowe Well Clyme to Heven*, A Study of the Prose Style of a Middle English Translation', *MLR*, 44 (1949), 465-75.

Hodgson, P., 'Walter Hilton and *The Cloud of Unknowing*, A Problem of Authorship Reconsidered', *MLR*, 50 (1955), 395-406.

Hodgson, P., *The Orcherd of Syon and the English Mystical Tradition*, Sir Israel Gollancz Memorial Lecture, Oxford UP, London, 1964.

Hodgson, P., and Liegey, G., eds, *The Orcherd of Syon, EETS*, OS, 258, 1966, I.

Hodgson, P., *Three 14th-Century English Mystics*, Writers and their Work, 196, British Book Centre, London, 1967.

Horstmann, C., 'Prosalegenden. Die legenden des MS. Douce 114', *Anglia*, 8 (1885), 102-196.

Horstmann, C., ed., 'Orologium Sapientiae or The Seven Poyntes of Trewe Wisdom aus MS. Douce 114', *Anglia*, 10 (1888), 323-89.

Horstmann, C., ed., *Yorkshire Writers. Richard Rolle of Hampole. An English Father of the Church and his Followers*, Swan, Sonnenschein, London, 1895-6, 2 vols.

Hübner, W., ed., 'The desert of religion', *Archiv*, 126 (1911), 58-74; 360-364.

Hutton, E., *The Franciscans in England 1224-1538*, Constable, London, 1926.

Inge, W.R., *Studies of English Mystics*, St Margaret's Lectures 1905, Murray, London, 1906.

Ingram, J.K., ed., *De Imitatione Christi, EETS*, ES, 63, 1893.

Jolliffe, P.S., *A Check-List of Middle English Prose Writings of Spiritual Guidance*, Subsidia Mediaevalia, 11, Toronto, 1974.

Jolliffe, P.S., 'Two Middle English Tracts on the Contemplative Life', *MS*, 37 (1975), 85-121.

Kane, G., *Middle English Literature: A Critical Study of the Romances, the Religious Lyrics, Piers Plowman*, Methuen, London, 1951.

Ker, N.R., 'The Migration of Manuscripts from the English Medieval Libraries', *The Library*, 23 (1942).

Ker, N.R., *Medieval Libraries of Great Britain. A List of Surviving Books*, Royal Historical Society, London, 2nd edn, 1964, 1-11.

Kirchberger, C., ed., *The Mirror of Simple Souls*, Burns & Oates, London, 1927.

Knowles, D., *The English Mystics*, Burns & Oates, London, 1927.

Knowles, D., *The English Mystical Tradition*, Burns & Oates, London, 1961.

Knowles, D., *The Religious Orders in England*, Cambridge UP, 1961-2, 3 vols.

Knowles, D., and Hadcock, R.N., *Medieval Religious Houses. England and Wales*, Longmans, London, 1953.

Lewis, C.S., *The Allegory of Love. A Study in Medieval Tradition*, Clarendon Press, 1936, repr. with corrections 1938 and later.

Little, A.G., *Studies in English Franciscan History*, Publications of the University of Manchester, Historical Series, 1917.

Lovatt, R., 'The Imitation of Christ in Late Medieval England', *Transactions of the Royal Historical Society*, 5th ser., 18 (1968), 97-121.

Moorman, R.H., *A History of the Church in England*, Adam & Charles Black, London, 3rd edn, 1973.

Morgan, M.M., 'A Talking of the Love of God and the Continuity of Stylistic Tradition in the Middle English Prose Meditation', *RES* n.s. 3 (1952), 97-116.

Morgan, M.M., 'A Treatise in Cadence', *MLR*, 47 (1952), 156-64.

Morris, R., ed., *The Pricke of Conscience (Stimulus Conscientiae)*, Published for the Philological Society, Berlin, 1863.

Myers, A.R., *England in the Late Middle Ages (1307-1536)*, The Pelican History of England, 4, Penguin, Harmondsworth, 1952.

Owst, G.R., *Preaching in Medieval England*, Cambridge UP, 1926.

Owst, G.R., *Literature and Pulpit in Medieval England*, Blackwell, Oxford, 2nd edn, 1961.

Pantin, W.A., *The English Church in the Fourteenth Century*, Cambridge UP, 1955.

Pepler, C. *The English Religious Heritage*, Blackfriars Publications, London, 1958.

Perry, G.G., ed., 'Religious Pieces in Prose and Verse from R. Thornton's MS', *EETS*, OS, 26, 1913.

Pfander, H.G., 'Some Medieval Manuals of Religious Instruction in England and Observations on Chaucer's Parson's Tale', *JEGP*, 35 (1936), 243-58.

Power, E., *Medieval English Nunneries c. 1275-1535*, Cambridge UP, 1922.

Renaudin, P., *Quatre Mystiques Anglais*, Editions du Cerf, Paris, 1945.

Robertson, D.W. and Huppé, B.F., *Piers Plowman and the Scriptural Tradition*, Princeton Studies in English, 31, Princeton UP, 1951.

Rogers, L.E., ed., *An Edition of British Museum MS Harley 2372 (Advice to Recluses)* (unpublished PhD thesis, Oxford, 1934).

Ross, W.O., ed., *Middle English Sermons*, *EETS*, OS, 209, 1940.

Salter, E., *Nicholas Love's 'Myrrour of the Blessed Lyf of Jesu Christ'*, Analecta Cartusiana, 10, ed. J. Hogg, Salzburg, 1974.

Sargent, M., 'The Transmission by the English Carthusians of some late Medieval Spiritual Writings', *Journal of Ecclesiastical History*, 27 (1976), 500-12.

Schleich, G., 'Auf den Spuren Susos in England', *Archiv*, 156 (1929), 184-94.

Schleich, G., 'Über die Entstehungszeit und den Verfasser der mittelenglischen Bearbeitung von Susos Horologium', *Archiv*, 157 (1930), 26-34.

Southern, R.W., *Western Society and the Church in the Middle Ages*, Penguin, Harmondsworth, 1970.

Thompson, E.M., *The Carthusian Order in England*, SPCK, London, 1930.

Thornton, M., *English Spirituality. An Outline of Ascetical Theology According to the English Pastoral Tradition*, SPCK, London, 1963.

Vaissier, J.J., ed., *A deuout treatyse called the tree & xii. frutes of the holy goost*, J.B. Wolters, Groningen, 1960.

Walsh, J., ed., *Pre-Reformation English Spirituality*, Fordham UP, 1966.

Ward, M., ed., *The English Way. Studies in English Sanctity from St. Bede to Newman*, Sheed & Ward, London, 1933.

Wells, J.E., *et al.*, *A Manual of Writings in Middle English 1050-1400*, Connecticut Academy of Arts and Sciences, New Haven, 1916; see the supplements 1-9 (1919-51).

Westra, M.S., ed., *A Talkyng of þe Loue of God*, Martinus Nijhoff, The Hague, 1950.

Wichgraf, W., 'Susos "Horologium Sapientiae" in England. Nach Handschriften des 15. Jahrhunderts', *Anglia*, 53 (1929), 123-33; 269-87; 345-73; and *Anglia*, 54 (1930), 351-52.

Wilson, R.M., 'Three Middle English Mystics', *E&S*, n.s. 9 (1956), 87-112.

Workman, H.B., *John Wyclif. A Study of the English Medieval Church*, Clarendon Press, 1926.

Zeeman, E., 'Continuity in Middle English Devotional Prose', *JEGP*, 55 (1956), 417-22.

Zeeman, E., 'Continuity and Change in Middle English Versions of the *Meditationes Vitae Christi*', *Medium Aevum*, 26 (1957), 25-31.

Literature on individual authors

Ancrene Wisse

The following edition has been used:

Tolkien, J.R.R., ed., *Ancrene Wisse*: with an Introduction by N.R. Ker, *EETS*, OS, 249, 1962.

There is also a modern English translation:

Salu, M.B., ed., *The Ancrene Riwle*: with an introduction by D.G. Sitwell, Burns & Oates, London, 1955.

Secondary literature:

Allen, H.E., 'The Origin of the Ancrene Riwle', *PMLA*, 33 (1918), 474-546.

Allen, H.E., 'Some Fourteenth Century Borrowings from Ancrene Riwle', *MLR*, 18 (1923), 1-8.

Allen, H.E., 'On the author of the Ancrene Riwle', *PMLA*, 44 (1929), 635-80.

Allen, H.E., 'Further Borrowings from "Ancrene Riwle" ', *MLR*, 24 (1929), 1-15.

Colledge, E., 'The Recluse. A Lollard Interpolated Version of the Ancrene Riwle', *RES*, 15 (1939), 1-15 and 129-45.

Crawford, S.J., 'The Influence of the "Ancrene Riwle" in the Late Fourteenth Century', *MLR*, 25 (1930), 191-2.

Dobson, E.J., *The Origins of 'Ancrene Wisse'*, Clarendon Press, 1976.

Fisher, J.H., 'Continental Associations for the Ancrene Riwle', *PMLA*, 64 (1949), 1180-9.

Grayson, J., *Structure and Imagery in Ancrene Wisse*, Univ. Press of New England, 1974.

Hackett, P., 'The Anchoresses' Guide', *Pre-Reformation English Spirituality*, ed. J. Walsh, Fordham UP, 1964, 67-80.

Käsmann, H., 'Zur Frage der ursprünglichen Fassung der *Ancrene Riwle*', *Anglia*, 75 (1957), 134-56.

Påhlsson, J., *The Recluse. A Fourteenth Century Version of the Ancrene Riwle*, Lunds Universitets Årsskrift, N.F., vol. 6, 1, 1911.

Paues, A.C., 'A Fourteenth Century Version of the *Ancrene Riwle*,' *Englische Studien*, 30 (1902), 344-6.

Samuels, M.C., 'Ancrene Riwle Studies', *Medium Aevum*, 22 (1953), 1-9.

Shepherd, G., ed., *Ancrene Wisse: Parts Six and Seven*, Nelson, London, 1959.

Talbot, C.H., 'Some Notes on the Dating of Ancrene Riwle', *Neophilologus*, 40 (1956), 38-50.

The Cloud of Unknowing *and its related tracts*

Middle English editions:

Hodgson, P., ed., *Deonise Hid Diuinite, and Other Treatises on Contemplative Prayer Related to The Cloud of Unknowing*, *EETS*, OS, 231, 1955.

Hodgson, P., ed., *The Cloud of Unknowing and the Book of Privy Counselling*, *EETS*, OS, 218, 1944, repr. (with corrections) 1958 and 1973.

Modernized editions with important introductions:

Gardner, J.E.G., ed., *The Cell of Self-Knowledge: Seven Early English Mystical Treatises Printed by Henry Pepwell in 1521*, Chatto & Windus, London, 1910 (contains the tracts: *Tretyse of þe Stodye of Wysdome, Pistle of Discrecioun of Stirings, Tretis of Discrescyon of Spirites*).

McCann, J., ed., *The Cloud of Unknowing, and Other Treatises*, with a commentary on the Cloud by Fr A. Baker, Burns & Oates, London, 6th edn, 1952.

Noetinger, M., ed., *Le Nuage de l'Inconnaissance*, A. Mame, Tours, 1925.

Underhill, E., ed., *A Book of Contemplation, the which is Called the Cloud of Unknowing, in the which a Soul is Oned with God*, ed. from BM. MS. Harley 674, Watkins, London, 3rd edn, 1934.

Wolters, C., ed., *The Cloud of Unknowing and other Works*, Penguin, Harmondsworth, 1978.

Secondary literature:

Burrow, J.A., 'Fantasy and Language in *The Cloud of Unknowing*', *EC*, 27 (1977), 283-98.

Coleman, T.W., *English Mystics of the Fourteenth Century*, Epworth Press, London, 1938.

Colledge, E., *The Mediaeval Mystics of England*, Murray, London, 1962.

Elwin, V., *Christian Dhyāna or Prayer of Loving Regard. A Study of 'The Cloud of Unknowing'*, SPCK, London, 1930.

Gardner, H.L., 'Walter Hilton and the Authorship of *The Cloud of Unknowing*', *RES*, 9 (1933), 129-47.

Hodgson, P., 'Walter Hilton and "The Cloud of Unknowing": A Problem of Authorship Reconsidered', *MLR*, 50 (1955), 395-406.

Hodgson, P., *Three 14th-Century English Mystics*, Writers and Their Work, 196, British Book Centre, London, 1967.

Hort, G., *Sense and Thought*, Allen & Unwin, London, 1936.

Jones, R.M., *The Flowering of Mysticism. The Friends of God in the Fourteenth Century*, Macmillan, New York, 1939.

Kendall, E.L., *A City not Forsaken. English Masters of the Spiritual Life*, Faith Press, London, 1962.

Knowles, D., 'The Excellence of *The Cloud*', *Downside Review*, 52 (1934), 71-92.

Knowles, D., *The English Mystics*, Burns & Oates, London, 1927.

Knowles, D., *The English Mystical Tradition*, Burns & Oates, London, 1961.

McCann, J., 'The Cloud of Unknowing', *Ampleforth Journal*, 29 (1924), 192-7.

Noetinger, M., 'The Authorship of the 'Cloud of Unknowing', *Blackfriars*, 4 (1924).

Pepler, C., *The English Religious Heritage*, Blackfriars Publications, London, 1958.

Sitwell, G., 'English Spiritual Writers: The Cloud of Unknowing', *Clergy Review*, 45 (1960), 385-94.

Underhill, E., *The Mystics of the Church*, J. Clarke, London, 1925.

Walsh, J., 'The Cloud of Unknowing' in: *Pre-Reformation English Spirituality*, ed., J. Walsh, Fordham UP, 1966, 170-81.

Walter Hilton

Middle English editions:

Horstmann, C., ed., *Yorkshire Writers*, Swan, Sonnenschein, London, 1895, I (contains the tracts *Of Angels' Song* and *Mixed Life*, 175-82 and 264-92 respectively).

Hussey, S.S., ed., *An Edition, from the Manuscripts, of Book II of Walter Hilton's Scale of Perfection* (unpublished PhD thesis, London, 1962). The text follows MS. BL. Harley 6579.

Kuriyagawa, F., ed. *Walter Hilton's Eight Chapters on Perfection*, Keio Institute of Cultural and Linguistic Studies, Keio University, Tokyo, 1967.

Wallner, B., ed., *An Exposition of Qui Habitat and Bonum Est in English*, C.W.K. Gleerup, Lund, 1954 (Hilton's authorship doubtful).

Wallner, B., *A Commentary on the 'Benedictus'*, C.W.K. Gleerup, Lund, 1959

(Hilton's authorship doubtful).

Wykes, B.E., ed., 'An Edition of Book I of *The Scale of Perfection* by Walter Hilton (unpublished dissertation, Ann Arbor, 1957). The text follows MS. BL. Harley 6579. For Hilton's translation of the *Stimulus Amoris* MS. BL. 2254, f. $1^r - 72^v$ has been used.

Modernized editions:

Gardner, J.E.G., *The Cell of Self-Knowledge*, Chatto & Windus, London, 1910 (contains the tract *Of Angels' Song*).

Hodgson, G.E., *The Sanity of English Mysticism: A Study of Richard Rolle*, Faith Press, London, 1926 (contains the tract *Of Angels' Song*).

Jones, D., *Minor Works of Walter Hilton*, Burns & Oates, London, 1929 (contains the works *Mixed Life, Eight Chapters on Perfection, Qui Habitat, Bonum Est, Benedictus*).

Kirchberger, C. ed., *The Goad of Love*, Faber, London, 1952 (modernized edition of the translation of the *Stimulus Amoris*).

Noetinger, M. and Bouvet, E., eds., *Scala Perfectionis par Walter Hilton*, A. Mame, Tours, 1923.

Shirley-Price, L., ed., *Walter Hilton. The Ladder of Perfection*, Penguin, Harmondsworth, 1957.

Underhill, E., ed., *The Scale of Perfection by Walter Hilton Canon of Thurgarton*, Newly edited from MS. Sources with an introduction, J.M. Watkins, London, 1923.

Secondary literature:

Coleman, T.W., 'Walter Hilton's "Scale of Perfection" ', *London Quarterly and Holborn Review*, 160 (1935), 241-5.

Coleman, T.W., *English Mystics of the Fourteenth Century*, Epworth Press, London, 1938.

Colledge, E., 'Recent Work on Walter Hilton', *Blackfriars*, 37, no. 435 (1956). 265-70.

Colledge, E., *The Mediaeval Mystics of England*, Murray, London, 1962.

Gardner, H.L., 'Walter Hilton and the Authorship of the "Cloud of Unknowing" ', *RES*, 9 (1933), 129-47.

Gardner, H.L., 'The Text of the Scale of Perfection', *Medium Aevum*, 5 (1936), 11-30.

Gardner, H.L., 'Walter Hilton and the Mystical Tradition in England', *E&S*, 22 (1937), 103-27.

Hodgson, P., *Three 14th-Century English Mystics*, Writers and their Work, 196, British Book Centre, London, 1967.

Hudson, A., 'A Chapter from Walter Hilton in Two Middle English Compilations', *Neophilologus*, 52 (1958), 416-9.

Hughes, A.C., *Walter Hilton's Direction to Contemplatives* (dissertation, Rome, 1962).

Hussey, S.S., 'Langland, Hilton, and the Three Lives', *RES*, n.s. 7 (1956), 132-50.

Hussey, S.S., 'The Text of the Scale of Perfection, Book II', *Neuphilologische Mitteilungen*, 65 (1964), 75-92.

Hussey, S.S., 'Latin and English in the Scale of Perfection', *Mediaeval Studies*, 35 (1973), 456-76.

Knowles, D., *The English Mystical Tradition*, Burns & Oates, London, 1961.

Knowles, D. and Russell-Smith, J., 'Walter Hilton', *DSAM*, VII, 1969, col. 525-30.

Milosh, L.E., *The Scale of Perfection and the English Mystical Tradition*, Wisconsin UP, 1966.

Noetinger, M., 'La Contemplation d'après Walter Hilton', *La Vie Spirituelle*, 9 (1923-4), 453-9.

Pepler, C., *The English Religious Heritage*, Blackfriars Publications, London, 1958.

Riehle, W., 'The Problem of Walter Hilton's Possible Authorship of the "Cloud of Unknowing" and its Related Tracts', *Neuphilologische Mitteilungen*, 78 (1977), 31-45.

Russell-Smith, J., 'Walter Hilton and a Tract in Defence of the Veneration of Images', *Dominican Studies*, 7 (1954), 180-214.

Russell-Smith, J., 'Walter Hilton', *The Month*, N.S. 22 (1959), 133-48.

Russell-Smith, J., 'Walter Hilton' in *Pre-Reformation English Spirituality*, ed. J. Walsh, Fordham UP, 1966, 182-97.

Sitwell, G., 'Contemplation in "The Scale of Perfection" ', *The Downside Review*, 67 (1949), 276-90 and 68 (1950), 21-34 and 271-89.

Sitwell, G., 'Walter Hilton', *The Clergy Review*, 44 n.s. (1959), 321-32.

Underhill, E., *The Mystics of the Church*, J.M. Watkins, London, 1925.

Underhill, E., 'Walter Hilton' in *Mixed Pasture*, Methuen, New York, 1933, 188-208.

Julian of Norwich

The following edition has been used:

Reynolds, F. (Sr Anna Maria), ed., *A Critical Edition of the Revelations of Julian of Norwich (1342-c.1416)*, Prepared from all the Known Manuscripts with Introduction, Notes and Select Glossary (unpublished PhD thesis, Leeds, 1956). Text follows MS. BL. Addit. 37790 (for the *Shorter Version*) and MS. Fond anglais no. 40 Bibliothèque Nationale, Paris (for the *Long Version*).

Modernized editions with important introductions or commentaries:

Glasscoe, M., ed., *Revelations of Divine Love*, University of Exeter, 1976.

Harford, D., ed., *The Shewings of Lady Julian*, transcribed and edited from BM. Add. MS. 37790, H.R. Allenson, London, 3rd edn, 1925.

Hudleston, R., *Revelations of Divine Love Showed to a Devout Ankress by Name Julian of Norwich*, Burns & Oates, London, 2nd edn, 1952.

Meunier, G., ed., *Juliene de Norwich Mystique Anglaise du XIVᵉ Siècle, Revelations de l'Amour de Dieu, Traduites par un Bénédictin de Farnborough*, Paris, 1925.

Reynolds, F. (Sr Anna Maria), ed., *A Shewing of God's Love. The Shorter Version of Sixteen Revelations of Divine Love by Julian of Norwich*, ed. and partially modernized from the 15th century manuscripts, Longmans, Green, London, 1958.

Tyrrell, G., ed., *XVI Revelations of Divine Love, Showed to Mother Juliana of Norwich, 1373*, with a Preface, Kegan Paul, London, 1902.

Walsh, J., ed. and transl., *The Revelations of Divine Love*, Burns & Oates, London, 1961.

Warrack, G., *Revelations of Divine Love recorded by Julian, Anchoress of Norwich A.D. 1373*, Methuen, London, 13th edn, 1949.

Wolters C., *Revelations of Divine Love*, Penguin, Harmondsworth, 1966.

Secondary literature:

Benvenuta, Sr Mary, 'Juliana of Norwich', *Dublin Review*, 176 (1925), 81-94.

Cabassut, A., 'Une dévotion médiévale peu connue: La dévotion a Jésus notre mère', *RAM*, 25 (1949), 234-45.

Chambers, F.P., *Juliana of Norwich. An Introductory Appreciation and an Interpretative Anthology*, Gollancz, London, 1955.

Coleman, T.W., *English Mystics of the Fourteenth Century*, Epworth Press, London, 1938.

Colledge, E., *The Mediaeval Mystics of England*, Murray, London, 1962.

Fairweather, W., *Among the Mystics*, Arno, Edinburgh, 2nd edn, 1968.

Jones, R.M., *The Flowering of Mysticism*, Macmillan, New York, 1939.

Kendall, E.L., *A City not Forsaken. Studies of English Masters of the Spiritual Life*, Faith Press, London, 1962.

Knowles, D., *The English Mystical Tradition*, Burns & Oates, London, 1961.

Lawlor, J., 'A Note on the "Revelations of Julian of Norwich" ', *RES*, n.s. 2 (1951), 255-8.

Molinari, P., *Julian of Norwich: the Teaching of a Fourteenth Century Mystic*, Longmans, London, 1958.

Pepler, C., *The English Religious Heritage*, Blackfriars Publications, London, 1958.

Reynolds, F. (Sr Anna Maria), 'Some Literary Influences in the Revelations of Julian of Norwich (c. 1342-post-1416)', *Leeds Studies in English and Kindred Languages*, 7 (1952), 18-28.

Reynolds, F. (Sr Anna Maria), 'Julian of Norwich' in *Pre-Reformation English Spirituality*, ed. J. Walsh, Fordham UP, 1966, 198-209.

Stone, R.K., *Middle English Prose Style: Margery Kempe and Julian of Norwich*, Studies in English Literature, 36, Mouton, The Hague, 1970.

Underhill, E., *The Essentials of Mysticism and Other Essays*, Dent, London, 1920.

Underhill, E., *The Mystics of the Church*, J.M. Watkins, London, 1925.

Walsh, J., 'God's Homely Loving. St. John and Julian of Norwich on the Divine Indwelling', *The Month*, 205, n.s. 19 (1958), 164-72.

Watkin, E.I., 'Dame Julian of Norwich' in: *The English Way: Studies in English Sanctity from St. Bede to Newman*, ed. M. Ward, Sheed & Ward, London, 1933, 128-58.

Wilson, R.M., 'Three Middle English Mystics', *E&S*, n.s. 9 (1956), 87-112.

Margery Kempe

Complete edition:

Meech, S.B. and Allen, H.E., eds, *The Book of Margery Kempe*, EETS, OS, 212, 1940.

Modernized edition:
Butler-Bowdon, E., ed., *The Book of Margery Kempe*, Jonathan Cape, London, 1936.

Secondary literature:
Bennett, H.S., *Six Medieval Men and Women*, Cambridge UP, 1955.
Brooks. B.G., 'Margery Kempe', *The Nineteenth Century and After*, 132 (1942).
Cholmeley, K., *Margery Kempe: Genius and Mystic*, Longmans, London, 1947.
Coffman, G., 'The Book of Margery Kempe', *Speculum*, 17 (1942), 138-41.
Colledge, E., *The Mediaeval Mystics of England*, Murray, London, 1962.
Colledge, E., 'Margery Kempe', in: *Pre-Reformation English Spirituality*, ed. J. Walsh, Fordham UP, 1966, 210-23.
Collis, L., *The Apprentice Saint: Margery Kempe*, Joseph, London, 1964.
Hirsh, J.C., 'Author and Scribe in The Book of Margery Kempe', *Medium Aevum*, 44 (1975), 145-50.
Jones, R.M., *The Flowering of Mysticism*, Macmillan, New York, 1939.
Knowles, D., *The English Mystical Tradition*, Burns & Oates, London, 1961.
McCann, J., 'The Book of Margery Kempe', *Dublin Review*, 200 (1937).
Stone, R.K., *Middle English Prose Style: Margery Kempe and Julian of Norwich*, Studies in English Literature, 36, Mouton, The Hague, 1970.
Thornton, M., *Margery Kempe: An Example in the English Pastoral Tradition*, SPCK, London, 1960.
Watkin, E.I., 'In Defence of Margery Kempe', in: *Poets and Mystics*, Sheed & Ward, London, 1953.
Wilson, R.M., 'Three Middle English Mystics', *E&S*, n.s. 9 (1956), 87-112.

Richard Rolle

Middle English and Latin editions:
Allen, H.E., *English Writings of Richard Rolle Hermit of Hampole*, Clarendon Press, 1931; contains, among other texts, *Meditations on the Passion, Ego Dormio, The Commandment, Form of Living*.
Amassian, M.G., 'An Edition of Richard Rolle's The Commandment' (unpublished dissertation Fordham University, 1967); text follows Cambridge University MS. Dd. v. 64.
Arnould, E.J.F., ed., *The Melos Amoris of Richard Rolle of Hampole*, Blackwell, Oxford, 1957.
Bramley, H.R., ed., *The Psalter or Psalms of David and Certain Canticles with a Translation and Exposition in English by Richard Rolle of Hampole*, Clarendon Press, 1884.
Deanesly, M. ed., *The Incendium Amoris of Richard Rolle of Hampole*, Publications of the University of Manchester, Historical Series, 26, London, 1915.
Faber, J., ed., *D. Richardi Pampolitani Anglosaxonis Eremitae, Viri in diuinis scripturis ac veteri illa solidaque Theologia eruditissimi, in Psalterium Dauidicum, atque alia quaedam sacrae scripturae monumenta (quae versa indicabit pagella) compendiosa iuxtaque pia Enarratio*. Colonia, ex officina Melchioris Nouesiani, Mense Martio, Anno M.D. xxxvi.
Harvey, R., ed., *The Fire of Love and the Mending of Life, translated by Richard*

Misyn, 1434-5, EETS, OS, 106, 1896.

Horstmann, C., *Yorkshire Writers,* Swan, Sonnenschein, London, 1895, I.

Lindquist, H., ed., *Richard Rolle's Meditatio de Passione Domini according to MS. Uppsala C. 494,* Skrifter utgifna af K. Humanistika Vetenskaps-Samfundet: Uppsala 19, 3, Uppsala, 1917.

Murray, E.M., *Richard Rolle's Comment on the Canticles,* ed., from MS. Trinity College Dublin 153 (unpublished dissertation, New York, 1958).

Perry, G.G., ed., *English Prose Treatises of Richard Rolle de Hampole,* ed. from Robert Thornton's MS. in the Library of Lincoln Cathedral, *EETS,* OS, 20, 1921 (contains the translation of the chapter on the *Oleum Effusum-*verse from the *Song of Songs*).

Perry, G.G., ed., *Officium de Sancto Ricardo de Hampole, EETS,* OS, 20, 1921.

Theiner, P.F., ed., *The Contra Amatores Mundi of Richard Rolle of Hampole,* University of California Publications, English Studies, 33, California UP, Berkeley, 1968.

Wilmart, A., ed., 'Le Cantique d'Amour de Richard Rolle', *Revue d'Ascétique et de Mystique,* 21 (1940), 131-48.

The as yet unedited *Emendatio Vitae* is contained in MS. Bodl. 16 (Summary Catalogue of Western MSS. in the Bodleian Library, Nr. 1859), f. 49^r – 78^r.

Modernized editions:

Comper, F.M.M., ed., *The Fire of Love or Melody of Love and the Mending of Life or Rule of Living,* translated by Richard Misyn from the 'Incendium Amoris' and the 'De Emendatione Vitae' of Richard Rolle, Hermit of Hampole, done into modern English, with an Introduction by E. Underhill, Methuen, London, 1914.

Harford, D., *The Mending of Life,* ed. from Cambridge University MS. Ff. v. 40, H.R. Allenson, London, 1913.

Harrell, J.G., ed., *Selected Writings of Richard Rolle,* SPCK, London, 1963.

Hubbard, H.L., ed., *The Amending of Life,* J.M. Watkins, London, 1922.

Noetinger, M., ed., *Mystiques Anglais. Le Feu de L'Amour. Le Modèle de la Vie Parfaite – Le Pater Par Richard Rolle L'Ermite de Hampole,* traduits par D.M. Noetinger, Tours, 1929.

Wolters, C., ed., *Richard Rolle. The Fire of Love,* Penguin, Harmondsworth, 1972.

Secondary literature:

Allen, H.E., 'On Richard Rolle's Lyrics', *MLR,* 14 (1919), 320-1.

Allen, H.E., *Writings Ascribed to Richard Rolle Hermit of Hampole and Materials for His Biography,* The Modern Language Association of America, Monograph Series, III, New York, 1927.

Arnould, E.J.F., 'Richard Rolle and the Sorbonne', *Bulletin of the John Rylands Library,* 21 (1937), 55-8.

Arnould, E.J.F., 'Richard Rolle of Hampole', *Pre-Reformation English Spirituality,* ed. J. Walsh, Fordham UP, 1966, 132-44.

Coleman, T.W., *English Mystics of the Fourteenth Century,* Epworth Press, London, 1938.

Colledge, E., *The Mediaeval Mystics of England,* Murray, London, 1962.

Comper, F.M.M., *The Life of Richard Rolle together with an Edition of His English Lyrics*, Dent, London, 1928.

Deanesly, M., 'The "Incendium Amoris" of Richard Rolle and St. Bonaventura', *The English Historical Review*, 29 (1914).

Everett, D., 'The Middle English Prose Psalter of Richard Rolle of Hampole', *MLR*, 17 (1922), 217-27; 337-50, and 18 (1923), 381-93.

Gilmour, J., 'Notes on the Vocabulary of Richard Rolle', *N&Q*, 201 (1956), 94-5.

Hahn, A., *Quellenuntersuchungen zu Richard Rolles englischen Schriften* (dissertation, Halle, 1900).

Hodgson, G.E., *The Sanity of English Mysticism: A Study of Richard Rolle*, Faith Press, London, 1926.

Hodgson, G.E., *Rolle and Our Daily Work*, Faith Press, London, 1929.

Hodgson, P., *Three 14th-Century English Mystics*, Writers and their Work, 196, British Book Centre, London, 1967.

Jones, R.M., *The Flowering of Mysticism. The Friends of God in the Fourteenth Century*, Macmillan, New York, 1939.

Kendall, E.L., *A City not Forsaken. Studies of English Masters of the Spiritual Life*, Faith Press, London, 1962.

Lehmann, M., *Untersuchungen zur mystischen Terminologie Richard Rolles* (dissertation, Jena, 1936).

Liegey, G., *The Rhetorical Aspects of Richard Rolle's Melum Contemplativorum* (unpublished dissertation, New York, 1954).

Middendorf, H., *Studien über Richard Rolle von Hampole unter besonderer Berücksichtigung seiner Psalmenkommentare* (dissertation, Leipzig, 1888).

Morgan, M.M., 'Versions of the Meditations on the Passion Ascribed to Richard Rolle', *Medium Aevum*, 22 (1953), 93-103.

Noetinger, M., 'The Biography of Richard Rolle', *The Month* (1926), 22-30.

Olmes, A., *Sprache und Stil der englischen Mystik des Mittelalters unter besonderer Berücksichtigung des Richard Rolle von Hampole* (dissertation, Göttingen, 1933).

Robbins, H.W., 'An English Version of St. Edmund's Speculum ascribed to Richard Rolle', *PMLA*, 40 (1925), 240-51.

Schneider, J.P., *The Prose Style of Richard Rolle of Hampole, with Special Reference to its Euphuistic Tendencies*, J.H. Furst, Baltimore, 1906.

Schnell, E., *Die Traktate des Richard Rolle von Hampole 'Incendium Amoris' und 'Emendatio Vitae' und deren Übersetzung durch R. Misyn* (dissertation, Erlangen, 1932).

Ullmann, J., 'Studien zu Richard Rolle de Hampole', *Englische Studien*, 7 (1884), 415-72.

Underhill, E., 'Ricardus Heremita', *Dublin Review*, 183 (1928), 176-87.

Wilson, R.M., 'Three Middle English Mystics', *E&S*, n.s. 9 (1956), 87-112.

MIDDLE ENGLISH WORD INDEX

*

INDEX OF NAMES AND TITLES

*